Mutant Narratives in Ecological Science Fiction

Posthumanism in Practice

Series editors: Matt Hayler (University of Birmingham, UK), Danielle Sands (Royal Holloway, University of London, UK) and Christine Daigle (Brock University, Canada)

Ways of thinking allied with "posthumanism" have received increasing interest across a number of disciplines, predominantly in philosophy and the humanities, but also in biology, law and ethics, and art theory and creative practice. Indeed, we contend that the field's potential implications extend to the majority of academic disciplines. Focusing on emerging trends, cutting-edge research and current debates, Posthumanism in Practice presents work in and across multiple disciplines that investigates how posthumanism can effect change.

The questions that posthumanism raises, of what it means to be human, the nature of our relationship with the world, our relative importance, our obligations, entanglements, potentials and limitations, speak to every aspect of life. This series will address questions such as: What are the implications and entailed effects of the revelations of contemporary science and philosophy? Can our laws, societies, and egos hold up to our becoming less special? What can we do, and how might thinking differently enable us to act differently?

Works in this series will pose these kinds of questions and offer practical answers, suggestions and provocations. The aim is to inspire work that isn't occurring often or loudly enough, and to promote a wide variety of voices which are left outside of the arenas where they might be most usefully and importantly heard. Disciplinary conversations also often remain siloed, but posthumanism is inherently an interdisciplinary concern; the field questions (but doesn't necessarily reject) the usefulness and stability of existing disciplinary boundaries. As such, this series will prioritize works which bring insights across those boundaries and which demonstrate the real-world potential and/or risks of posthumanist ideas.

Editorial Board:
Megen de Bruin-Molé (University of Southampton, UK)
Emily Jones (University of Essex, UK)
Yoriko Otomo (Director of Global Research Network)

Pedro Oliveira (Independent Researcher)
Rick Dolphijn (Utrecht University, Netherlands)
Isabel Galleymore (University of Birmingham, UK)
Craig N. Cipolla (Tufts University, USA)
Stefan Herbrechter (Heidelberg University, Germany)
Simone Bignall (University of Technology, Sydney, Australia)
Olga Cielemęcka (University of Turku, Finland)
Dominique Chen (Waseda University, Japan)
Mickey Vallee (Athabasca University Canada)

Mutant Narratives in Ecological Science Fiction

Thinking with Embodied Estrangement

Kaisa Kortekallio

BLOOMSBURY ACADEMIC
LONDON • NEW YORK • OXFORD • NEW DELHI • SYDNEY

BLOOMSBURY ACADEMIC

Bloomsbury Publishing Plc, 50 Bedford Square, London, WC1B 3DP, UK
Bloomsbury Publishing Inc, 1385 Broadway, New York, NY 10018, USA
Bloomsbury Publishing Ireland, 29 Earlsfort Terrace, Dublin 2, D02 AY28, Ireland

BLOOMSBURY, BLOOMSBURY ACADEMIC and the Diana logo are trademarks of
Bloomsbury Publishing Plc

First published in Great Britain 2024
This paperback edition published 2025

Copyright © Kaisa Kortekallio, 2024

Kaisa Kortekallio has asserted her right under the Copyright, Designs and Patents Act, 1988, to be identified as Author of this work.

For legal purposes the Acknowledgments on pp. x–xi constitute an extension of this copyright page.

Cover design: Kaisa Kortekallio
Cover image: *Violin Dancer*, Ahmad Odeh/Unsplash

All rights reserved. No part of this publication may be: i) reproduced or transmitted in any form, electronic or mechanical, including photocopying, recording or by means of any information storage or retrieval system without prior permission in writing from the publishers; or ii) used or reproduced in any way for the training, development or operation of artificial intelligence (AI) technologies, including generative AI technologies. The rights holders expressly reserve this publication from the text and data mining exception as per Article 4(3) of the Digital Single Market Directive (EU) 2019/790.

Bloomsbury Publishing Plc does not have any control over, or responsibility for, any third-party websites referred to or in this book. All internet addresses given in this book were correct at the time of going to press. The author and publisher regret any inconvenience caused if addresses have changed or sites have ceased to exist, but can accept no responsibility for any such changes.

A catalogue record for this book is available from the British Library.

A catalog record for this book is available from the Library of Congress.

ISBN: HB: 978-1-3502-9684-8
PB: 978-1-3502-9680-0
ePDF: 978-1-3502-9677-0
eBook: 978-1-3502-9678-7

Series: Posthumanism in Practice

Typeset by Newgen KnowledgeWorks Pvt. Ltd., Chennai, India

For product safety related questions contact productsafety@bloomsbury.com.

To find out more about our authors and books visit www.bloomsbury.com and sign up for our newsletters.

For my niches, in construction and destruction

Contents

Acknowledgments   x

1 Introduction: Literary Scholars in the Anthropocene   1
2 More-than-Human Reading and Experiential Change   23
3 Mutant Figures and Reading Bodies   77
4 Readerly Choreographies and Paolo Bacigalupi's Climate Fiction   109
5 Embodied Estrangement and Jeff VanderMeer's *The Southern Reach*   143
6 Conclusion: More-than-Human Reading and Subjective Experience   187

References   195
Index   211

Acknowledgments

Academic publications are collective achievements, and this book is no exception. My heartfelt gratitude goes out to my brilliant mentors Merja Polvinen and Bo Pettersson, who carefully guided my thought process into the form of a doctoral dissertation, completed in 2020 at the University of Helsinki. Thanks to their generous and persistent cultivation efforts, the Thing was also well prepared for its rebirth as a fully-fledged Book.

Along the way, I was helped and encouraged by multitudes of colleagues, friends, and peers—Aino-Kaisa Koistinen, Vesa Kyllönen, Jari Käkelä, Mika Loponen, Laura Oulanne, Anna Ovaska, Hanna-Riikka Roine, Esko Suoranta, Essi Varis, and Päivi Väätänen being particularly consistent forces. Esko gains a special mention for the crucial act of introducing me and my work to Matt Hayler at a moment when my mind was light-years apart from any publishing aspirations. It is certain that this book would not have happened without Esko's intervention. Another remarkable influence was that of the NARMESH research group—Marco Caracciolo, Susannah Crockford, Shannon Lambert, and Gry Ulstein—whose keen interest and expertise in narrative theory and Anthropocene fiction I got to tap in my six-month visit to Ghent University in 2019–20. Pieter Vermeulen also kindly offered his vision on how to reintroduce the work for wider audiences.

I am grateful to Christine Daigle, Matt Hayler, and Christine Sands for their courage and insight in kicking up the Posthumanism in Practice series and including my book as one of its first items. I also want to thank Ben Doyle, Laura Cope, and other Bloomsbury Academic staff for their kind and professional manner during the publication process. Comments and suggestions from both the editors and anonymous reviewers helped to smooth out the wrinkles. Any wrinkles (or outright errors) that remain are of course my own.

Special thanks to the more-than-human patches of earth that let me in and nourished me: The University of Oulu Botanical Garden in Kaijonharju, The University of Helsinki Botanical Garden in Kaisaniemi, the little yard and big woods in Metsälä, the garden in Lippajärvi, Träskända Park, Mustarinda woods, Aatamila farm, and Keuruu Ecovillage.

Most of the research presented in the book was carried out on funding from the Helsinki University Research Fund (2014–18). Part of the research was also conducted in the consortium project *Instrumental Narratives: The Limits of Storytelling and New Story-Critical Narrative Theory* (2018–22), funded by the Academy of Finland (no. 315052). The manuscript for this book version was prepared during a research period in the School of Resource Wisdom at the University of Jyväskylä (2021–22), and additional funding for the editing phase was received from Suomen Tietokirjailijat ry. I gratefully acknowledge this financial and institutional support.

An earlier version of the section 5.2, "From Cognitive Nihilism to Ecological Monstrosity," appeared in *Collateral* 16 (2019), under the title "Turning Away from the Edge of Madness. Kinesis, Nihilism, and Area X." Parts of section 4.1, "Moving with the Figures of Bacigalupi's 'The People of Sand and Slag'," have also been published in "Dancing with the Posthumans: Readerly Choreographies and More-than-Human Figures" (*Partial Answers* 20, no. 2, 2022).

The third-party copyrighted material displayed in the pages of this book are done so on the basis of "fair dealing for the purposes of criticism and review" or "fair use for the purposes of teaching, criticism, scholarship or research" only in accordance with international copyright laws, and is not intended to infringe upon the ownership rights of the original owners.

1

Introduction: Literary Scholars in the Anthropocene

At the time of writing this introduction, in October 2022, the World Wildlife Fund reports that the wild animal populations of the world have diminished by 69 percent since 1970. More locally, in Finland, the Parliament—led by a left-green government—is debating whether to commit to the nature restoration measures agreed on by the European Parliament. More locally still, neighbors are busy insulating their houses and hoarding firewood for the coming winter, expecting fearsome inflation and power shortages due to the war in Ukraine.

All of these events are features of the same global environmental catastrophe. Climate change and biodiversity loss, the two overarching developments, are joined and exacerbated by other developments, such as chronic overuse of land and water, chemical pollution, and ocean acidification. Such developments have been described in terms of planetary boundaries—thresholds defined by the scientific community to illustrate the limits of the Earth's vital systems (Rockström et al. 2009). Out of nine thresholds, five have been breached at the time of writing (Persson et al. 2022). This is a catastrophe created by the collective actions of the human species—and an era dubbed as the *Anthropocene*.[1]

What should one do, as a literary scholar, at a time like this? What to make of all the cultural responses to environmental disasters, global and local, and of the political dramas and struggles linked to them? Should one try and make sense of these movements with the inherited toolkits of the trade—close reading, cultural criticism, or ecocriticism? Should one join those who invent new modes and devices of analysis and interpretation—new materialism, posthumanism, or empirical reading studies? Or should one refrain from literary analysis altogether and focus instead on outlining broad developments in culture, such as the formative power of fossil fuels? Should one remain on the political level and highlight how the destructive agency of humans is unequally distributed between different factions of humanity, to better cultivate responsible actions—or commit to a far-reaching philosophical strategy and aim at destabilizing the whole paradigm of anthropocentrism?

Going against the whole tradition of ecocriticism, literary critic Timothy Clark (2015) severely questions the power of literature and literary criticism to reimagine environmental relations. Clark argues that the current state of environmental destruction—climate change, mass extinctions, and wide-scale exploitative land use, all collectively signified by the concept of the Anthropocene—is not the doing of individual humans or even societies, but of the emergent, destructive agency of the human species as a whole. If literary critics cannot think on the scale of destructive human organicism, Clark argues, but restrict themselves to analyses on the smaller scales in which intentionality and rationality still play some part, they latently contribute to the status quo and thus also to the destruction. The ecocritical aim of rethinking "environmental imaginations" (Buell 1995) in order to foster cultural change is in the danger of becoming a "diversionary side-show, blind to its relative insignificance" (Clark 2015: 21; see also Colebrook 2014: 178). The nonconscious, noncultural entity that is the human species is not impressed or transformed by the ideas of literary writers or critics.

Clark is not alone in his critique of liberal humanist values and methods. Long before the introduction of the term *Anthropocene*, developments in twentieth-century Western science and philosophy gave rise to a deep crisis of humanist thinking.[2] Evolutionary theory and cognitive science have made it more and more difficult to figure the human according to Enlightenment ideals of autonomy, rationality, and *human exceptionalism*, that is, the idea that humans are, by their nature or by divine will, allotted a privileged position among other inhabitants of the Earth. As Cary Wolfe (2010: xv) notes, "'the human' is achieved by escaping or repressing not just its animal origins in nature, the biological, and the evolutionary, but more generally by transcending the bonds of materiality and embodiment altogether." Giving up these escapist traditions and moving into systems thinking has been a difficult task that continues in the twenty-first century.

A humanist response to the Anthropocene cannot be an easy one, as rethinking humans and humanity from a systemic perspective requires humanist scholars to question some of their basic assumptions. Clark, for one, is particularly suspicious of critical appeals to subjective experience, such as David Abram's phenomenological approach to animist perception or Ursula Heise's work on spatial and local experience. He sees this kind of work as inherently bound by "terrestriality," defined as "that 'normal' prereflective sense of scale inherent to embodied human life on the Earth's surface, [which] forms a kind of transcendental, one that both underlies and exceeds any view that it is merely our social context that determines our understanding of ourselves" (Clark 2015: 33).[3] For Clark, if we are to take the Anthropocene seriously, we can no longer trust everyday experience as the basis of ethical decisions—yet we are bound by it, due to our embodied condition.

I am sympathetic to the way in which Clark interrogates naturalized notions of individualism and personal freedom, but do not fully agree with his conclusion that readings focusing on subjective experience have become unuseful to environmental modes of criticism. Despite all the destruction human collectives have caused on the Earth, I believe cultural currents—in literature and elsewhere—can still affect and transform them. With cognitive narratologist Erin James (2015: 208), I am convinced that both literary and nonliterary narratives can "reveal perceptual points of difference, clarify the interests of those who imagine and inhabit an environment in a specific way, and expose readers to different or opposing points of view." Moreover, James claims that the cognitive process of inhabiting storyworlds has political potential: narratives can "open channels of communication about the way that people perceive and inhabit their environments and encourage an environmental awareness that may help to craft more equitable, just, and nonpartisan environmental policies" (James 2015: 208).

I see James's focus on the cognitive force of literature as a convincing and pragmatic response to the problem of the human scale. While Clark's strategy is to introduce in his readings a wider scale frame from which to discuss the relentless material destruction brought on by humanity at large, James's strategy is to stick to human experience, as bound by local environmental and cultural contexts. Her focus on human experience as necessarily limited gives rise to a multiperspectival view of environmental knowledge and action. A third strategy, employed by Marco Caracciolo (2021: 12), would combine the planetary and experiential scales and "strive to translate science into the human-scale, embodied language of everyday perception" via the method of careful formal analyses of complex Anthropocene-era literary artifacts. For Caracciolo, fictional narratives can provide a way out of the linear thinking of destructive anthropocentrism by evoking "mesh-like" patterns of experience and affect: "Strategies developed in the seemingly rarefied domain of fiction have the potential for trickling down to concrete cultural attitudes toward the nonhuman" (Caracciolo 2021: 23). Caracciolo thus shares both James's cultural optimism and her econarratological approach.

Whereas Clark offers the literary scholars of the Anthropocene the position of a detached analyst, James the task of politically engaged diplomacy, and Caracciolo the work of interpreting cultural and material complexity from a place of privilege, the only role I can personally and wholeheartedly subscribe to is that of a *medium*—a figure that carefully attends to the ongoing turmoil, with all capacities and sensibilities available to them, and generates affective and creative responses. Crucially, this task requires the whole body of the scholar—not just a few functions of their brain or their academic persona. Moreover, a medium for the Anthropocene would need to be in touch not only with human cultures but also with the nonhuman matters and forces driving environmental change. To be able to do so, they would need to cultivate skills and capacities that may be described as *posthuman* or *more-than-human*.

This book explores how to grow into the role of a medium for the Anthropocene. In cultivating the necessary skills and capacities, I have felt the need to begin from the basics: embodied experience and ecological relationality. This need stems from a deep-seated skepticism of currently dominant modes of experience and inquiry, that is, human exceptionalism and reductionist materialism. Detecting, unraveling, and abandoning such modes requires deliberate acts of decomposition, and cultivating new modes requires suitable nourishment. For those, I call upon ecological science fiction and, in particular, *mutant narratives*.

Mutant narratives unfold in environments that are transformed: post-epidemic, postindustrial, post-catastrophical spaces. Such spaces are inhabited by transforming bodies: hybrids, mutants, and diseased and contaminated plants and animals. Through such spaces and figures, mutant narratives tackle the problem of human-centered thinking and the exploitation of natural environments, in ways that are deeply troubling and conflicted. They reach for a new ecological understanding, for "ecology after Nature" (Morton 2010), but they are also constrained by the human-centered conventions of both the science fiction genre and late modernity more generally. Thus, they participate in cultural transformation by being uneasy hybrids, hardly viable, first adaptations to radically changed environments. Mutants always carry both the risk of failure and the chance of success.

The driving question of this book is whether conscious engagement with mutant narratives can give rise to more-than-human modes of experience. In short, the book tests the malleability of readerly experience, stretching its limits and opening it up to more-than-human influences. This strategy can be characterized as speculative and experimental: it begins by provisionally accepting a potential state of things (reading can be both embodied and more-than-human) and proceeds by enacting that state as carefully as possible. The whole operation can be seen as analogous to science fictional world-building that considers fictional worlds as "laboratories" for fleshing out ideas and theories. The aim is to provide an alternative to the detached mode of reading that currently dominates literary studies. I do not intend to prove the detached mode as untrue or wrong: rather, I argue that other modes are equally possible, and that both human cognition and literary theory are far more flexible than they are usually presented to be.

In this strategic and experimental operation, the corpus of science fictional narratives is considered in terms of dynamic programs rather than as inert objects. Drawing from the systems-theoretical work of N. Katherine Hayles (1999, 2018), the reader and the narratives are considered to form *cognitive assemblages*, temporary collective systems of cognizers and devices that give rise to thought, feeling, and action. Even as I write my analyses and discussions using the first person singular (rather than first person plural, third person plural, or the passive voice), this view of reading maintains that the cognition involved always goes beyond the personal: it is constituted by a multitude of actors, some human and some nonhuman, some accessible to the consciousness of the human participant, and some not.[4]

Through outlining the humanist values and meanings at play in mutant narratives, this book presents a series of posthumanist critiques: a posthumanist critique of experientiality (in Chapter 2), a posthumanist critique of character (in Chapters 3 and 4), and a posthumanist critique of reading (in Chapter 5). Similar critiques have been made before (see, e.g., Grosz 1994; Hayles 1999; Vint 2005; Morton 2007; Neimanis 2017; Varis 2019b; Vermeulen 2020), but bringing them together in the context of mutant narratives grounds them in the practice of reading contemporary science fiction.

1.1 Mutant Narratives as Responses to the Crisis of Humanism

Science fiction is caught between scientific ideas and humanist form, which lends it a generative tension. It generally adopts a systemic view of the human, but as popular literature, most of it tends to conform to the traditions of realist expressive strategies (Roberts 2005; Stockwell 2000; McHale 2018). While the realist and naturalist movement of the late nineteenth century was remarkable particularly in its aim for "objective" and "scientific" ways of representing reality, contemporary Western mainstream literature has also been shaped by modernist and postmodernist cultural currents that seek to narrate the "inner" experience of the subject and the epistemological ruptures brought on by the limited human condition.

The contemporary, broadly realist style—the style generally experienced as "natural" and unmediated—tends to present human experience as distinctly opposed to nonhuman life, as bound by individual bodies and persons, and narratable through coherent, rational subjects. This unquestioned baggage of the realist tradition is, I claim, at the core of the now-dominant form of human subjectivity, naturalized to the extent that we experience it as self-evident—like the air we breathe (see also Rossi 2012; Kukkonen 2019).

Science fiction is an established arena for testing the boundaries of the realistically depicted human subject. The genre has been producing mutations of humanist forms—robots, androids, mutants, and hybrids—since its beginning in the late nineteenth century. As such, it has always been attuned to the crisis of humanism. In the mature genre of today, the best works of science fiction make use of this tradition in self-reflective modes that have the potential to turn the readers' attention to the ways in which reading shapes thought and experience (Polvinen 2023). Ecological science fiction in particular produces hybrid figures and hybrid narratives that negotiate the contradiction between systemic view and humanist form.

Ecological science fiction can open routes and draw models for coping with radical environmental change. While science fiction is not necessarily *environmentalist*, it has always been profoundly interested in environments and environmental knowledge. In *Trillion Year Spree*, Brian Aldiss and David Wingrove (2001: 4) characterize science fiction as a literature of epistemology: "the search for a definition of mankind and his status in the universe which will stand in our advanced but confused state of knowledge (science)." They further argue that science fiction has potential value as environmental literature because "the greatest successes of science fiction are those which deal with man in relation to his changing surroundings and abilities: what might loosely be called *environmental fiction*" (Aldiss and Wingrove 2001: 8, emphasis in original). Examples of this kind of loosely environmental science fiction range from classics such as H. G. Wells's *The War of the Worlds* (1898), Stanislaw Lem's *Solaris* (1961), and Frank Herbert's *Dune* (1965) to contemporary fiction such as Margaret Atwood's *Oryx and Crake* (2003), Kim Stanley Robinson's *Mars* trilogy (1992–5) and *Science in the Capital* trilogy (2004–7), and Nnedi Okorafor's *Lagoon* (2014).

As Chris Pak (2016: 6) notes, Aldiss's and Wingrove's emphasis on environmentality highlights how science fiction "explores two major themes that are essential to the mode: our relationship to the environment, and the way our abilities—our technologies—allow alteration of both the environment and the range of environments made available to us." As such, the mode of science fiction is interested in human action at a species level, as both environmental and technological, as well as our perceptual and physical access to new environments (implied by Pak's phrase, "the range of environments made available to us"). Pak's own treatise on the theme of *terraforming* (geoengineering human-habitable planets), *Terraforming: Ecopolitical Transformations and Environmentalism in Science Fiction* (2016), demonstrates this interest, as do such recent volumes as Ursula Heise's *The Sense of Space and the Sense of Planet* (2008), Eric Otto's *Green Speculations* (2012), the collected volume *Green Planets* (2014, edited by Gerry Canavan and Kim Stanley Robinson), and Tom Idema's *Stages of Transmutations* (2019). Such research has rapidly proliferated in recent years and while my list only covers a fraction of it, we can infer that science fiction provides ample material for studying environmental imaginations.

Science fictional imaginations also develop and discuss visions of humanity and human nature. The entanglements of humans and technology have always formed a central theme for science fiction, and technologization has been both celebrated and contested in genre fiction. Some strains of science fiction present technology, and the extensive resource use required by the manufacture and development of high technology, as inherent in human nature.

Take, for example, the trope of the *galactic empire*. Developed in the so-called Golden Age science fiction of the post–Second World War years and since popularized by *Star Wars* and *Star Trek*, galactic empire stories imagine humanity extending beyond the Earth and the solar system to inhabit and exploit outer space. The humanity presented in these fictions can be seen as the inherently destructive and consuming human aptly portrayed by Claire Colebrook (2014) and Timothy Clark (2015). However, in the grand scheme of galactic empire stories, the ruination of Earth is typically presented as a sad but inevitable minor step on the way to the galactic age. These stories thus perpetuate imperialist notions of Western civilization and expansion, often revolving around conflicts in war, trade, and politics, which, as Iain M. Banks's extensive post-scarcity Culture series demonstrates, often unfold into complete fictional universes. In the mature genre of today, postcolonial critique has reached the galactic empire, with works such as *Rogue One: A Star Wars Story* (2016) and *Altered Carbon* (Richard K. Morgan 2002, Netflix adaptation 2018) focusing on the exploited underclasses and ecological devastation produced by imperialist and colonialist projects. Even more pointedly, works such as William J. Gibson's *The Peripheral* (2014) and Cory Doctorow's *Walkaway* (2017) tackle the extreme polarization of wealth and power inherent to the project of galactic empire.[5]

The analyses presented in this book focus on a selection of Anglo-American ecological science fiction that stays on Earth: Greg Bear's novel *Darwin's Children* (2003); Paolo Bacigalupi's short story "The People of Sand and Slag" (2004) as well as his novel *The Windup Girl* (2009); Jeff VanderMeer's *The Southern Reach* novel trilogy (*Annihilation*, *Authority*, and *Acceptance*, all published in 2014); and N. K. Jemisin's novel *The Fifth Season* (2015). These twenty-first-century science fiction narratives are profoundly different from galactic empire stories, but the backdrop of the galactic empire imaginary is a necessary context for them. This is mostly due to their origin and publication in the context of American science fiction.

The narratives studied imagine specific places such as the United States in the near future (in *Darwin's Children*), Bangkok in the twenty-third century (in *The Windup Girl*), a remote area off the coast of the Gulf of Mexico (*The Southern Reach*), and a continent on a far-future Earth (*The Fifth Season*), and they engage with the environmental crises relevant to their imagined locations. In this way, they reflect many themes salient to the first decades of the twenty-first century: the rising awareness of climate change and environmental destruction, increasingly complex entanglements of technological and biological forms, and, indeed, the Anthropocene—a conception of human kind as both an overbearing planetary force and thoroughly embedded in nonhuman environments (see, e.g., Colebrook 2014; Clark 2015; Vermeulen 2020).

The narratives portray humanity in a drastically different way from the galactic empire stories, presenting situations in which human societies and individuals are influenced, infected, and transformed by nonhuman forces. If there is, at times, mastery over nature, it is presented as partial and as particular to systemic conditions. Contrary to the galactic empire imaginary, these works do not portray humanity as a unified agent with a specific internal nature. Rather, the narratives destabilize and reconfigure humanist ideas of human agency and exceptionality by drawing on scientific models and ideas, such as coevolution, climate modeling, and bioengineering.

Ecological science fiction can also develop scientific models and ideas further by considering how they would pan out in speculative scenarios, or by asking how certain scientific findings might bear on human lives and societies. Greg Bear's *Darwin's Children*, continuing the storyline of the multiple-award-winning *Darwin's Radio* (1999), speculates on a planetwide evolutionary leap in humans, caused by the stress that overpopulation puts on the planetary ecosystem. Bear's novel thus fleshes out particular ideas in evolutionary theory, asking how environmental changes effected by human action might affect the biological makeup of the human species.[6]

As part of *The Broken Earth* trilogy, N. K. Jemisin's novel *The Fifth Season* imagines what human and more-than-human life would look like on a planet undergoing a geologically unstable era. At first glance, Jemisin's worldbuilding seems fantastic, but as one reads further the geological conditions are explained in a science-fictional manner. As Jemisin explores a time span of thousands of years and drastically changing environments, she can engage in envisioning evolutionary adaptations such as specific predatory behaviors triggered by volcanic ash (in nonhuman animals) and sensory capabilities tuned to perceiving the movements of the earth (in humans).

Paolo Bacigalupi's short stories and novel *The Windup Girl* critically explore exploitative and instrumental relations to nonhuman nature, constructing fictional worlds in which biological life is largely shaped by human design and politics. *The Windup Girl*, in particular, has been connected to real-life political struggles with transnational agribusiness companies such as Bayer and Monsanto. The story is commonly interpreted as a warning against the capitalist appropriation of biological life, figuring fully instrumentalized ecosystems as extremely impoverished and destructive to human and nonhuman life alike (see, e.g., Selisker 2015). Bacigalupi also builds on contemporary climate change scenarios, fleshing out futures in which sea levels have risen, weather patterns are highly irregular, and mass extinctions have wiped out the majority of nonhuman species.

By introducing a strangely transformative natural area, Jeff VanderMeer's *The Southern Reach* speculates about the implications of ecosystemic events that are inherently unknowable. The trilogy brings together environmental change and embodied experience, thus fleshing out how coevolution unfolds on the level of embodied cognition. VanderMeer's style emphasizes the affectivity and subjectivity of environmental relations, using the narrative strategies of Weird and horror fiction to challenge scientistic and rationalist notions of environmental knowledge. As such, *The Southern Reach* engages with notions of embodied and enactive cognition (e.g., Varela, Thompson, and Rosch 1992; Noë 2004), as well as with cognitive science of perception more generally (e.g., Metzinger 2003).

Despite the scientific influences, the characterization and focalization in these works are couched in humanist traditions of depicting human minds and bodies.

Even when foregrounding the themes of nonhuman agency and environmental entanglement, they reiterate hierarchical patterns in which human characters stand out from the background constituted by other life-forms.[7] What emerges, in each work, is an uneasy, internally conflicted hybrid of coevolutionary and humanist conceptions of human and nonhuman life. Focusing on this conflict in reading experience, as it unfolds, is a central tactic for unraveling the themes of posthumanist subjectivity.

Mutant narrative is a conceptual shorthand that loosely holds the confusing and effective hybridity that drives such works. Mutant narratives are uneasy hybrids of human-centered and posthumanist narratives that contain potential for ecological understanding. The term *mutant* carries its Latin present tense (from Latin *mutantem*, nominative *mutans*, "changing;" present participle of *mutare*, "to change") from grammar to cultural and experiential significance. Not only are these narratives in the ongoing process of change, but they can also *afford* change.

Moreover, mutant narratives arise from environmental relations that are technological on a systemic level: for example, the mutant generation of Greg Bear's *Darwin's Children* springs from conditions brought on by modern overpopulation and planetwide stress on ecosystems, and figures in Paolo Bacigalupi's work tend to be either bioengineered or otherwise enmeshed in capitalist systems of production. Thus, and crucially for the posthumanist ethos developed in this book, mutant narratives do not figure nature as separate from human action or culture. Instead, they give rise to environmental imaginations that locate human activity on a systemic level and thus also foster conceptions of human agency as more-than-human.

1.2 Staying with the Human

Science fictional figurations of human bodies enmeshed with nonhuman actors have often been discussed through the term *posthuman* (e.g., Hayles 1999; Graham 2002; Vint 2006). The need for terms such as posthuman stems from a peculiar point in history where there is a conscious struggle for a different kind of humanity, and where the questions are mostly posed in terms of an apparently natural-scientific worldview that nevertheless is constructed on humanist values of human exceptionalism and mastery. Posthumanist philosophers such as Elaine Graham (2002), Cary Wolfe (2010), and Rosi Braidotti (2013) argue that in order to develop a sustainable way of living, humanity needs to change—not only at the level of political and economic practices, but also at the level of subjective experience. The logic is that in order to act differently, we need to perceive of ourselves differently. In order to become posthuman, we should be able to imagine ourselves *as* posthuman.

However, most theories of the posthuman tend to deconstruct the ideas of individual subjectivity, consciousness, and rationality—aspects that are (presumably) necessary both in the construction of a relatable fictional character and in subjective experience. While such deconstructions are important exercises in more-than-human imagination and potentially transformative for the theoreticians themselves, engaging with the theoretical figurations of the posthuman requires such motivation and expertise that they cannot reach beyond academic discussion. Following Donna Haraway's (2016) critique, I find that the term *posthuman* produces a deceptively easy break with the human (as the masterful subject of Enlightenment visions), and therefore choose to use other terms such as *more-than-human* (when referring to the material and experiential enmeshment with nonhuman actors and environments) and *mutant* (when referring to science fictional renditions of enmeshed subjectivity). That said, I find the discourse on the posthuman highly valuable for the discussions of embodiment and materiality.

Critics have also noted that posthumanist and new materialist approaches, such as material ecocriticism, tend toward the erasure of all boundaries between mind and matter, human and nonhuman, and human scale and global scale, thus making detailed analysis of their relations difficult (see, e.g., Weik von Mossner 2017a: 10–11; Hayles 2018: 65–7; Faassen and Vermeulen 2019; Vermeulen 2020: 84–103). Hayles (2018: 65–6) makes the further critique that new materialisms do not recognize or discuss cognitive processes or consciousness. The dismissal of cognition in new materialist theorization, Hayles (2018: 66) claims, weakens "the case for materiality" as it "erases the critical role played by materiality in creating the structures and organizations from which cognition and consciousness emerge."

As conceptual work that crosses boundaries without erasing them and potentially also changes social practices, certain ideas by Donna Haraway are essential. While Haraway herself steers clear from the term *posthuman*, her work informs posthumanism, particularly the kind working with feminist "situated knowledges." Throughout her career, Haraway has demanded materialist and practical approaches to more-than-human ethics, discussing the troubling entanglements between humans, nonhuman animals, and technology. She is also keen on creating calls for action, complete with catchy slogans. One of the latest slogans, introduced also as the title of a collection of essays, is "staying with the trouble."

> In urgent times, many of us are tempted to address trouble in terms of making an imagined future safe, of stopping something from happening that looms in the future, and of clearing away the present and the past in order to make futures for coming generations. Staying with the trouble does not require such a relationship to times called the future. In fact, staying with the trouble requires learning to be truly present, not as a vanishing pivot between awful or edenic pasts and apocalyptic or salvific futures, but as mortal critters entwined in myriad unfinished configurations of places, times, matters, and meanings. (Haraway 2016: 1)

"Staying with the trouble" marks the ethical and practical starting point as well as the ongoing process of this book. The present is a complex situation, and while escape to "awful or edenic pasts and apocalyptic or salvific futures" is tempting, beginning from the current situation can be judged as more responsible. In this book, choosing to engage critically with science fictional characters means not just staying with the trouble but also *staying with the human*—in all its artificiality and toxicity.

Staying with the human involves attention to present dynamics of embodied experience—both with regard to readerly and scholarly subjectivity, and to the material-cultural networks that enable and constitute such subjectivity. The mode of this attention is phenomenological, as it focuses on the process of experience unfolding in living subjectivity.

Whatever experiential changes reading in embodied modes might provide, mutant narratives do not present a blueprint for the New Human, and reading them will not automatically upgrade your subjectivity into posthuman modes.[8] As has been noted in the ongoing posthumanist debate, the dream of replacing the troublesome Human with another, improved model (the posthuman) is an inherently modern and humanist one, tied to the logic of progress and individuation (e.g., Hayles 1999, 2006; Callus, Herbrechter, and Rossini 2014; Raipola 2014; Haraway 2016). This dream, prominent in both speculative fiction and transhumanist literature, often involves either the hope of humanity transcending its biological limits (e.g., Kurzweil 2005; see Wolfe 2010: xv) or humanity blending with the nonhuman in harmonious modes of cohabitation (e.g., Abram 1996). Like the human, the posthuman should be regarded as "a historically specific and contingent term rather than a stable ontology" (Hayles 2006: 160), while also recognizing the fact that the term is constantly being rethought and redefined in both academic and artistic discourse.

Whereas the "human" has since the Enlightenment been associated with rationality, free will, autonomy, and a celebration of consciousness as the seat of identity, the posthuman in its more nefarious forms is construed as an informational pattern that happens to be instantiated in a biological substrate. There are, however, more benign forms of the posthuman that can serve as effective counterbalances to the liberal humanist subject, transforming untrammelled free will into a recognition that agency is always relational and distributed, and correcting an overemphasis on consciousness to a more accurate view of cognition as embodied throughout human flesh and extended into the social and technological environment. (Hayles 2006: 160–1)

Ivan Callus, Stefan Herbrechter, and Manuela Rossini (2014: 107) have noted that in this search for meaning, "criticism needs to determine the posthumanist value of any instantiation of the posthuman and the various constructions that are made of its coming, origins and ends." My exploration of particular science fictional narratives aims to do just that: to determine what these narratives contribute to posthumanist modes of cultural transformation, and more specifically to the reconfigurations of agency and cognition suggested by Hayles earlier. It does not claim that mutant narratives will give rise to new kinds of posthuman subjects or open up new posthuman worlds of meaning. It does claim that they can help readers in learning to experience the current world in richer and more nuanced ways and encourage them to stay with the troubling feelings of comfort-seeking denial, overwhelming pain brought on by ecological knowledge, and utter confusion with the strangeness of the more-than-human world. I propose, and hope to demonstrate throughout the book, that such experiential learning requires special attention to the bodily aspects of experience, as well as to the narrative strategies and techniques at play in the formation of such experience.

1.2.1 Combining Posthumanism and Enactivism

Reading literature entails skillful engagement with affective narrative techniques, in which readerly experience is organized, moment to moment, in collaboration with the narrative techniques and strategies (Caracciolo 2014c; Kukkonen 2019; Polvinen 2023). In this book, I defend a view that considers such engagement as both embodied and ecological, involving bodily dispositions and experiential backgrounds. As readers attune to fictional figures and events, their experience shifts and changes in accordance with the textual design.

Reading mutant narratives is only one example of such readerly dynamics. Still, in this book I argue that while much of contemporary literature, particularly literature in realist modes, supports and naturalizes certain experiential habits such as human-centered perception and trust in the continuity of persons, mutant narratives have the potential to estrange such experiential habits—that is, they give rise to *embodied estrangement*. Reading mutant narratives evokes bodily feelings that are strange and uncomfortable. This is important, because rehearsing such strange feelings has the potential to gradually develop readers' sensitivities to the unfamiliar and the unknown, and thus strengthen their capabilities for responding to rapidly changing socioecological environments. By disrupting naturalized modes of engaging with the text, mutant narratives can also make readers aware of their cognitive and affective force and thus encourage an understanding of fictional narratives as affective and more-than-human technology.

In searching for ecological and dynamic understandings of human cognition and subjectivity, I draw on two broad strains of thought: posthumanism and enactivism. Posthumanist theory guides me to consider subjectivity as part of more-than-human ecologies, while the enactivist approach enables me to focus on the embodied and environmental aspects of subjective experience.

Posthumanist approaches to cultural imaginaries have in recent years begun to reconfigure the human-centered assumptions that give shape to our current theoretical understanding of human cultures. While posthumanism (if we can imagine such an entity) is a formidable tangle of bristly threads of thought, most of those threads discuss "the embodiment and the embeddedness of the human being in not just its biological but also its technological world" and the potential new modes of thought that can be developed after the realization of this "prosthetic coevolution" (Wolfe 2010: xv; see also Foucault 1984; Braidotti 2013; Nayar 2014). Posthumanist feminist and new materialist approaches in particular emphasize that cultural imaginaries operate on material and bodily levels, and thus they also develop methodologies that can attend to such materiality (see, e.g., Neimanis 2017).

The embodied cognitive approach, and particularly the enactivist perspective on literature and cognition, is a similarly recent and potent challenge to conventional notions of mind, matter, and bodily action, as it insists that cognition is not the property of brains, but of entire embodied organisms (see, e.g., Varela, Thompson, and Rosch 1992; Gallagher and Zahavi 2007; Noë 2015; Kukkonen 2019; Polvinen 2023). In light of Wolfe's (2010) definition earlier, the cases in which the embodied cognitive approach proposes new modes of thought could even be called posthumanist (e.g., Clark 2004; Varela, Thompson, and Rosch 1992).[9]

The shared interests of these two approaches, especially the complementary notions of *material agency* and *embodied cognition*, give rise to the theoretical discussions as well as the practical method in this book. Building on enactivist and posthumanist approaches to literature, this book assumes an exploratory and speculative attitude to readerly experience. By asking what happens to readerly experience when reading is assumed to be both embodied and environmental, it attends to the ways in which literature evokes bodily feelings, impressions, and experiential changes. In the book, the two approaches are synthesized into a method of *more-than-human reading* that trains such environmental and more-than-human aspects of readerly engagement. I argue that repeated engagements with literature can shape readers' habitual patterns of feeling and perception.

1.2.2 Embodied Estrangement and More-than-Human Reading

Having mentioned "potential" so many times already, the question remains: what can readers actually do with mutant narratives? What happens in the process of reading them, with or without the historical perspective I have provided earlier? My claim is that even without a historical perspective, reading mutant narratives can estrange one's embodied experience of self and world and facilitate alternative modes of experience. This claim builds on the traditional claim that science fiction effects *cognitive estrangement*—that is, it can defamiliarize and reconfigure naturalized notions about everyday environments and open up space for new kinds of thought and experience (Suvin 1979; McHale 2010; Haraway 2016).[10] The ovearching claim I develop throughout this book is that the cognition in "cognitive estrangement" should not be considered as merely cerebral, rational, or detached from the body—rather, the experientiality of contemporary science fiction supports the view that estrangement can and does take place on the level of embodied experience. I refer to such a mode of estrangement as *embodied estrangement*.

In my mind, cognitive estrangement needs to be reconfigured to better serve the contemporary notions of embodied, embedded, extended, and enactive cognition, which have been widely adopted in literary studies but not quite as eagerly in science fiction studies (but see Polvinen 2023). In its traditionally rationalist mode, the notion of cognitive estrangement cannot grasp the philosophical and political implications of the affective aspects of science fictional texts, such as immersion and flow, weird modes of temporality, spatiality and embodiment, and the material and aesthetic feel of the text itself. As I have argued elsewhere, following Sherryl Vint (2005), the material and bodily aspects of science fiction need to be recognized not merely as background and flavor, but as important modes of cognitive influence (Kortekallio 2019, 2022).

I propose that the notion of embodied estrangement can help to focus the analysis of science fiction (and, especially here, of mutant narratives) on the material and affective aspects of texts that estrange and reconfigure the readers' experience of empirical reality. Thinking in terms of embodied estrangement allows us to reflect on specific moments of strange bodily feelings experienced while reading, and discuss how they participate in the interpretive processes of reading science fiction.

Such moments involve specific cognitive assemblages of text, reader, and context. For instance, feeling the exploitative force of capitalist biopower becomes possible through imaginatively enacting the puppet-like movements of the central figure in Paolo Bacigalupi's *The Windup Girl*, and engagement with Jeff VanderMeer's *Annihilation* reconfigures the plant and animal life in the environment as slightly too conscious for comfort. The locus of such experiences is a particular human body—yet, in a posthumanist context, that body has to be thought of as entangled with and constituted by other bodies and patterns of meaning.

Bodily feeling, as a phenomenological concept, should not be simply equated with *emotions* (see Ratcliffe 2010). Bodily feelings vary from emotionally neutral sensations to deeply emotional bodily experiences. Bodily feeling and *affect* can be used as partly overlapping concepts, but whereas bodily feeling is tied to an individual body, affect can be considered as a collective or cultural phenomenon that informs feeling (cf. Ahmed 2004; Seyfert 2012; Vermeulen 2014). Feeling is more akin to physical exercise: the more you do it, the readier you become to do it again. As works of fiction prompt readers to affectively engage in the twists and turns of plots as well as with their materially evocative elements such as rhythms and sensory impressions, they participate in the moment-to-moment production of subjectivity.

In the crossroads of enactivist and posthumanist approaches, I find that the locus of research is necessarily the experiential self, in all its complexity. For this reason, I write my analyses in the first person singular. I find that only as an experiential self in active engagement with my surroundings can I give a proper account of the reading experience. Perhaps surprisingly, a posthumanist sensitivity to nonhuman things cultivates, in my lived body, a somewhat humanist sensibility: that only as a human can I explore the world. The posthumanist mode of engagement, however, estranges and reconfigures what it is to be that human. I find that I am not merely a subject, a sociocultural creature, but also an organism, an assemblage of nonhuman forces, and a node in a vast network of interacting entities. As that node, I can explore the network. Moreover, I find that the first-person approach is necessary for effectively communicating the experiential changes that occur during reading.

I propose that the combination of posthumanist and enactivist approaches enables a literary scholar to conduct *first-person, more-than-human exploratory work* that investigates the constitution of readerly experience by attending to the bodily feelings that arise during the reading event, especially when such experience is deliberately altered by the affective technologies of both fiction and theory. This is the gist of *more-than-human reading*. From the perspective of more-than-human reading, one could ask, for example: What happens to reading if one considers the reading body as a more-than-human collective, in which the text is one participant? What happens to reading if one practices sensitivity to the dynamic constitution of one's experiential states, such as moods or bodily feelings, in engagement with physical environments as well as with the virtual environments of fiction? The core activity of more-than-human reading is to *experience, recognize, and describe bodily feelings and responses during the reading experience*, and this activity is contextualized by a complex view of embodied subjectivity and reading as a bodily practice.

I suggest that this mode of exploration can complement existing approaches such as ecocriticism or narrative studies by developing (1) a certain phenomenological awareness of one's material and embodied implicatedness in the reading process, (2) a certain phenomenological awareness of the more-than-human extratextual materialities emerging as salient in particular reading events, and (3) an understanding of the human subject as part of collaborative, more-than-human, ever-shifting networks. Moreover, mingling and mixing with posthumanist feminist thinking can bring a healthy dose of the experimental attitude to cognitive literary studies. Especially when operating within the enactivist framework that emphasizes the conception of the cognizing subject as a skillful animal exploring its environment, it seems logical that a scholar engaging in such thinking would consider themself an active, creative, dynamically affected, and mutable being, and systematically explore that experiential configuration.

1.3 Outline

Each chapter of the book is structured around reading a particular work of recent American ecological science fiction. In Chapter 2, I show how Greg

Bear's *Darwin's Children* (2003) downplays the radical potential brought on by its mutant protagonist by naturalizing the strangeness of mutant embodiment as just another step in the progress of human evolution. In Bear's novel, the activation of a retrovirus inherent in the human genome brings forth a whole generation of genetically altered children. The novel foregrounds the nonhuman entities and processes inhabiting and constituting the human body, constructing humans as multispecies ecosystems or, in Bear's analogy, "spaceships for bacteria" (Bear 2003: 376). The novel encourages readers to empathize and identify with a mutant figure, but eventually undermines the transformative aspects of such engagements by naturalizing the initially strange aspects of mutant embodiment and presenting an affective vision of universal humanity that is grounded on familial unity.

In Chapter 2, I also outline an approach that brings forth the embodied experientiality of reading. The key idea is that different texts evoke and cultivate different kinds of experientiality, and repeated engagement with any particular type of text trains the reader in attuning to the experiential qualities particular to that type. As demonstrated by the reading of Bear's novel, science fiction can estrange human-centered experiential structures. In the chapter, I also introduce the method of *more-than-human reading*, which draws on both posthumanist and enactivist approaches and focuses on analytical reading as a bodily skill.

In Chapter 3, I discuss how mutant figures complicate bodily reading by estranging naturalized forms of embodied experience. I begin with a brief overview of mutant narratives and mutant figures in the wider context of twentieth- and twenty-first-century Anglo-American science fiction. Mutant figures are considered, from the perspective of embodied cognition, as potential sites for contesting the habitual experiential patterns that separate minds from bodies and humans from nonhumans. In reading mutant figures, I focus primarily on their bodily affectivity rather than their psychological aspects, which further develops the method of more-than-human reading. As a means of considering how more-than-human reading benefits from focusing on *kinesic* and *kinetic* aspects of readerly engagement (Sheets-Johnstone 2011; Bolens 2012; Cave 2016), the chapter discusses N. K. Jemisin's novel *The Fifth Season* (2015).

In Chapter 4, I analyze Paolo Bacigalupi's short story "The People of Sand and Slag" (2004) and the novel *The Windup Girl* (2009) from a more-than-human perspective and introduce the concept of *readerly choreography*. Bacigalupi utilizes bioengineered figures to demonstrate and criticize how capitalist power dynamics shape human and nonhuman bodies, and turns readers toward their own affective engagement with fictional figures by employing blatantly manipulative narrative strategies. His stories strategically employ violent affects and gendered stereotypes to further their environmentalist and anticapitalist agenda. I argue that focusing on such readerly choreographies, or genre-typical patterns of bodily feelings evoked in reading, amplifies the experientiality of the narrative and enables interpretations that are sensitive to the more-than-human aspects of the reading process.

The joint theoretical contribution of Chapters 3 and 4 is a posthumanist reevaluation of how we read characters. Engaging with the previous work in cognitive literary studies, I argue that theories of literary character lean disproportionately on a historical conception of human minds as disembodied or individually bounded, and on an evaluation of fictional characters based on the fullness of their "inner lives," that is, their "roundness" (see, e.g., Hochman 1985; Vermeule 2010). I propose that reading "flat" and type-based characters as affective figures can contribute to a posthumanist understanding of human minds as collective and more-than-human.

In Chapter 5, I focus on literary strategies of estranging ecological experience with the help of Jeff VanderMeer's *The Southern Reach* trilogy (*Annihilation*, *Authority*, and *Acceptance*, all published in 2014). The trilogy combines elements of science fiction, horror, and Weird fiction into intense figurations of mutant bodies, nonhuman agency, and more-than-human experience. I consider *The Southern Reach* trilogy in the context of Weird and New Weird fiction and propose that it gives rise to experiential change that could be described as *embodied estrangement*. In VanderMeer's work, the defamiliarization of human bodies and perception is a means of navigating nonhuman agency and more-than-human ecologies. I argue that *Annihilation* in particular offers its readers a readerly choreography that allows them to live through bodily feelings associated with encountering the monstrous nonhuman, and thus enables them to move closer to an acceptance of *groundlessness* as a lived condition. *Authority* and *Acceptance*, on the other hand, develop an understanding of embodied experience as more-than-human by their use of haunting experiential motifs. *Acceptance*, in particular, also invites its readers to experience embodied estrangement as an ongoing part of everyday life. With such mutant narratives, there is no escape from the troubling conventions of human exceptionalism, exploitation of othered bodies, and human embodied condition.

Gathering together the threads of the whole book in Chapter 6, I present the practices of more-than-human reading and writing as means of practicing posthumanist sensitivities. The final chapter sets the central argument in the larger context of the ongoing socioecological transformation. I propose that a more-than-human take on readerly experience configures the human-centered and destructive aspects of Anthropocene cultures as collective, more-than-human, material, and bodily habits that can be gradually estranged and reconfigured by bodily practices. Reading mutant narratives is one such bodily practice.

Notes

1. *Anthropocene* denotes a geological epoch that follows the Holocene, an epoch that is marked by the fact that human activity and agency have made a geologically significant trace on the Earth's crust (Crutzen and Stoermer 2000). The term is also widely adopted by scholars in the humanities and social sciences, as well as by artists and journalists, to denote the unprecedented impact humanity has made on the natural world in the industrial age (see, e.g., Chakrabarty 2009; Ghosh 2016). In criticism, the term has been accused of rendering invisible both the differences within and between human populations (see Palsson et al. 2013; Malm 2018) and nonhuman agency (see Alaimo 2016: 143–68).
2. The crisis of humanism is the driving force behind many contemporary philosophical approaches such as the different critiques of classical humanism (see Soper 1985; Sheehan 2003) and interdisciplinary work in fields such as ecocriticism, posthumanism (see Wolfe 2010; Nayar 2014), cognitive literary studies (see Zunshine 2006; Cave 2016; Kukkonen 2019), Darwinist literary studies (see Carroll 2004; Boyd 2009), human animal studies (see Wolfe 2010), and feminist philosophy of science (see Haraway 1991; Åsberg, Koobak, and Johnson 2011). Lately, much of the conversation has revolved around the concept of the Anthropocene, delineating the crisis of humanism as inseparable from the global ecological crisis (see, e.g., Trexler 2015; Clark 2015; Weik von Mossner 2016; LeMenager 2017; Vermeulen 2020; Caracciolo 2021). For a discussion specifically on the complex relations of Enlightenment, humanism, and posthumanism, see Wolfe (2010: xii–xxxiv).
3. In another context, Clark (2015: 148) also refers to the phenomenon of terrestriality as "the phantasm of normality." Terrestriality is thus bound not only to the condition of human embodiment, but also to the naturalized conceptions of such a condition.
4. In the book, I use both *readers* and the first person singular to refer to reading experience. *Readers* is used in instances when I discuss the experience provided by the fictional narrative in question on a more general level. In sections that discuss reading using the first person singular, I am referring to reading as it unfolds in my

particular embodied experience. In these instances, I provide some context for the specific material and environmental actors that participate in the experience.

5   On the interplay between imperialism, advanced capitalism, and misanthropy especially relating to *The Peripheral*, see Vermeulen (2019: 165–71).

6   As a hard science fiction novel that purposefully discusses scientific developments by means of fictional narrative, *Darwin's Children* also explicitly builds on the evolutionary-theoretical notions of symbiogenesis (Margulis and Sagan 2002) and punctuated equilibrium (Eldredge and Gould 1972).

7   Moreover, most of the narratives I discuss feature female figures written by male authors, and those figures tend to reiterate gendered stereotypes. Chapter 4 delves into this theme.

8   Experimental *mutant identities* or *mutant subjectivities* are a matter of their own. There are several individuals and groups of people who deliberately expose themselves to nuclear radiation with the aim of altering their subjectivity. I have no knowledge of whether mutant narratives are involved in such experiments. See, for example, "The Woman who Ate Chernobyl's Apples" (https://www.atlasobscura.com/articles/the-woman-who-ate-chernobyl-s-apples/); Joseph Masco, *The Nuclear Borderlands: The Manhattan Project in Post-Cold War New Mexico* (Princeton, NJ: Princeton University Press, 2006), and Magdalena E. Stawkowski, "'I Am a Radioactive Mutant': Emergent Biological Subjectivities at Kazakhstan's Semipalatinsk Nuclear Test Site." *American Ethnologist*, 43(1) (2016): 144–57. I thank Alison Sperling for bringing these sources to my attention.

9   While both posthumanism and enactivism are relatively recent movements in themselves, they draw on the long histories of feminist, phenomenological, and systems-theoretical inquiry, among others.

10 Throughout the book, *defamiliarization* is used to denote narrative techniques and *estrangement* to denote experiential change.

2

More-than-Human Reading and Experiential Change

How could mutant narratives help their readers develop modes of more-than-human experience and thus take part in the larger project of building ecologically viable cultures? I argue that such development can be aided by the practice of more-than-human reading. In this chapter, I outline the practice, showing how it differs from close reading and human-centered modes of reading. To begin with, I suggest that we let go of two presuppositions: considering science fictional narratives as (more or less accurate) representations of reality and assuming that reading is similar to viewing something from the outside. Rather, we may think of them as *systems to think and feel with*—instead of vision, more suitable cognitive metaphors for the act of reading could be *inhabiting a space* or *operating a vehicle*.

The anti-representational stance invites attention to the many ways in which readers act together with the narratives they read. Every science fictional narrative invites the reader to adopt what Donna Haraway calls a "generous but suspicious" receptive posture: a willingness to accept the existence, internal logic, and affective appeal of the fictional world, and an awareness of its fictionality, in the best cases laced with a curiosity about the construction and ideological weight of the world (Haraway 1992: 326; see also Polvinen 2023). As such, science fictional narratives promise to develop the metanarrative skills of the reader, making it easier to question the sincerity or naturality of any kind of story, be it framed as fictional, journalistic, scientific, or political.

Both Hayles and Haraway invite attention to the particular bodies, environments, and contexts that participate in reading situations. Careful studies of particular bodily experiences can inform narrative theory in ways that universalizing strategies cannot. In the context of this book, they can develop a more detailed understanding of the material and more-than-human aspects of narrative.

2.1 Starting Points

Two basic ideas inform my approach to experience and reading. Firstly, I start from the premise that cognition is not just embodied but *enactive*, that is, it is shaped in constant interaction with its environments. Secondly, and entwined with the first premise, all experience and action take place in *existentially groundless* circumstances.

2.1.1 Enactive Minds

The *embodied mind* is a concept that travels over disciplinary borders—between philosophy of mind, cognitive science and neuroscience, psychology and sociology, technology studies, as well as research on arts, culture, and literature, in what is sometimes called cognitive humanities.[1] It suggests that the human mind is embodied and embedded in the world and hence is not reducible to neurological functions in the brain—or to any other object-like definition. As mentioned already, the enactivist framework in particular considers minds as dynamic processes rather than stable objects: meaning and experience emerge in the continuous reciprocal interactions of the brain, the body, and the world. This is a model in which minds, bodies, and environments are constituted by each other in a way that renders all three concepts somewhat different from their traditional connotations.[2]

Perhaps the most widely influential notion presented by the contemporary enactive approach is that there can be no "entirely inert, inactive perceiver" (Noë 2004: 12)—the kind of cerebral *cogito* much of Western philosophy and much of twentieth-century cognitive science are grounded on. The "4E" paradigm of cognition focus on *embodied, embedded, enactive,* and *extended* aspects of cognition (Menary 2009; Stewart, Gapenne, and DiPaolo 2010), and the enactive approach in particular promotes the idea that many cognitive actions involve *skillful activity* (Noë 2004; Gallagher and Zahavi 2007). For example, perceiving "isn't something that happens in us, it is something we do" (Noë 2004: 216; see also O'Regan and Noë 2001).[3] Thus neural activity is considered necessary but not sufficient for perceiving or having perceptual experience—rather, in the enactive approach, perceiving is "realized in the active life of the skilful animal" (Noë 2004: 227).

Alva Noë (2004: 78) asks his readers to consider a commonplace event: seeing a circular plate from an oblique angle (e.g., a clock on the wall). The plate looks elliptical, even though you know it is in fact circular. Noë argues that one perceives both the (actual) circular shape and the (apparent) elliptical shape simultaneously, and thus the *potential for bodily movement* is already present in the act of perception. The example also highlights the role of *appearances* in perception. According to Noë, perception is always permeated by variations of perspectival properties, such as the varying ellipticality of the perceived plate. These variations are how we find out about an object as we move with it: therefore, temporary appearances do not obscure "the true nature" of physical reality but, on the contrary, they are what our knowledge of physical reality is based on (Noë 2004: 86; see also Gibson 1979).[4] In Noë's (2015: 10, emphasis in original) more recent articulation, seeing, as well as other kinds of perception, is "the *organized activity* of achieving access to the world around us."

The enactive approach could be characterized as the exploration of "the active life" of Noë's (2004: 227) "skilful animal." This entails maintaining an awareness of the whole embodied and situated being as the subject of cognition (Thompson 2007), and thus reconfiguring the models of mind developed in the more cerebral approaches (most prominently, computationalism and connectionism). The generative dilemma in the center of this conception is an epistemological and a methodological one: if minds are dynamic processes rather than stable objects, how should one study them? Evan Thompson (2009) stages the initial dilemma of enactive thought between representation and experience:

> It is one thing to have a scientific representation of the mind as "enactive"—as embodied, emergent, dynamic, and relational; as not homuncular and skull-bound; and thus in a certain sense as insubstantial. But it's another thing to have a corresponding direct experience of this nature of the mind in one's own first-person case. In more phenomenological terms, it's one thing to have a scientific representation of the mind as participating in the "constitution" of its intentional objects; it's another thing to see such constitution at work in one's lived experience. (Thompson 2009: 78)

The solution to this dilemma, first presented in the seminal book that first introduced the term *enactive cognition*, *The Embodied Mind*, and since developed independently by both Varela and Thompson, has been to engage in contemplative practices of the Buddhist kind while also continuing to study neural processes by means of objective science. Thompson reports that Francisco Varela believed first-person investigation of the enactive mind to be crucial for the development of this line of thought. Without it, he thought, neurophilosophers would "fall prey to one or another extreme view—either denying experience in favor of theoretical constructions or denying scientific insight in favor of naive and uncritical experience" (Thompson 2009: 78). This dilemma is alive in the field of neurophenomenology, in which experiential accounts of cognizing are combined with neuroscientific experiments, as well as in experiential research of contemplative practices (see Varela 1996; Thompson 2014).

For a literary scholar, this dilemma is not necessarily quite as difficult to resolve. Literary research is made in the first person by default—as a field, it is dependent on the analytical readings made by skilled and trained individuals who develop their collective knowledge through established academic procedures. The ambiguous and subjective qualities of cultural phenomena are not only accepted but celebrated, even with the perpetual argument over the social, economic, and philosophical value of such a mode of knowledge. The work done in the development of reception theory and reader-response criticism shows that personal experience is highly relevant to literary studies (see Richards 1929; Barthes 1974; Iser 1978, 1993; Fish 1980; Jauss 1982; Rosenblatt 1995), even if the experience in question is rarely ascribed to the scholars themselves, or to a specific embodied subject of any kind. Contemporary approaches in literary studies that draw on cognitive science and philosophy of mind (as well as from affective science and affect theory) can critically build on such traditions. Insights found in feminist and ecocritical approaches can also contribute to the understanding of embodied cognition and narrative (see, e.g., Warhol 2003; Easterlin 2012; Troscianko 2014; James 2015; Weik von Mossner 2017a).[5]

For the second-generation approach to literature and cognition, reading is always a bodily practice, and it necessarily involves some amount of experiential change. Fictional texts, as well as nonfiction, contain various suggestive cues that guide the embodied reader to adopt stances, positions, and attitudes toward the texts themselves, the imaginative realities they evoke, and the experiential realities of everyday life. According to the enactivist approach, this action is reciprocal: texts provide cues and guidance, but readers are always actively involved in the meaning-making process (see Caracciolo 2014c; Kukkonen and Caracciolo 2014; Polvinen 2023). Therefore, and against the grain of much research associated with cognitive science, the enactivist approach to literature and cognition considers any claims about linearly causal "effects" of literature on readers too narrow in scope. Rather, the interest literature holds for the enactivist framework lies in its capability to move readers on the level of the whole cognitive system, that is, the embedded and extended subject.

From a posthumanist perspective, the embedded and extended subject found in enactivist theory can also be viewed as *more-than-human*. By considering experience as interplay between cognizers, their backgrounds, and their environments (Caracciolo 2014c), it already diverts from the traditionally narrow focus on cognition and narrative as primarily social and psychological phenomena. The notion of situated embodiment necessarily accepts and includes more-than-human materiality and brings forth the bodies, spaces, substances, and processes co-constituting lived experience.

As I will discuss in the sections that follow, posthumanist approaches to literature take this material aspect of reading further. They acknowledge nonhuman elements both in the textual design and in the situations in which meanings are generated, such as the reading event. Moreover, they approach fiction with the conviction that humanity, as both a conceptual entity and a biological species, is constituted by complex networks of human and nonhuman beings. Informed by systems theory and allied with critical humanist approaches (including feminism, postcolonialism, monster studies, critical race studies, and disability studies), posthumanist studies of literature display the patterning of humanity and nonhumanity in the texts they discuss.

Whereas the cognitive approach to literature, and especially the more scientifically oriented strands of it, tends to construct general theories about universally shared or biologically basic cognitive patterns of "the reading mind," the posthumanist approach tends to criticize universalizing practices and articulate the genealogies of specific social imaginaries and material instances of meaning-making.[6] Due to this difference in positioning, they also tend to support very different takes on academic writing: the cognitive approach prefers to distance the author from the text, whereas the posthumanist approach sees the two as irrevocably entangled. Combining the two approaches thus entails a significant tension. In my view, the tension is a generative one: the combination orients research toward questioning both evolutionary-biological and social-constructionist assumptions about "human nature," and toward conducting detailed, contextualized readings of texts and cultural patterns. Both approaches challenge the scholar to articulate how the biological/material and the social/cultural are entangled in human meaning-making practices. A combined approach must thus remain reflective at all times, restraining itself from generalizations that come too easily.

2.1.2 Groundlessness

Crucially, when operating within enactivist and posthumanist frameworks, neither the reading bodies nor their environments can be considered stable: rather, they should be considered dynamic and processual. This is not only a theoretical matter, but an existential state with wide-ranging philosophical and cultural consequences, which will become more and more relevant as major environmental upheavals continue to transform human and more-than-human lifeworlds.

In *The Embodied Mind*, Francisco Varela, Evan Thompson, and Eleanor Rosch discuss how nineteenth- and twentieth-century developments in both evolutionary studies and cognitive science have highlighted the profound instability of human life. In Western thought, the realization of instability has not been easy: despite the broadly accepted science-based view that sees individuals and species as being shaped by the flows of developmental and evolutionary change and recognizes human cognition as a limited and somewhat unreliable way of making sense of the world, Western individuals still tend to *experience* themselves as stable, free agents navigating largely predictable worlds—that is, as "liberal humanist subjects" (see, e.g., Hayles 2006: 160). Varela, Thompson, and Rosch describe the result of this cognitive dissonance as *cognitivist nihilism*, defined in Nietzschean terms as "the situation in which we know that our most cherished values are untenable, and yet we seem incapable of giving them up" (Varela, Thompson, and Rosch 1992: 128).

Since the 1990s, the notion of existential instability has received increasing attention. The belief in grounded worlds and selves has become harder and harder to hold on to, even in the West: Europe and the United States have seen multiple societal and economic crises (e.g., the collapse of the Soviet Union, the 2008 financial crisis, the 2020–23 Covid-19 pandemic, and the 2022 Russian attack on Ukraine) and the ecological devastation linked to climate change (e.g. heat waves in Southern and Central Europe, Hurricane Katrina, the California wildfires, and loss of common bird and insect species), which severely undermine the notion of a stable environment, and, arguably, the notion of a stable self too.

Varela, Thompson, and Rosch (1992) also claim that the emerging realization of existential instability gives rise to a sense of *groundlessness*.[7] According to them, the articulations of both science and poststructuralist philosophy have failed to produce a positive model of groundless experience—one that does not rely on either a pregiven world or a permanent self but accepts change as an ontological and experiential principle. What is missing in the Western tradition, for the authors, are *experiential practices*. As a starting point for developing such practices, and means for coping with existential instability, they propose a framework of enactive cognition.

While I will not attempt a comprehensive review of philosophical approaches to existential instability, I will include posthumanist perspectives on processual ontology, material agency, and more-than-human subjectivity. *The Embodied Mind* briefly mentions the poststructuralist work on rethinking subjectivities, but it does not discuss or criticize it at length. It advocates a science-based broad view of selfless cognition and mutual enfoldment of self and world, and the "second-generation" cognitive framework developed in the last twenty years tends to follow its lead. However, if we wish to develop models and practices that cultivate groundless modes of lived experience, it is necessary to learn from approaches that work with situatedness, particularity, and the more-than-human world. In this book, I draw on posthumanist feminisms and new materialisms.

2.2 More-than-Human Subjectivity

Enactivist and posthumanist approaches to literature are rooted in enactivist and posthumanist conceptions of embodiment, subjectivity, selfhood, and agency. Both strains of theory revolve around various modes of change, such as adaptation, coevolution, niche construction, materialization, becoming, and performativity. As living beings and cognitive agents, embodied subjects are generated in ongoing reciprocal interaction with their environments. Outlining enactivist and posthumanist conceptions of subjectivity will pave the way to a working understanding of what takes place in subjective experience and bodily activity—such as reading.

2.2.1 From Gendered Subjectivity to More-than-Human Subjectivity

If mutant narratives contain the potential for estranging and reconfiguring one's embodied experience, it would seem that they do so only when encountered in attentive and responsive ways. A posthumanist outlook makes it possible to view human subjectivity as something both culturally and materially produced, and also to experientially attend to such production as it unfolds. I argue in this chapter that it enables a scholarly reader to open up to the potentially transformative engagements with mutant narratives.

Personal experience is, however, a challenge to posthumanist practices. If posthumanist practices seek to unhinge the notion of a stable, sovereign humanist subject, what else is there to work with? What is the locus of experience? Posthumanist scholars too work from specific situated standpoints centered on some forms of experiential selfhood, but how do they distance such standpoints from the forms of subjectivity they critically target?

Posthumanist feminism (or *feminist posthumanism*, or plural forms of both terms) provides partial answers to the challenge. Judith Butler's *performative gender* and Rosi Braidotti's *materialist theory of becoming* are particularly influential in posthumanist feminist theorization of subjectivity, and reviewing them lays the ground for the methodological considerations at the core of this chapter. With its deep roots in critiques of humanistic ideals and androcentrism, feminist theory helps us to delve deeper into topics relevant to both posthumanism and cognitive literary studies: bodily materiality, cultural construction of embodied experience, and the dynamics of subjective and collective change (see Åsberg, Koobak, and Johnson 2011; Braidotti 2013: 24–6; Neimanis 2017: 10–12). Reviewing Butler's and Braidotti's materialist notions of subjective change also provides context for Donna Haraway's (1992, 2008, 2016) technique of *figuration* and its potential for cognitive literary studies.

Posthumanist feminism draws on the history of *poststructuralist feminism*. Poststructuralist feminism has advanced the idea that gendered identities and subjectivities, along with the experiential understanding of one's embodiment, are produced through participation in linguistic communities. This idea opposes the conception of subjects preceding language and claims that there are no fixed or stable identities (Nayar 2014: 17; see also Callus, Herbrechter, and Rossini 2014).

The poststructuralist feminist conception of subjectivity has been problematized by *the material turn* in feminism, which holds on to the social constructivist view but questions the primary role of language in the production of identities and subjectivities. Instead, it foregrounds the material elements that participate in the formation of bodies and identities, including biological, technological, economic, and ecological elements (see Barad 2003; Alaimo 2010; Bennett 2010; Åsberg, Koobak, and Johnson 2011). In their introduction to the collection *New Materialisms*, Diana Coole and Samantha Frost (2010) describe new materialism as a turn away from linguistic and discursive forms of social constructivism, for which "overtures to material reality are dismissed as an insidious foundationalism" (Coole and Frost 2010: 6). New materialists consider matter and its forms as active in themselves, not as blank slates subjected to human inscription of meaning. While subscribing to this notion, Coole and Frost acknowledge the value of social constructivist analyses of power, and propose a hybrid form of critical thinking, *critical materialism*, that appreciates the dynamicity and force of both social and material processes (Coole and Frost 2010: 27).

I admire Coole and Frost's aim toward a balanced approach and hope, in this section, to develop similar balance between notions of *bodily materiality* and *performative gender*. The tension between these notions, in feminist theory, is bound to the same major themes as certain discussions in the cognitive framework: how could we think of minds and bodies without rigid dualist scaffoldings and how should we account for the biological and physical dynamics at work in human life?

The notion of performative gender is often traced back to the work of Judith Butler. For Butler (1990: 112), "gender ought not to be conceived as a noun or a substantial thing or a static cultural marker, but rather as an incessant and repeated action." Repetitive performative action shapes the physical contours of human bodies, in a process that Butler calls *materialization*. One learns, mostly unwittingly, to express gender: to walk like a woman, to stand like a man, to compose one's face in socially acceptable expressions—and, through repetition, these movements of the body, as well as gender categories, become stabilized. Rather than discussing predetermined subjects, this approach discusses events in which all participants are produced, shaped, and turned. The notion is broadly accepted in contemporary societies, and its cultural impact is a prime example of how conceptual work can shape both society and embodied experience.

According to some critics, including Rosi Braidotti (2002: 33; see also Gatens 1996), Butlerian gender theory "tacitly assumes a passive body on which special codes are imprinted." Braidotti traces this model of gender to the social-psychological roots and Anglo-American historical context of gender theory and claims that poststructuralist feminism, in the European context at least, generally employs a more dynamic and interactive notion of embodiment (Braidotti 2002: 32–3). Braidotti herself develops an approach she calls a *materialist theory of becoming*. In this theory, bodies already contain forces and intensities that ground the processes of subject formation and cannot be performatively shaped into just any form. The most prominent intensities lie in sexual difference, but Braidotti also brings up differences in other material groundings of bodies, such as location, language, or ethnicity (Braidotti 2002: 21, 27):

> Feminists cannot hope … merely to cast off their sexed identity like an old garment. Discursive practices, imaginary identifications or ideological beliefs are tattooed on bodies and thus are constitutive of embodied subjectivities. Thus, women who yearn for change cannot shed their old skins like snakes. This kind of in-depth change requires instead great care and attention. It also needs

to be timed carefully in order to become sustainable, that is to say in order to avoid lethal shortcuts through the complexities of one's embodied self. (Braidotti 2002: 26)

Braidotti (2002: 7) stresses that subjectivity should not be confused with individualism or particularity as, for her, subjectivity is a "socially mediated process" and the "emergence of new social subjects is always a collective enterprise, 'external' to the self while it also mobilizes the self's in-depth structures." She has characterized subjectivity as *fictional choreography*: a slowly changing network of habitual patterns and responses, materializing through repetitive action but mutable through careful imaginative work (Braidotti 2002: 22).

Braidotti's theory of experiential change informs my understanding of more-than-human reading in that it presents subjectivity as something not only socially and culturally mediated but also embedded in particular material and bodily situations. Within such a notion of subjectivity, it becomes possible to consider reading as a means of slow cultural and personal transformation. In Chapter 4, I will build on Braidotti's notion of fictional choreography to theorize how fiction suggests *readerly choreographies*. For now, I will focus on explicating a more general level of experiential change.

While Butler and Braidotti disagree on the issue of bodily materiality, I find their views on subject formation mutually complementary rather than oppositional. From a pragmatic perspective, the two views achieve two different sets of effects: Butler's gender performativity agitates subversive performative play in spite of traditional gender roles, whereas Braidotti's bodily materiality encourages one to attend to the complexities and contradictions of one's already-sexed bodily state—and, perhaps, to slowly move toward new forms of subjectivity, in a mode resonating with Haraway's (2016) *staying with the trouble*. Thus, while Butler compellingly describes how subjects emerge in performative social processes and how identifying this dynamic can serve the emancipatory aims of feminism, Braidotti's account of subjectivity is more sensitive to the material constraints placed by the specific histories of individual and collective bodies. Both insights are valuable and necessary for a rounded and grounded view of processual subjectivity.

Through theorizing experiential change with the help of feminist thinkers, I aim to zoom in on the microlevel of experiencing specific events, such as reading a novel. In such events, the material, bodily, and social structures of gendered experience and feeling are iterated or creatively altered (see Warhol 2003). Viewed together, Butler's and Braidotti's work gives rise to a notion of embodied subjectivity as a network of habitual patterns, thoroughly entangled in material processes and social imaginaries.⁸ Carrying this complex notion with me into particular readings, I hope to articulate the experientiality of reading in terms of minute changes in the habitual patterns of bodily feeling.

Despite this background in feminist theory, the main context of analysis in this book is not *gendered* subjectivity as such. Rather, my strategy is to build on feminist theorizing of gendered subjectivity and experiential change and apply it to other aspects of embodied subjectivity, particularly those related to human exceptionalism, thus enabling movement from these dominant figurations into more-than-human directions. From a posthumanist feminist perspective, "human" is a category as material-discursively constructed as "gender" (see Braidotti 2013; Hellstrand 2016). As feminists before me, I will focus my analyses of the category of "human" on border cases: figures that just barely, if at all, "pass as human" (see Koistinen 2015; Hellstrand 2016). Staying at the fuzzy and fluctuating borders of humanity makes it easier to see how the human and the nonhuman leak into each other, constituting each other as well as the boundary between.

One way to understand the material and transformative aspects of feminist conceptual work is to think of concepts as *figurations*, that is, as "material-semiotic knots" (Haraway 2008: 4–5) or "dramatizations of becoming" (Braidotti 2013: 164) that become part of our lived experience. Astrida Neimanis (2017: 5) describes figurations as "embodied concepts ... already here, semi-formed and literally at our fingertips, awaiting activation." In her helpful analysis of Haraway's figurations, Michelle Bastian (2006) describes figuration both as a technique for meaning-making and as the patterns of meaning that result from using such technique.

We might also think of figurations as a kind of *affective technology*. In her feminist take on narratology that draws on the work of Butler, Robyn Warhol (2003: 24) describes narrative techniques as "devices that work through readers' bodily feelings to produce and reproduce the physical fact of gendered subjectivity." In Warhol's (2003: 10) model, the body is understood "not as the location where gender and affect are expressed, but rather as the medium through which they come into being." For Warhol, feelings are always socially and culturally constructed to some extent, and bodily events such as crying over a sentimental novel are considered in terms of *generating* rather than *expressing* feelings.⁹

Butler's notion of performative gender is an apt example of successful feminist figurative work, at least in the pragmatic sense, as it has become widely accepted among the younger generations of contemporary Western societies.

Performative gender has nourished the use of linguistic markers of variating sexual identities and orientations (cis, trans, etc.), and it has materialized in lived bodies not only at the intersubjective level of habitus and gesture, but often also at the sociotechnological level of anatomical modification. One of the main theoretical ideas in this book is that literature can do similar figurative work. I will get back to this in later sections.

2.2.2 The Enactivist View of Organismic Selfhood

Posthumanist feminist views on subjectivation are largely compatible with the second-generation approach to cognition. Even if the constituent theoretical traditions are quite different, both strains of thought arrive at the same challenge: how can the theoretical understanding of human subjectivity be reconfigured in ways that can account for its dynamic emergence in material environments? The paradigm cases for both traditions aim to challenge static models with dynamic ones: the second-generation cognitive approach seeks to develop models of perception and cognition that focus on the entire living organism rather than just the brain, and the posthumanist approach seeks to replace notions of detached, essentialized human subjects with more-than-human, processual subjectivities.

Enactivism is concerned with living beings and their dynamic relationships with environments. Cognition is characterized in terms of bodily processes that involve embodied experience and coupling with environments. But how do the basic notions of enactive theory compare with the principles of posthumanist feminist performativity introduced earlier?

The enactivist view draws on evolutionary biology. For enactivists, "organism and environment are mutually enfolded in multiple ways, and so what constitutes the world of a given organism is enacted by that organism's history of structural coupling" (Varela, Thompson, and Rosch 1992: 202). *Structural coupling*, a systems-theoretical term here applied to the biological context of coevolution, refers to developments in which organisms of a species coevolve with organisms of another species, or with other features of their environment such as habitats. A well-known example to illustrate a "history of structural coupling" is the capacity of the microbes in human guts to digest lactose from bovine milk—a capacity still lacking in regions of the world not accustomed to breeding cattle (see Nuismer 2017).

Whereas coevolution usually refers to evolution of anatomical traits such as the digestive abilities of gut flora, the emphasis of the enactivist approach—and the more elaborate term *mutual specification of organism and environment*—is on how perception and cognition are shaped in coevolutionary processes. Richard Lewontin's famous example of bee-and-bat senses highlights this aspect:

> Our central nervous systems are not fitted to some absolute laws of nature, but to laws of nature operating within a framework created by our own sensuous activity. Our nervous system does not allow us to see the ultraviolet reflections from flowers, but a bee's central nervous system does. And bats "see" what nighthawks do not. We do not further our understanding of evolution by general appeal to "laws of nature" to which all life must bend. Rather, we must ask how, within the general constraints of the laws of nature, organisms have constructed environments that are the conditions for their further evolution and reconstruction of nature into new environments. (Lewontin 1983, cited in Varela, Thompson, and Rosch 1992: 202)

Moreover, Varela, Thompson, and Rosch bring the notion of mutual specification to the level of individual perceivers in asking how experiential worlds are both constrained by the biological histories of structural coupling and constantly being reconfigured in everyday perceptual actions. This work has been carried on by cognitive scientists and philosophers such as Daniel Hutto, Michelle Maiese, Giovanna Colombetti, and Alva Noë.

In the enactivist framework, then, living is never merely static existing but an ongoing process of self-regeneration, or *autopoiesis*, in metabolism and movement: "Living beings are autonomous systems that actively generate and maintain their identities" (Colombetti and Thompson 2008: 55–6). In living activity, the organism is generated as a *self*. Michelle Maiese calls this kind of basic identity "sensorimotor subjectivity" and argues that it necessarily involves an egocentric, spatial, and temporal structure (Maiese 2015: xi):

> To stay alive, the living system must establish itself as a unity located in space, and also must make sense of the world and renew itself in order to survive. Self-regeneration and metabolism propel a living organism forward in time, beyond its present condition and toward a future moment when the organism's needs might be satisfied. Thus, the basic sense that "I am here now" is rooted in the dynamic space-time process of autopoiesis. (Maiese 2015: xii)

It would seem, then, that enactivism upholds the conception of a central self based on biological organization, a necessarily stable point of reference incompatible with postmodern notions of fluid boundaries and discursively produced subjects. On a closer look, we have to (1) distinguish between the biological self and the cultural subject and (2) admit reciprocal feedback between these levels, and dynamic change in the overall organization of self-centered experience.

Thus, even if the conception of selfhood that enactivism sketches seems to promote stability by being rooted in individual biological bodies, the conception is not, in fact, based on any essential quality but rather on the principle of *activity*. Living beings "don't just passively process pre-existing information from the world but they bring forth or enact their own cognitive spheres in ongoing, continuous reciprocal interaction with their environment" (Colombetti and Thompson 2008: 55–6). Such continuous reciprocal interaction—be that metabolism, niche construction, social interaction, or reading—is where bodies, as living beings and cognitive agents, are generated. There is no neutral, object-like self. Rather, selves adapt and change. This is also for the simple reason that maintaining a self necessarily involves *care* and *desire*—for the organism itself and for its immediate environment.

> Among living animals like us, this egocentric, spatio-temporal orientation is bound up with the capacity for perception, movement, and intentionality. Indeed, one's awareness of oneself as a single coherent being consists not only in proprioceptive awareness of one's body, but also in the awareness of oneself as the author and source of movement. And in my view, the reason why the body serves as a point of convergence of perception and action is that the body is *the locus for desiring and caring*. From the time that we are infants, everything that appears to us *as* something is necessarily *valenced*. Objects or events attract or repulse us, we are provoked by what strikes us, and we experience ourselves as affected by our surroundings. For objects and events to matter, there must be a sense of an "I" or "me" to whom they matter. (Maiese 2015: xii, emphases in original)

Enactivism begins from acknowledging the phenomenological truth of there being a sense of self in its minimal formulation: the sense of being a body, and an "author and source of movement" (see also Sheets-Johnstone 2011). But a self is not the body: rather, it is a mode of organization, realized in the ongoing process of activity—that is, *life*. It is this dynamism that also makes enactivism compatible with poststructuralist approaches to subjectivity. Enactivism acknowledges that while biological organization is guided by relatively stable organismic and species-specific patterns, most likely including a minimal sense of the body as "the locus for desiring and caring," selfhood is also something that emerges from the varying contextual circumstances of the living being, which may well include social and cultural aspects.

In the enactivist framework, the logic of self-renewal in continuous reciprocal interaction with environments is described as a basic dynamic in all lifeforms. Yet it is also realized at the level of sociocultural subjectivity—which can be considered an ongoing material process of self-renewal. To rephrase Butler's and Braidotti's feminist thinking in enactivist terms, the notion of *materialization* elucidates the reciprocity between a living body and its environment. By constraining its actions according to social expectations and integrated belief systems, the living being enacts its cognitive sphere and, in effect, modifies its environment (e.g., the gendered practices in social situations). An environment is always already an experiential sphere or a *lifeworld* (Husserl 1970; see also Thompson 2007: 34–6). As Butler's and Braidotti's theorization effectively illustrates, these experiential spheres are never merely individual, but always collectively constituted, maintained, and renewed.

On the basis of such a view of enactive subjectivity, one can consider reading a process that *participates in the materialization of lived bodies*—like the patterns of physical exercise, gender expression, or eating. Engaging in repetitive patterns of reading, as described by Robyn Warhol (2003), may be considered not only as gradual change in the individual, but also as collective and ecological activity. The term *niche construction* provides a helpful image of such activity: an individual organism actively modifies its immediate environment (mental and cultural as well as physical) and thus effects changes in the living conditions of the future inhabitants of the environment (Laland and Brown 2006; Kukkonen 2019; see also Caracciolo 2016: 50–1).

With this slow material change in mind, we can consider how the notion of performativity is used to reconfigure the phenomenological method. Such phenomenology bridges the apparent gap between organismic selfhood and subjectivity.

2.2.3 More-than-Human Meanings

The term *more-than-human* dates back to the work of philosopher David Abram (1996). Drawing from Maurice Merleau-Ponty's phenomenology of the body and anthropological research in indigenous experience, Abram has developed a more-than-human approach to phenomenology.[10] He argues for a conception of human experience and perception that coemerges with the nonhuman environment. Before its more recent posthumanist usages, Abram used *more-than-human* to denote how experiential "lifeworlds" emerge in the interaction of humans and nonhumans.

Abram focuses particularly on the more-than-human aspects of language, arguing that nonhuman sounds are integral to the expressiveness of human language:

> If language is always, in its depths, physically and sensorially resonant, then it can never be definitively separated from the evident expressiveness of birdsong, or the evocative howl of a wolf late at night. The chorus of frogs gurgling in unison at the edge of a pond, the snarl of a wildcat as it springs upon its prey, or the distant honking of Canadian geese veeing south for the winter, all reverberate with affective, gestural significance, the same significance that vibrates through our own conversations and soliloquies, moving us at times to tears, or to anger, or to intellectual insights we could never have anticipated. Language as a bodily phenomenon accrues to all expressive bodies, not just to the human. (Abram 1996: 80)

Abram's take on phenomenology includes a participatory view of perception that will be developed in Chapter 3 in the context of enactivist theory. At this stage, however, I merely want to point out that Abram's more-than-human view of language opens up implications that he does not follow up—namely, the role of technological and cultural participants, such as literature and media. More keen on discussing orality, Abram presents a highly skeptical view of the technology of writing, arguing that the consolidation of language to alphabetical signs has severed the living relation between human experience and nonhuman nature. Abram's thinking, while insightful in its observations about perception, does not contribute much to posthumanist analyses of literature and reading.

Another more-than-human approach to phenomenology shows more promise. Possibly the most detailed posthumanist practice available for a cognitively bent scholar, the *posthuman feminist phenomenology* of Astrida Neimanis (2017), investigates lived experience beyond the comfortable boundaries of naturalized human subjectivity.

Neimanis's consistent project in the last decade has been the reimagination of human bodies as "bodies of water." This phrasing should be understood in a materialist sense: Neimanis has explored how water connects the lived human body to other bodies of water, such as rain, rivers, oceans, fish, and plant life. In her work, rethinking embodiment from an aquatic perspective becomes a way of amplifying the significance of water in the constitution of lived bodies. In its ethical rethinking of nonhuman bodies, Neimanis's practice resembles other posthumanist feminist conceptual work, such as Donna Haraway's (2008) *companion species* or Stacy Alaimo's (2010) *trans-corporeality*. Moreover, it provides an opening for considering literature as a participant in embodied experience, or as an affective technology.

2.3 More-than-Human Reading: A Model

In practicing more-than-human reading, one becomes aware of the material connections and cooperative loops salient to particular reading events. More-than-human reading could also be described as *embodied, experiential,* and *environmental close reading*. The method is informed by enactivist approaches to literature (Caracciolo 2014c; Kukkonen 2014; Troscianko 2014; Polvinen 2023), as well as the posthumanist approaches introduced earlier. My readerly awareness is thus shaped by two sets of theoretical constraints, the enactivist one dealing with the *experientiality of fiction* and the posthumanist one with *materiality*.

Lived experience is crucial to both of these approaches. The studies made in the second-generation cognitive framework construct a specific kind of reader: one who engages in reading emotionally and affectively without losing their interpretative abilities. The posthuman feminist phenomenological approach, on the other hand, is aimed particularly at developing more-than-human modes of engagement: environmental perception, attention to the dynamics of nonhuman materialities, and awareness of one's bodily entanglement with nonhuman things and processes.

My method, in its shortest formulation, is to become a reader who can incorporate and perform these relational and attentional skills, and articulate the resulting reading experience in enactivist and posthumanist terms. This is a somewhat circular process, as it both begins and ends in a more-than-human conception of embodied experience. I accept this circularity and stress that the focus of the methodology should not be seen to be on whether more-than-human embodied experience is *possible*—I begin from the assumption that it is—but on what exactly happens to reading when it is considered as bodily and more-than-human. The focus is thus on the particular process of reading science fictional texts in a more-than-human mode, and on the particular experiential dynamics that can be identified in the process.

As phenomenologist Matthew Ratcliffe (2010: 363), suggests, the body can be something through which we feel something else, or relate to the world, and bodily feelings can mediate that relating. In bodily performance, such as dance or sports, the feeling body "makes itself present via proprioception, kinesthesia, and even interoception" (Colombetti 2014: 122), while the focus of experience is on aspects of the surrounding world and not the body itself. I suggest that the reading body can also be such a performative body, present in the experience of reading but not the primary intentional object of awareness. Moreover, like other bodily skills, the skills of more-than-human reading can be consciously trained.

I have decided on this methodological aim of developing readerly skills on the basis that, despite the vast variety of theoretical frameworks and approaches, first-person readings still form the heart of literary research. A literary scholar is, first and foremost, an expert reader: a person trained in awareness to texts and their particular effects, in identification of context and tradition as well as linguistic phenomena. A literary scholar is someone who develops their sensibilities regarding the texts they encounter. Theory is a way for developing those sensibilities. Thus, I propose that synthesizing the enactivist understanding of the experientiality of fiction and the posthumanist feminist understanding of performative materialization into a more-than-human method can train a professional reader in the cultivation of the cognitive skills necessary to the task of first-person enactive engagement with literary works.

More-than-human reading involves a set of skills. I propose some theoretical and practical starting points for developing each skill. The skillset is by no means complete: I encourage all readers to expand on it and experiment with it. At this point, more-than-human reading is more a proposal than a fully-fledged method, and developing it further requires collective effort.

The first skill I describe is *close reading*. As an interpretative tradition, close reading is attuned to the particularities of the text, and thus it is often thought that contextualist approaches (such as posthumanist, feminist, or ecocritical approaches) are incompatible with the method. I will argue that this is not the case: close reading can involve attention to both contexts and subjective experience. In my mind, paying special attention to the affective aspects of readerly experience is key to more-than-human reading.

Close reading is a base for all the other skills needed to develop more-than-human reading: exploring embodied experience, interlacing readerly experience with environmental experience, amplifying bodily feelings, feeling the appeal of figurations, and dancing with the text (as suggested by its readerly choreography).

2.3.1 Read Closely and with Feeling

When aiming to figure out how literature can give rise to new and strange experiences, beginning from the experiences of actual readers would seem like a reasonable starting point. However, empirical studies of readerly experience surprisingly rarely inform either psychological theory or narrative theory. Even more rarely is the study of experience systematically included in the *methodology* of studying minds or reading. There appears to be a rift between the mind of the "lay" reader, immersed in the experience, and the mind of the theoretician, positioned in a detached space somewhere above or outside experience. As Troscianko (2013) and Polvinen (2017, 2023) have argued in the context of empirical reading studies, the lack of sufficient attention to readerly experience can lead researchers to uncritically adopt common presumptions about reading, which in turn can lead to "flawed experimental data about the exact [experiential] processes involved" (Polvinen 2017: 140).

In addition to neglecting the nuances of first-person readerly experience, "first-generation" approaches to readerly cognition often fail to include affect in their models of embodied sense-making. Affect is habitually separated from cognition and screened out from literary analysis. Reflecting the longer and wider history of conceiving thought only in terms of rationality, this tendency might be traced back to influential critiques made by the New Critics, especially "The Affective Fallacy" by William K. Wimsatt and Monroe Beardsley (1967). Wimsatt and Beardsley identify a trend in literary criticism, which they describe as "the affective fallacy": "a confusion between the poem and its results (what it is and what it does)" (Wimsatt and Beardsley 1967: 21). Affective fallacy, the authors continue, "begins by trying to derive the standard of criticism from the psychological effects of the poem and ends in impressionism and relativism" (Wimsatt and Beardsley 1967: 21). Their primary target is a particular kind of "romantic reader psychology" (Wimsatt and Beardsley 1967: 34) that focuses solely on the emotional experience of the critic, thus losing sight of the text itself. This kind of analysis, the authors claim, cannot get beyond the personal into the objective.

> The report of some readers … that a poem or story induces in them vivid images, intense feelings, or heightened consciousness, is neither anything which can be refuted nor anything which it is possible for the objective critic to take into account. The purely affective report is either too physiological or it is too vague. (Wimsatt and Beardsley 1967: 32)

It is undoubtedly true that focusing on the affective experientiality of narrative cannot meet the ideals of objective criticism. Such an approach does not treat the text as an object, but as a participant in experience. Contrary to popular belief in literature departments, literary theorists in the 1930s were already concerned with striking a careful balance between affectivity and analysis. Louise Rosenblatt, to give just one example, emphasized that the reader draws from their past experiences and identity: "each reader is unique, bringing to the transaction an individual ethnic, social, and psychological history" (Rosenblatt 1995: xix). As a result of this transaction, "literary experiences" are formed: aesthetic experiences that are based simultaneously on the text, the reader, and the reading environment. For Rosenblatt, the purpose of teaching literature is to develop the transaction between the reader and the text, and thus support the enhancement of literary experiences.[11]

The New Critical concern that the text and its detailed analysis are lost in the throes of scholarly passion is also left ungrounded in the current research climate. The second-generation cognitive critics seek to bring back affect, but not without losing their reflective and analytical capabilities, that is, their readings are not "purely" affective, as Wimsatt and Beardsley would put it. Troscianko (2014), Polvinen (2023), Kukkonen (2019), and others are developing *enactive reading styles* that systematically include experientiality (including affectivity) in their theoretical models. I will illustrate the notion of an enactive reading style with the help of an empirical example.

In an empirical phenomenological study on reader-response conducted by Don Kuiken, David S. Miall, and Shelley Sikora (Kuiken, Miall, and Sikora 2004; Sikora, Kuiken, and Miall 2011), the participants read a long poem. During and after reading, the participants filled in a structured questionnaire and provided commentaries on the text and their reading experience. Analyzing these responses, the authors identified several styles of reading, including a style of reading they call "expressive enactment" (Sikora, Kuiken, and Miall 2011: 263). In the responses of this style, readers described "transformations of meanings central to readers' experience of the poem," often referring to their bodily feelings and autobiographical memories, and using sensory language, metaphors, and expressions that blurred the boundaries between the fictional characters and the readers themselves.

The authors describe such a mode of engagement in terms of readers working with affective themes. Such themes recur throughout each reader's commentary, but they are constantly modified (or "enacted") as the participant develops his or her initial intuition about the personal relevance of the theme. This results in a movement "toward increasingly intricate and intimate personal understandings and progressive articulation of initially vague and inexpressible convictions" (Kuiken, Miall, and Sikora 2004: 193). The authors point out that expressive enactment differs from other modes of reader response in that it combines personal reflection with engagement with the formal features of the text (Sikora, Kuiken, and Miall 2011: 267). The transformative process of working with an affective theme takes the form of a loop that alternates between personal reflection and engaging with particular passages of the text, gradually getting deeper into the theme.[12]

Kuiken's, Miall's, and Sikora's study suggests that through this kind of dynamic engagement, reading can turn out to be a self-transforming process. Other empirical studies on readerly cognition suggest that reading fiction can help to effect changes in self-perception (Kuiken, Miall, and Sikora 2004; Sikora, Kuiken, and Miall 2011), personality traits (Djikic et al. 2009), environmental perception (Kuzmičová 2016), and behavior (Kaufman and Libby 2012). Studies focusing on reading groups also suggest that reading fiction is both affective and reflective, that interpretations develop over time, and that, at least in supportive environments, it can provide transformative experiences to readers (see Fialho, Zyngier, and Miall 2011; Longden et al. 2015; Polvinen and Sklar 2019; Meretoja, Kinnunen, and Kosonen 2022). Moreover, as reading is not only social but environmental too, physical surroundings also matter to reading experience: the bare rooms of research facilities might not be optimal settings for imaginative thinking and emotional engagement, and thus studies completed in such environments cannot capture the richness of readerly experience (Kuzmičová 2016).

Such studies offer insights into the dynamics of affective reading in general, but they can also inspire the development of more-than-human reading by providing examples of affective and enactive reading. From the enactive perspective, the crucial point is that the transformative effects of reading are not the doing of narratives in themselves, and neither are they products of imagination or personal will only. Rather, experiential and behavioral change requires active, skillful engagement with texts.

Merja Polvinen (2016, 2017) presents a helpful model for balancing the affective and critical aspects of close reading. In her work, the *double vision of fiction* is a mode of reading that allows emotional engagement and immersion but is simultaneously aware of fiction as an artifact (Polvinen 2016: 30). By foregrounding such a mode of engagement, Polvinen (2017: 139, 148) critiques some of the "apparently common-sense concepts" that empirical studies of reading often adopt, such as the notion of reading as immersion or transportation and the assumption that readers' emotional engagements with fiction can be reduced to "empathic identification with characters."

Countering such oversimplified views of readerly engagement, Polvinen (2017: 148) argues that "fictions are interactive cognitive environments that require from readers a combination of skills that is much more complex than traditionally computational cognitive sciences assume," and that both empirically and theoretically oriented studies of literature should "sharpen their own conceptual and theoretical apparatus" to better to attend to reading as skillful activity.

For a literary scholar, skillful reading entails striking a particular balance: an awareness of both the textual design and one's own experiential background, and the ability to tease out the dynamic processes between the two. Only by implementing such an awareness can a scholar distinguish between the experientiality of their personal reading and the experientiality of someone else's. Moreover, as we shall see in Section 2.3, experientiality is permeated by the contexts and intertexts salient to a particular reader. Professional reading thus requires focused attention and metacognitive skills. Caracciolo (2014a: 388) sees the interpretations formed during reading as "mostly pre-reflective (in the sense that readers make meaning without being aware of their own meaning-making activity)" whereas "the 'virtuoso' interpretations of literary criticism are maximally reflective." Professional readers thus need to balance their personal and pre-reflective experiences with more general and reflective views of the texts they read.

This is a balance that is necessarily achieved through careful practice.[13]

2.3.2 Explore Embodied Experience

Experience is "not an easy target for research, due to its dynamic, multisensory, situated, and uniquely subjective character" (Varis 2019b: 2; see also Caracciolo 2014b: 6, 14; Nagel 1974: 437). Broadly speaking, the term "experience" can encompass anything that falls under conscious attention, including thoughts, feelings, memories, impressions, and sensory experiences in all modalities. The boundary between conscious experience and nonconscious cognition is, however, remarkably porous and prone to change depending on mental habits, attention, and verbalization, among other factors. Echoing the entire history of phenomenology, psychologist Russell T. Hurlburt insists that experience as experienced in the moment, or *pristine experience*, is not the same as verbalized experience or experience when reflected upon after the fact, which both fall under the umbrella of *broad experience* (Caracciolo and Hurlburt 2016: 58–9, 77–8; see also Hurlburt 2011). Even when scholars such as Hurlburt develop methods for studying pristine experience empirically, it is highly questionable whether such a momentary form of experience can be captured in any consistent way.

While my explorations of the experientiality of science fiction draw on moments of pristine experience, my articulation of them necessarily becomes broad experience. While I wholeheartedly appreciate rigorous phenomenological practices that seek to observe experience in its purest form, learning to bracket all presuppositions, my practice points in a different direction. I accept that experience, including moments of pristine experience, is laced through with presuppositions and forces that arise from cultural and more-than-human environments. The experience I describe in this book is thus messy and conflicted, and quite often the description of experience is yoked to serve broader arguments. My aim is thus not to defend the truthfulness or repeatability of these particular experiences but to demonstrate that human cognition is flexible enough to allow for experiential exploration of many kinds.

However, my exploration of readerly experience is grounded in the analysis of narrative strategies and techniques that can be traced in the texts studied, and thus it also potentially opens to other readers. As a bridging concept between readerly experience and those narrative strategies and techniques, I draw on *experientiality*. Experientiality is a narrative-theoretical concept that refers to "the quasi-mimetic evocation of real-life experience" that takes place in reading events (Fludernik 1996: 12). While Fludernik's original use focuses on the textual properties of the narrative, Caracciolo (2014c) reformulates experientiality as a network between the reader, the text, and the environment:

> Even if engaging with narrative does involve mental representations of some sort, its experientiality cannot be understood in representational, object-based terms. Instead, we should think of experientiality as a kind of network that involves, minimally, the recipient of a narrative, his or her experiential background, and the expressive strategies adopted by the author. At the root of experientiality is, then, the tension between the textual design and the recipient's experiential background. (Caracciolo 2014c, 30, see also 9–11, 114)

The primary benefits of Caracciolo's networked model, for the purposes of this book, are its dynamicity and flexibility. The model views experientiality as a changing phenomenon and allows both textual analysis and historicizing/contextualizing approaches. Moreover, in presenting the model as a network, Caracciolo enables one to discuss the interactions between textual design and the embodied, active reader.

2.3.3 Connect Readerly Experience and Environmental Experience

When we have developed a working understanding of readerly experience as affective and embodied, we can turn to figuring out how such experience is linked to the perceptions and actions salient for life in the wider world. This means both figuring texts as "cognitive environments" and grasping how lived environments can participate in the reading process.

For cognitive linguists and philosophers such as George Lakoff and Mark Johnson (1980, 1999), the structures and dynamics of embodied experience give rise to verbal and abstract thinking. Recent contributions to cognitive science and philosophy have taken a step further, claiming that the embodied sense-making processes of humans connect them to nonhuman sense-making—through shared developmental histories, humans share sensory and cognitive abilities with animals and plants (see, e.g., Thompson 2007; Currie 2011; Ryan 2012; Chamovitz 2013). In this wider view, cognition is reconfigured as "know-how." Remembering, for example, can be understood as "the capacity to re-enact embodied procedures, often prompted and supported by external items" or "a kind of knowing what to do in familiar circumstances" (Hutto and Myin 2013: 30). A pine tree knows how to grow its roots toward water and nutrients; an arctic fox knows where and how to jump to catch a mouse it hears scuttling under the snow.

Much of cognitive literary studies builds on the idea that humans make sense of fictional and actual environments by using largely the same cognitive skills and resources. A particularly influential idea is that everyday cognition already involves an imaginative or "simulative" aspect, in which the mind responds to the environment in nonrational, bodily ways and creates experiential models of the people it encounters, whether they are actual or fictional. As neuroscientist Vittorio Gallese (2011: 197) explains, "our brain–body systems are equipped with a pre-rational, non-introspective process—embodied simulation—generating a physical, and not simply 'mental,' experience of the mind, motor intentions, emotions, sensations, and lived experiences of other people, even when narrated." For literary scholars, the embodied simulation view provides a chance to discuss making sense of fiction in terms of making sense of the world. In Alexa Weik von Mossner's (2017b: 556) words, "we also map the movements, sensations, and emotions of fictional people onto our own bodies."

While I appreciate the general idea that the experience of both environments and fiction is partly "a pre-rational, non-introspective process," I am not convinced that the process necessarily constructs "models" in the mind of the experiencer. Rather, I draw on the somewhat simpler idea, advanced by enactivist thinkers such as Alva Noë (2004), that experience deals in bodily feelings and actions that do not necessarily involve mental representations. While I agree with Weik von Mossner that the readers' understanding of their own bodies necessarily organize their understanding of fictional bodies, I want to leave room for strange and unstructured bodily feelings that do not exist in relation to such an organization: hauntings, impressions, atmospheres, and such. I also want to draw attention to the limitations of the simulation model by foregrounding readerly awareness of fictionality (see Sections 3.1 and 4.1).

Many cognitive literary scholars, including Caroline Levine (2015), Terence Cave (2016), and Merja Polvinen (2023), have turned to affordance theory to characterize how cultural practices participate in cognitive dynamics. Coined by the ecological psychologist James J. Gibson (1979), the term *affordance* refers to specific potentials for action provided by features of the environment—a tree might afford climbing, utilization as firewood, or aesthetic enjoyment; a coffee cup might afford holding and drinking coffee, or storing your collection of rare coins; the face of a friend affords social and physical engagement of many sorts, such as eye contact or a kiss on the cheek. As should be clear from these examples, affordances are flexible and somewhat improvisational, but also limited in situation-specific ways. Not only do they offer resources for action, but they place constraints, too—you cannot possibly hold your coffee in a living tree (although you might craft a cup out of one), and you cannot use your friend's face for firewood.

Cognitive literary studies propose that the skills and tendencies trained in daily environmental engagements are also utilized in reading literature. In producing cultural meanings, "we tend to reutilize in various ways the meanings that are already there, as part of our physical engagement with the world … human cultures find affordances in the combination and modification of the embodied patterns of our interaction with the world" (Caracciolo 2014a: 389; see also Caracciolo 2021). Fiction provides us with multiple affordances, ranging from engaging emotionally with fictional people and events to using a book as an ad hoc serving tray. While the notion of affordance is practical, it does not help to explain how our experiences with fiction are patterned, or how they unfold in time. Moreover, as Varela and others (1992: 203) point out, the notion of affordance rests on the separation of the environment and the experiencer—and on the view that both of them are somewhat stable. Enactivist thought presents both environments and experience in more dynamic ways.

In Alva Noë's (2015: 5–6, 11–18) terms, daily encounters with physical environments do not only provide human cognizers with affordances for action but also *organize them* in structured activities. They train them in negotiating possible and suitable encounters, in living with and thinking with the multiplicity of bodies around them. While *affordance* focuses on the features of the object or the environment in question, *organized activity* considers the action of engaging with such features. For Noë, organized activities are

> primitive and natural; they are arenas for the exercise of attention, looking, listening, doing, undergoing; they exhibit structure in time; they are emergent and are not governed by the deliberate control of any individual; they have a function, whether social or biological or personal. And they are (at least potentially) pleasurable. (Noë 2015: 5–6)

If we view engagement with fiction as such an organized activity, similar to driving a car or cooking dinner, we realize that it is largely habitual and pertains to the whole lived body rather than just the brain or a neural network. While reading, as Warhol (2003) and Kukkonen (2019) also point out, people fall into habitual patterns of expectation, response, and feeling. Moreover, all fiction provides affordances for thinking, feeling, articulating, and organizing one's experiential world. I argue that mutant narratives offer particular kinds of affordances—namely, affordances for reconfiguring one's habitual patterns of perception and environmental engagement, and thus modifying one's lived environment. This is an inherently enactive and affective process.

2.3.4 Amplify Your Bodily Feelings

The links between experience and environment are by no means simple. Neither are they unchangeable. On the contrary, many actions and attitudes can affect embodied and environmental experience. In my view—and in posthumanist philosophy more generally—unraveling the inherited forms of human-centered thinking requires us to intentionally modify the patterns of our experience.

In Caracciolo's enactivist formulation, experientiality already assumes that any reading happens within an embodied, spatial, and temporal context. This contextual stance affords meaningful entanglement with the posthumanist approach, a path recently explored also by Caracciolo (2021). Focusing on the entanglement of reader, text, and environment, I adopt a posthumanist-phenomenological stance on experiential knowledge. But as Astrida Neimanis (2017) reminds us, this kind of knowledge is never immediate or transparent, but neither is it purely ideatic or theoretical. A person knows her lived body, but only "partially and through different kinds of sensory apparatuses and amplifiers" (Neimanis 2017: 30).

In Neimanis's posthuman feminist phenomenology, introduced earlier, experiential change can be purposefully aided and explored by engaging with nonhuman materialities, scientific practices, and artworks. The crucial elements I wish to adopt from Neimanis's practice are (1) the conception of human bodies as radically open to and partially constituted by forces usually conceived as "outside" individual embodiment and (2) a readiness to explore such processes of constitution. For my approach, such "outside" forces also include literature, and fiction more widely. This dynamic and material view of embodiment shapes how I attend to the practice of bodily reading.

Neimanis's approach complements both the humanist tradition of phenomenology and the feminist understanding of bodily material change by providing a more-than-human conception of embodiment. While this conception is not altogether new to phenomenology, Neimanis's approach focuses especially on describing lived bodies that are augmented, dispersed, and mediated through their access to the "sensory apparatuses" of science and technology. She further extends this cybernetic relationality to our mediated knowledge about pollution and ecosystems:

> Could we not imagine a similar sort of reconfiguration—one that stretches and disperses our bodies—when we read how our human wastes and emissions are transforming entire oceanic ecosystems? By paying attention to the measurement of water levels in aquifers, reservoirs, or lakes, might our own thirst be imagined as a more extensive, collaborative gullet? (Neimanis 2017: 59)

Taking seriously the notion that all knowledge, including scientific knowledge, is both embodied and mediated, Neimanis thus challenges the idea of "purely human" embodied knowledge. In addition to technological devices and mediated information, Neimanis (2017: 61) also figures artworks and stories as *amplifiers* of more-than-human modes of embodied experience.

This step into the realm of artifice and fictionality provides an opening for cognitive theories of narrative. The notion of amplification contributes to the understanding of fiction's affective powers by capturing how they raise and intensify bodily feelings particular to engagement with nonhuman materialities such as water currents. By amplifying those bodily feelings, art and fiction can guide our attention to the otherwise downplayed more-than-human aspects of embodiment.[14] As cognitive literary critic Terence Cave puts it when discussing his practice of kinesic reading, which is attuned to bodily feelings:

> Once one begins to notice such effects in literature and indeed elsewhere, reading becomes subtly different: kinesic reading brings to the surface something you always already felt when you read the text properly, but somehow ignored for

the sake of supposedly "higher," more intellectual or aesthetic pleasures. (Cave 2016: 29)

The practice of amplification can thus help to attend to reading-related bodily feelings that are otherwise too vague, or considered secondary in approaches that do not focus on the bodily aspects of reading. Moreover, as Cave (2016: 41) also suggests, such amplification also requires the professional reader to purposefully *slow down* her attention and responses, as many of the kinesic and affective effects of reading happen slightly faster than conscious reflection (see also Section 3.2). Bodily reading in the posthuman feminist phenomenological mode would thus require that the professional reader attend both to the material forces and effects of literature and to her own active and skillful responses to those forces and effects—to "give our minds the opportunity to learn how to move in ever new kinds of constellations" (Polvinen 2023: 151). Moreover, the relationship between the reader and the literature cannot be figured as a one-directional subject–object relation, but rather as "thinking with" (Neimanis 2017; see also Cave 2016; Haraway 2016) or "mutual enfoldment" (Varela, Thompson, and Rosch 1992).

In the case of professional readers such as literary scholars, *theoretical frameworks and assumptions* also participate in lived experience and the formation of meaning, and thus they should be discussed not just as mere tools but as aspects of the experiential background of the reader. Feminist scholars such as Haraway (1991, 1992) and Grosz (1994), and especially new materialists such as Neimanis, stress that such cultural structures of meaning should be considered as material.

Taking my cue from both Neimanis and the enactivist framework, I encounter fictional narratives as affective artifacts that participate in the formation of more-than-human experience. What this means in terms of my reading method is that I complement the minimal network of experientiality with an awareness of the nonhuman forces and actors present in the act of reading. This view is indebted to both phenomenology and philosophy of technology (e.g., Merleau-Ponty 2002; Ratcliffe 2010; Hayles 1999, 2018), both of which also inform the enactivist conception of *organized activity* (Noë 2015: 5–6; 11–18; see also Sections 2.2, 3.2, and 4.1). However, the method of more-than-human reading is not phenomenological in the strict sense, but closer to the often autoethnographical explorations of experience undertaken in posthumanist criticism.

Posthumanist feminism informs the *performative* aspect of more-than-human reading: by emphasizing how bodily material change takes place in everyday actions such as walking and watching television, feminist thinkers such as Butler, Braidotti, and Warhol foreground performativity in the simple sense of habitually acting out bodily routines. Through their critical practices, however, they also foreground performativity as a conscious mode of generating experiential change. More-than-human reading involves the exploration of both these modes of performativity in the context of bodily reading: on the one hand, it attends to how science fictional narratives inform readerly engagements that tend to escape attention, such as identification with protagonists or imaginative construction of space; on the other hand, it seeks to consciously live through those moments of readerly engagement, and explore how they guide and shape embodied experience. Critical reading thus becomes a mode of performative experiential change.

2.3.5 Feel the Appeal of Figurations

Whereas Neimanis thinks and feels with water, and the scientific and theoretical apparatuses that amplify her embodied experience of water, a literary scholar thinks and feels with literature, and with the theoretical apparatuses relevant to the embodied experience of literature. Thinking with *figurations* (Haraway 1997; Bastian 2006) helps us grasp how readerly bodies are *partially constituted by literature in moment-to-moment interactions*—in similar ways that they are partially constituted by water, nutrients, bacteria, gendered habits, or ideology. Literature itself can be figured as partially constituted by nonhuman forces: it is one outcome of the entanglement of human and nonhuman actors and forces.

Thinking in figurations is helpful for considering how fiction might inform embodied experience, as posthumanist feminist thinkers also use the term to refer to affective experiential patterns of meaning in fictional contexts or "performative images that can be inhabited" (Haraway 1997: 11). Braidotti (2013: 164), following Deleuze, even characterizes figurations as "conceptual personae." In the analytical sections of *Metamorphoses*, Braidotti (2002) foregrounds science fiction narratives, such as David Cronenberg's films and the *Alien* film series, as potential counter-imaginaries. Through comparative and diffractive readings, she draws out the often complex and ambiguous political implications of the figurations of popular culture, claiming, for example, that the popular figuration of the cyborg "evokes simultaneously the triumphant charge of Schwarzenegger's *Terminator* and the frail bodies of those workers whose bodily juices—mostly sweat—fuel the technological revolution" (Braidotti

2002: 18). Braidotti also claims that our current figurations do not adequately respond to the lived experience of people in rich countries.

> There is a noticeable gap between how we live—in emancipated or post-feminist, multi-ethnic societies, with high technologies and telecommunication, allegedly free borders and increased control, to name just a few—and how we represent to ourselves this lived familiarity. This imaginative poverty can be read as the "jet-lag" problem of living simultaneously in different time-zones, in the schizophrenic mode that is characteristic of the historical era of postmodernity. Filling in this gap with adequate figurations is the great challenge of the present. And I cannot think of a bigger one for the future. (Braidotti 2002: 6)

Similar imaginative poverty can be diagnosed in the context of the ongoing ecological catastrophe, and the cultural shift toward the ecological reconstruction of societies. There are few popular figurations that respond to the particular need of fleshing out such (actual and potential) lived conditions that academic thinkers have diagnosed as *Anthropocene disorder* (Clark 2015) or *fossil subjectivity* (Salminen and Vadén 2015). On the other hand, artists are constantly engaged in this figurative work, reworking notions such as the *posthuman* in experiential forms for nonacademic audiences, and generally amplifying and intensifying underlying trends in the collective imagination. In Finland-based performative arts, for example, posthumanist methodology is developed by such works as Tuija Kokkonen's *Performance by Non-Humans* (2010–), Saara Hannula's *The Bodybuilding Project: An Introduction* (2014), and *Humanoid Hypothesis* (2015–16) by the Toisissa tiloissa/Other Spaces collective.

This book follows such posthumanist and feminist work in suggesting that contemporary science fiction is a fertile site for the emergence of popular figurations. The "science-fictional metamorph," to give an example that comes remarkably close to my discussion of mutant figures, has been foregrounded as a potentially feminist figuration that may be able "to shift our conceptual reality slightly, and to challenge the stability of established ontologies and structures for determining difference and belonging" and, more specifically, "challenge the notion of the human as a contained, universalized subject" (Hellstrand 2017: 26, 27). While Hellstrand's politically oriented analysis mostly considers how metamorphing fictional bodies reconfigure conceptualizations and bodily markers of sameness and otherness, my analysis focuses more on how fictional bodies materially participate in the embodied experience of readers.

2.3.6 Dance! (Readerly Choreography)

How do all these theoretical conceptions and suggestions finally come together in the practice of reading? I propose that the aptest metaphor for the practice of more-than-human reading is *dance*—in the specific sense of *moving in response to a choreography*.

As feeling bodies, readers live through echoes of bodily movements and rehearse the affective patterns associated with them. Through repetition, these affective patterns can shape the habitual movements and feelings of readers (Warhol 2003). According to Giovanna Colombetti, "kinetic portrayals" in visual arts and music

> can effectively evoke specific emotions because they reproduce bodily movements analogous to those we often experience in our body when we feel the portrayed emotions—a piece of music that feels "angry" (think heavy metal) arguably feels so because it mimics the kinesthetic character of anger, with its sense of bodily upsurge and frantic impulse to shake and kick. (Colombetti 2014: 120)

While Colombetti does not discuss literature, the point about kinetic portrayals easily extends to it. Moreover, the point lends itself well to the analysis of repetitive and genre-typical forms of replicating the kinesthetic character of feelings and emotions, such as the thrill of the chase scene or the evocation of sublime feelings in romantic nature writing, or in certain forms of science fiction and horror (see also Chapters 5 and 6). The affective force of kinetic portrayals also echoes Robyn Warhol's (2003: 24) notion of narratives as "devices that work through readers' bodily feelings" (see also Section 2.1). Warhol's performative model of feeling, along with the other cognitive-narratological work discussed earlier, describes the basic dynamic in what I would call *readerly choreography*: the experience of patterned bodily feeling, arising in enactive engagement with specific designs of kinesic and kinetic cues in a narrative (see also Kortekallio 2022).

The notion of readerly choreography comes close to Karin Kukkonen's (2019) *designed sensory flow*, which develops the second-generation approach to literature and cognition by drawing on the framework of *predictive processing*. Through this concept, Kukkonen explains how readers make sense of the text by predicting its flow and adjusting their predictions according to the actual encounter as it unfolds, that is, according to the *sensory flow* of the text. Through the notion of *design*, Kukkonen distances her theory from the kind of cognitive literary theory that describes readerly engagement with fiction merely in terms of imitations or echoes of real-world experience. In *designed sensory flow*, elements of real-world experience are fictionalized, and readerly predictions of elements such as character action or plot events also draw from culturally established models (Kukkonen 2019: 20; see also Iser 1993). Whereas *designed sensory flow* targets the processual and temporal aspects of bodily reading, *readerly choreography* is more tuned to describing schematic and spatial aspects such as the affective patterns, kinetic portrayals (Colombetti 2014), and kinesic styles (Bolens 2012) that particular fictional bodies afford to readers.

Readerly choreography thus aims to capture the sense of what it feels like to enactively attend to the bodily experientiality of a narrative as it unfolds, with a focus on reading singular fictional figures within their generic and environmental contexts.[15] Drawing on posthumanist feminist theory, such affectively experiential narrative patterns can be characterized as figurations. While posthumanist feminist theory often discusses figurations as "embodied concepts" (Neimanis 2017: 5), the term is also often used to refer to culturally established and mediated "knots" of meaning such as the cyborg or the lab mouse (Haraway 1992, 2008).

The notion of readerly choreography builds on enactivist theory by focusing on readerly experience as *organized activity* (Noë 2015), which is often habituated but sometimes estranged and reorganized. Noë (2015) argues that art and philosophy can stop our habitual organized activities and *display* them to us. His primary example is the relationship between dance and choreography. While dancing is natural to us, as an organized activity we are "lost in," choreography is designed to induce reflection.

> To stage a dance is to put into view this organized activity within which we are, by nature, embedded but within which we are, as we tend to be, lost. Choreography casts light on one of the ways in which we are organized, that we are organized by dancing. (Noë 2015: 14)

A new choreography can thus make us stop our "absorption" in dancing and make us consciously reflect on how it participates in our lives. Dancing, as other organized activities, is "level 1" activity, and choreography, as other artistic and philosophical practices, is "level 2" activity (Noë 2015: 29). Importantly, however, level 2 affects level 1 not only by affording reflection, but also by informing the habitual patterns of activity. Noë suggests that the existence of choreographies

> loops back down and shapes how we think about dancing, and thus how we dance, even when we are by ourselves or in our most intimate settings. In a world in which dance has been *represented*, it is not generally possible to dance in a way that is insulated from dance's image, that is, from choreography's model of

ourselves as dancing. Watch people dance, and you see them perform; they cite and sample the postures, attitudes, steps, and styles that they have consumed. It is as if their spontaneous, free, untutored forays into dancing are shaped by a culturally shared motion bank. (Noë 2015: 31, emphasis in original)

What I suggest about readerly choreographies is analogous to Noë's suggestion about regular choreographies. I propose that all narratives, intentionally or not, suggest experiential patterns in which to affectively and corporeally enact them. In most cases, enacting these patterns feels natural, and as readers we "go with the flow," empathizing with characters and immersing in the events. Readers "perform the moves" without realizing that those moves are informed by long histories of narrative production and reception, that is, a kind of "culturally shared motion bank." Sometimes, however, a narrative suggests a readerly choreography that turns our attention to the affective and corporeal dynamics of reading. My readings in Chapters 4 and 5 detail such experiences.

Thus, this prompting of reflectivity does not mean that readers would necessarily be disengaged from the narrative, or that they would cease feeling and shift completely to a disembodied analytical mode of reading (see also Polvinen 2016, 2017). On the contrary, the kind of reflective engagement readerly choreographies suggest requires readers to *feel with* the narrative.

2.4 Lived Experience and Reading Greg Bear's *Darwin's Children*

Some texts are more suitable to more-than-human reading than others. This is because different texts evoke and cultivate different kinds of experientiality, and because repeated engagement with any particular type of text trains the reader in attuning to the experiential qualities particular to that type. With mutant narratives, the particularity lies in the oscillating dynamic of defamiliarization and familiarization, especially in relation to human bodies. Mutant narratives defamiliarize aspects of human embodiment normally taken for granted, such as reproduction, sensory perception, or the functions of hormonal glands. They also attune their readers to strange and diverse forms of embodied experience, thus familiarizing them. Through the oscillation of these defamiliarizing and familiarizing effects, mutant narratives contest and possibly reconfigure the culturally established modes of relating to our environments. In this section, I consider such oscillation in more detail.

Greg Bear's *Darwin's Children* (2003) was published as a sequel to the Nebula-award-winning *Darwin's Radio* (1999).[16] Both novels were marketed as thrillers that draw on evolutionary and epidemic anxieties, with taglines such as "The Next Great War Will Start Inside Us" and "More Evolved, More Dangerous" on the book covers. Formally and stylistically, *Darwin's Children* is a conventional popular novel. Content-wise, it is radical and ambitious, as it speculates on established theories of evolutionary biology. This tension between form and content affords a chance to discuss how reading the novel both estranges and naturalizes embodied experience.

The novel presents a scenario in which ancient retroviral elements in the human genome are activated, due to complex environmental changes on a global scale. This results in a global pandemic and a generation of strange children. The retroviral elements are named SHEVA, and the children are labeled with various tags, *Homo sapiens novus*, *virus children*, and *Shevites* being the more polite ones. Moreover, the novel draws on the biological theory of *symbiogenesis* (Margulis and Sagan 2002; Gilbert, Sapp, and Tauber 2012) to present a vision of a universal humanity joined by communication that is both biological and spiritual (see also Idema 2019: 79–100).[17]

The inclusion of spiritual speculation in the novel is a brave move from Bear, given his reputation as a hard science fiction writer. Moreover, it is combined with a careful construction of a plausible biological model that explains the emergence of a new clade of humans.[18] Perhaps for this reason, Bear has added a "Caveats" section at the end of the novel. In the caveats, he describes the speculations as "based on empirical evidence" but "remarkably and uniquely difficult to present scientifically, since it's necessarily anecdotal" (*Darwin's Children*, hereafter *DC*: 457). For him, the experience is personal, but in a way that goes beyond personal:

> Epiphany is not limited to our conscious selves, or even to human beings.
>
> Imagine epiphany that touches our subconscious, our other internal minds—the immune system—or that reaches beyond us to touch a forest, or an ocean ... or the vast and distributed "minds" of any ecological system. (*DC*: 458)

On a first glance, such epiphany seems like a perfect experiential image of ecological interconnectedness. However, despite the author's ecological and even more-than-human aspirations, *Darwin's Children* ultimately reiterates and supports human-centered experientiality. Much of this has to do with the novel's strategic use of familial affect.

Darwin's Radio features a love triangle between epidemiologist Christopher Dicken, molecular biologist Kaye Lang, and archaeologist Mitch Rafelson—as well as the controversial SHEVA pregnancy of Dr. Lang. The scientist characters justify the extensive theoretical exposition in the novels, help construct a complex dramatization of science and politics in a time of crisis, and provide emotional tension. The emergency measures enforced by the US health officials to control the "plague"—segregation of sexes and abortion of all fetuses—force Lang and Rafelson to leave their homes and careers and live their life in hiding. At the end of the novel, their child Stella is born.

Darwin's Children begins by describing the situation twelve years after the events of the first novel. The family is still in hiding, and Stella has grown into a rebellious teenager who vehemently claims that she is not like her parents—she is "a part of something worthwhile, something not human" (*DC*: 242). In the hope of finding other Shevite children, she runs away from home, thus asserting herself as a mutant rather than a human. This theme of *teenage mutant rebellion* is developed throughout the novel.[19] Adolescent Shevites are depicted in stark contrast to their parent generation, and they repeatedly use "human" as a derogatory term.[20] They develop their own language and culture, including songs and games that involve "signs and smells and spit, eyes that twirl and brows that knit" (*DC*: 206).

The mutant adolescents of *Darwin's Children* thus present readers with a challenge to and a reconfiguration of naturalized notions of humanity. Moreover, the novel presents them with a situation and several relatable characters that they can affectively engage in imagining. This much can be agreed on—but in a particular reading situation, some aspects of the novel are bound to emerge as more powerful than others.

I have argued that fiction participates in the lived experience of readers through evoking experientiality, and more precisely by evoking bodily feelings. The experientiality of actual reading situations comes together in the crossing of textual cues, bodily responses, and the readers' personal backgrounds. In developing the method of more-than-human reading through the following reading of *Darwin's Children*, I aim to describe some of the bodily feelings and perceptual dynamics suggested by the text. Enacting the embodied reader model, I adopt the strategy of least resistance. I am interested in the novel as a system that produces experientiality through *affective devices* (see Caracciolo 2014c; Warhol 2003: 24), and therefore I approach it like I would a rollercoaster ride, a gym device, or a new winter coat. Getting acquainted with any of these devices involves a fair amount of adaptation, even surrender, as my body finds the appropriate positions and movements through which I can employ them.

Along with the immediate perceptions linked to the bodily experientiality of reading the novel, I pay attention to the affective alignments the novel invites me to take up. Bringing together these various aspects of reading experience, I wish to portray experientiality as a complex, temporal, and situated phenomenon. This broad approach to readerly experience lays ground to the more focused readings in later chapters.

2.4.1 Amplification of Affect, Attention, and Sensory Perception

As both phenomenologists (Heidegger 19271996; Ratcliffe 2010) and enactivist cognitive philosophers (Thompson 2007; Colombetti 2014) have argued, human beings are always in a mood of some kind, and there is thus no cognition untainted by affect. The ubiquity of affectivity prompts the enactivist literary scholar to ask how affect, emotion, and perception are evoked and entangled in reading experience.

Darwin's Children, like most realist novels, invites a particular human-centered mode of engagement: an emotional attunement to the dramatic life events of the fictional characters, and to their personalities. This kind of engagement is considered normal and natural, not strange at all. While reading, I am under what Marco Caracciolo (2016) has called a "character-centered illusion"—a willing imagining of fictional characters as quasi-people, whose lives and emotions I can sympathetically and empathetically engage with. The novel constantly presents affordances that enable this kind of engagement, which are also the basic elements of a modern realist novel: small dramatic scenes of interpersonal engagements and personal worries, as well as descriptions of everyday environments, objects, and habitual patterns. Even when scientific analysis or theoretical work is presented, as focalized through an individual scientist character working on a specific problem, the analysis is laced with an attunement to the social realities of the scientific and familial communities of the individual.

During the reading event, these affordances exercise particular aspects of my emotional and social cognition: the ones linked to interpersonal relationships. Feeling through the fictional exhaustion, stress, and love of the characters, I also relive some of the emotional states connected to the past events of my personal life—stressful relationships, difficult choices, and painful feelings. In this way, my personal background shapes the experience of reading the novel, thus playing into the dynamic of narrative experientiality. A reader in a different mental state (myself, at another time, included) would attend to different aspects of the novel. However, even based only on the style and techniques of the novel, bracketing the themes and topics as well as the personal backgrounds of particular readers, it can be argued that the novel invites its readers to employ their social and emotional skills, and prompts in its readers emotional and social responses.

In literary studies focusing on cognition and affect, such responses are often discussed in terms of empathy, sympathy, or *mind-reading*, that is, the mental activity of making sense of the hypothetical minds of others (see Zunshine 2006; Keen 2007; Vermeule 2010). Such processes of sense-making also involve our capability to make sense of the bodily gestures and expressions of others (Bolens 2012; Cave 2016). To some extent, we make sense of fictional minds and bodies in the same way we make sense of actual people. Cognitive literary studies generally agree on this point, but here I want to suggest that making sense of fictional people also affects our moment-to-moment perceptions and impressions of the actual people in our lives.

Darwin's Children constructs a specific style of social perception. Every new character is introduced, when entering a scene, with a brief but meticulous description of their bodily appearance. The introductions are very similar in style and tone, independent of the focalizing character, serving to ease the reader into a socially shared mode of observation.

> Jurie wore brown oxfords, wool slacks, a dark blue shirt with a broad collar, and a sleeveless, cream-colored knit sweater, all clean but rumpled. At fifty-five, his features were still youthfully handsome, his body lean. He had the kind of face that would have fit well right above the collar of an Arrow shirt in a magazine ad. Had he smoked a pipe, Dicken would have thought him a cliché scientist. His body was too small, however, to complete the Oppenheimer effect. Dicken guessed his height at barely five feet three inches. (*DC*: 218, as focalized by Christopher Dicken)
>
> Cross was in her middle sixties, portly, her short-cut, scraggly hair brilliantly hennaed, her face jowly, her neck a landscape of hanging wrinkles. She possessed a voice that could carry across a crowded conference hall, yet carried herself with the poise of a ballet dancer, dressed in carefully tailored pant suits, and somehow could charm the butterflies out of the skies. (*DC*: 290, as focalized by Kaye Lang)

Such descriptions help me to imagine the characters as fictional people embedded in their lifeworlds (and estimate their personality and social status based on their appearance), but they also subtly affect my perceptions outside the reading situation. Through this conventional device, the novel guides me to mimic the narrative perspectives and enact similar modes of attention: to take note of the facial features, expressions, clothing, and habitual patterns of movement in the people I encounter. While some effects of such shifts in focus probably escape my attention, others I become aware of—the appeal of hands, for example. After introductions, the descriptions in the novel often focus on hands as both a sign and a product of a person's life choices, for instance when readers learn that Mitch's callused hands are a product of years of archaeological digging, yet in absence of that work, they go smooth (*DC*: 4, 27), or when introductory handshakes are minutely described (*DC*: 214 *et passim*). Accordingly, in social situations throughout the reading week, my awareness of the hands of others is heightened.

By guiding my attention in this way, reading participates in my life. In a normal reading situation, most of such participation would be left unnoticed by readers, myself included, as it feels like such a natural part of everyday experience. It is only when the narrative diverges from this naturalized mode that its experiential effects come properly to the fore.

In *Darwin's Children*, such a *defamiliarization of embodied experience* happens primarily through the mutant perspective of the adolescent Shevite character Stella. This perspective is also narrated in a realist manner, but the sensory aspects portrayed are slightly different from conventional presentations of human perception. For example, the Shevites navigate their social world with smell as well as sight. In the passages focalized by Stella, introductory descriptions of people include olfactory perceptions:

> Stella could see that these children had lived lives different from her own. They all smelled lonely and left out, like puppies pulled from a litter, whining and searching for something they had lost. Beneath the loneliness and other emotions of the moment lay their fundamentals: Will smelled rich and sharp like aged cheddar. Kevin smelled a little sweet. Mabel smelled like soapy bathwater, steam and flowers and clean, warm skin. (*DC*: 58)

As I keep reading the novel, I experience the foregrounding of olfactory perceptions bleeding into my everyday life. During the reading week, my perception of the odors of food, spaces, weather, and human bodies is more fine-grained than usual. This is also one of the more persistent effects of reading the novel: since the first reading, I have paid more attention to my olfactory environments, and to the knowledge acquired via smelling. The issue of scents also emerges in everyday conversations. September is mushroom season, and the house I live in is often filled with the odors of drying mushrooms, and describing these odors is a common topic in kitchen talk. While such serendipity might seem trivial, in this particular case it is bound to feed back into the amplification of my olfactory experiences.

Such reciprocity of reading and lived experience highlights how literature can take part in the dynamic organization of our lives, and also the fact that such participation cannot be easily separated from other experiences not directly related to reading. Noë (2015: 8–9) notes that organized activities take place on a level of attention that is not quite conscious—they are habitual, and they feel natural enough to escape our notice. My enhanced experience of scents is just barely strange enough to cross the threshold of my conscious attention. Staying with that moment of subtle strangeness guides me to attend also to the less obvious changes, such as the increased attention of people's hands mentioned earlier. The amplification of sensory perception in the process of reading can thus be said to involve a fair amount of feedback between readerly experience and other lived experience.

The defamiliarization of embodied experience on the narrative level and the experiential estrangement it gives rise to contain potential for a wider destabilization of established habits of perception and experience. Later in the book, I will argue that most narratives involving mutant embodiment are geared to enable such a destabilization, and thus they can also be of help in developing new perspectives on embodied experience. The particular case of *Darwin's Children*, however, makes an exception to this general tendency, as it systematically naturalizes the potentially estranging effects of readerly attunement to mutant embodiment.

2.4.2 Naturalization of Mutant Embodiment by Realist Means

Despite their appearance in a novel characterized as science fiction, Bear's techniques for representing character and social perception are part of the long trend of realist narration. This is essential to the way they shape my daily perceptions. Riikka Rossi (2012) has claimed that realist literature utilizes our everyday frames of reference in evoking Barthesian "reality effects," and that these effects can be considered as cognitive. According to Rossi, realism encourages the reader to employ a nonreflective attitude toward the storyworld, that is, to interpret it *as if* it was the actual world and not a fictional construct. While this in no way implies that realist texts could not convey or evoke critical attitudes toward, say, societal problems, realist techniques tend to work toward hiding the representational and reality-shaping powers of narratives.

Science fiction often uses realist techniques for its production of plausibility. Both realist and science fictional texts seek to create a sense of "documentary verisimilitude" by using detailed description and literal language (Roberts 2005: 15; Stockwell 2000: 196; see also Mandala 2010; McHale 2018). For Roger Luckhurst (2007: 215), Bear's use of a realist style is tied to his status as a writer of "hard" science fiction, which emphasizes "rigorous technological and scientific extrapolation in blunt, instrumental prose." Even when the features of the storyworld are outlandish, a realist style of narration guides the reader to accept it as natural, as in the case of Stella's sophisticated sense of smell. A Shevite sense of smell is not typically part of any human reader's experiential background, and thus it probably gives rise to an initial feeling of strangeness in readerly experience. Yet the estranging effect is short-lived, as the realist style of narration smooths over the difference and naturalizes the sensory abilities of the mutant figure.

The experiential plausibility of the character Stella is created through framing her as an ordinary adolescent middle-class girl who resists the authority of her parents, goes to school, and gradually finds her place in the social life of her peers. Readers learn trivial things about her dietary preferences and the repetitive duties of daily life. Compared to the occasional science fiction texts that are experimental, and thus challenging in both their storyworlds and their narrative techniques (I'm thinking of Ann Leckie's *Ancillary Justice*, 2013, or Catherynne Valente's *Radiance*, 2015), *Darwin's Children* limits its challenging aspects to the diegetic level of the storyworld.

I propose that the realist techniques used in *Darwin's Children* to naturalize social behavior also serve to downplay the transformative potential of mutant embodiment. Presenting Stella as just another ordinary girl, whose perspective can be presented in the same style as any normal human, encourages the reader to keep on reading with a "natural attitude"—as if human experience, even when mutated, is transparently communicated through realist techniques. With its realist style, *Darwin's Children* also effectively hides the narrative techniques that temporarily shape readers' perceptions and affects, presenting itself as a transparent window to a plausible reality rather than as a construction of a speculative fictional world.

Crucially, the naturalizing effect also extends to the levels of society and species. In *Darwin's Children*, the Shevite sense of smell and the ability of intentionally producing scents serve as the basis of a whole culture, including idiosyncratic styles of communication. The sociality of the Shevites entails some potential for posthumanist subversion, as the novel envisions social practices that are strange and potentially threatening to normal humans. The young Shevites share moods and desires biochemically, through scent and spit, and enter into modes of social decision-making that are fluid enough to be called anarchist. Toward the end of the novel, I encounter descriptions of everyday life in the Shevites' commune:

> She took her tray from the food line and walked into the refectory, large and quiet, twelve workers off duty, none speaking, gesturing and facing and flashing, pleasant odors of cocoa and yogurt and jasmine—someone was being *very* pleasant—mingled together and out of context at this distance, like words pulled out of a conversation and tossed together randomly, the discourse going on at the old wooden tables and benches. (*DC*: 423, emphasis in original)

The Shevites are portrayed as having a remarkable capacity for social bonding and group formation, engaging in animated "discourse" even while they are silent. Even if the particulars of the narrated situation (communication by "gesturing and facing and flashing" as well as producing "pleasant odors of cocoa and yogurt and jasmine") are unfamiliar, the everyday frame of animated lunchtime conversation is familiar. This is a technique Bear uses throughout the novel, as is also shown by the example about introductions mentioned earlier.

Shevites are thus constructed as relatable despite their strangeness. According to Seo-Young Chu (2010), the sociality of Shevites makes them utopian, to the extent of becoming a model for global subjectivity:

> Addicted to multimedia information, profoundly dependent on live connections, at home in social-networking sites, Bear's Shevites science-fictionally personify many of the ways in which globalization has been affecting humanity in the late-twentieth- and early-twenty-first centuries. At the same time, Bear's Shevites personify the ways in which globalization is asking—even requiring—humanity to change if we are to avoid destroying ourselves and our planet. Generous, democratic, peaceful, and devoted to consensus decision making, Shevites would be exemplary citizens in a globalized world. (Chu 2010: 115–16)

According to Chu, such virtues—generosity, democracy, peacefulness, and consensus decision-making—serve as a moral blueprint for the global community. Chu also notes that the evocation of global subjectivity is a common function for mutants in science fiction. "To make humanity recognizable as a single species," Chu (2010: 110) writes, "is to call attention to the fact that human beings are physical organisms." Following Chu's line of thought, we can say that *Darwin's Children* naturalizes the Shevite's virtues as features of their specific genetic makeup, itself produced through the mysterious ends of evolution (personified in the novel as Gaia). Due to their status as physical organisms, the Shevites thus come to represent a potential new form of humanity.

From an enactivist perspective, the acknowledgment of humanity's shared evolutionary background (and a potential evolutionary future) provides opportunities for discussing the shared aspects of lived experience, as, for example, the sensory capabilities and tendencies discussed earlier. From a posthumanist feminist perspective, however, this kind of universalization is problematic, since it erases the unshareable and untranslatable differences between different human individuals and cultures, and between humans and other species (see Hellstrand 2016; Haraway 2016).

Most other mutant figures of contemporary science fiction foreground the risky and horrifying aspects of humans as physical organisms, such as disease, contamination, deformation, and all kinds of anxieties related to sexual reproduction (see Section 3.1). In Bear's naturalized figuration of the mutant, those aspects are diminished. Shevites are superhuman rather than posthuman—capable of communicating with the previous edition of humanity, *Homo sapiens*, and willing to do so. Compared to other recent renditions of mutated humans, such as Peter Watts's radically modified bleeding-edgers (in *Blindsight* and *Echopraxia*), Octavia E. Butler's predatory Clayarks (in the Patternist series), or Margaret Atwood's ironic Crakers (in *Oryx and Crake*, *The Year of the Flood*, and *MaddAddam*), Shevites are untypically safe, obedient, and comprehensible. While *Darwin's Children*, as a conflicted and hybrid text, can definitely be considered a *mutant narrative*, it ultimately does not challenge its readers to enact more-than-human modes of experience. Rather, it is an example of a text in which radical themes—symbiogenetic evolutionary theory, the emergence of a new strain of humans, and the subsequent societal changes—are downplayed by conventional form. Moreover, the novel presents an overarching unifying theme that affectively embraces difference and encloses it under the wide umbrella of universal humanity. A central device in this process is Bear's utilization of *nonconscious affective communication*.

2.4.3 Nonconscious Affective Communication

In *Darwin's Children*, Bear's vision of universal humanity is intertwined with his interpretation of cognitive and evolutionary theories. In the course of the novel, evolution emerges as a purposeful pattern that humans can tap into by using their intuitive skills, primarily dreams, visions, and prayers. Networks of *communication* emerge on all levels of the systems Bear envisions, from the biological to the social and the cosmic, and Shevites represent a leap in evolution after which humans are able to grasp such networks. While Bear's cosmic vision draws on complex theoretical understanding, I propose that its affective appeal is based on an evocation of a bodily feeling that is ultimately simple: the desire for familial warmth and comfort. I argue that Bear evokes such a bodily feeling by his realist depiction of intersubjective relations and then enlarges them to encompass the entire human species.

On the biological level, Bear envisions a network of communicating biological entities within human bodies, which the novel explicitly refers to as "minds." Closing her eyes, Stella can "feel the warmth behind her eyelids, the sun passing over her face, the suspended redness, and below that the rising up of all her minds, all the parts of her body that yearned" (*DC*: 388).[21] In this description of bodily experience, the "rising up of all her minds" is entwined with the experience of feeling the sunlight on her face: it is Stella's whole living and lived body that cognizes and reaches toward its environment. Reading the description, I feel a humming warmth in my face, chest, and stomach, and this feeling easily associates with the bundled affects of warmth, life, and desire.

The bodily feeling of rising toward warmth is something that even a unicellular organism would appreciate (see Thompson 2007: 157). The "yearning" of Stella's bodily minds could be understood in enactivist terms as *autopoiesis*: her body consists of mind-like living systems, such as the neuronal system and the immune system, which are already capable of enacting and renewing their identities. Enactive philosophy, as well as the philosophy of biology that precedes it, describes this basic dynamic of living systems as "essentially affective and protentional or forward-looking," as the living system "opens outward into space because its metabolism propels it forward in time, and this forward trajectory is fueled by want, concern, and need" (Thompson 2007: 156; see also Jonas 1966: 86). Bear's presentation of the biological level of Stella's body as affectively oriented, "yearning," is thus grounded on systems-biological theories of organismic intention, and so are the affects of warmth that emerge at the level of readerly experience. Moreover, as Stella *experiences* the biological level of her body as yearning, the novel suggests that affective experience can transcend the boundaries between the systemic levels (biological, social, and cosmic) and, by so doing, perform a communicative function within the body of an organism.

At the social level, in Shevite practices of "fever-scenting" (*DC*: 23 *et passim*) and "spit-calming" (*DC*: 201 *et passim*), collective moods are cultivated, maintained, and communicated by intentionally sharing pheromones and other psychoactive chemicals that Shevite bodies emit. The Shevites' olfactory abilities are also associated with their ability to communicate even in their sleep, as the pheromones function without the need for waking consciousness. Such nonconscious communication often also includes changes in the patterns of freckles on the cheeks of the Shevite individuals. In the course of the novel, the ability to communicate while sleeping is highlighted periodically at dramatic turning points: at the end of the first chapter, at the end of the first part (in a novel composed of three parts), and twice during the last chapter of the last part.

> "Got to go," he murmured. Stella's cheeks produced waves of golden freckles. Mitch smiled.
> Even asleep, his daughter could say good-bye. (*DC*: 5)
> In a blur of growth and young time, she tried to forget. And even in their sleep, her friends could soothe her. (*DC*: 184)
> Moments later, suckling her son, Stella relaxed and slept. Her cheeks kept showing patterns. Even asleep, the new mother could sign her love. (*DC*: 452)
> Kaye's face did not change expression, but Stella saw the tiny freckles darken under her mother's eyes. Even now, Kaye could show her love. (*DC*: 455)

The Shevites' nonconscious communication is presented as highly affective, as it is used to greet and soothe others, and to show love. The last of the quotations shows how nonconscious affective communication is also depicted as an ability that can be adopted by regular humans such as Stella's non-Shevite mother, Kaye, who not only develops Shevite-style freckles but uses them to nonconsciously communicate her emotions. In focusing on such intuitive abilities, Bear's novel presents mind-reading skills and social attunement as natural abilities that are, in principle, shared by all humans. The shared nature of such natural abilities supports the novel's naturalization of the mutant figure and the subsequent vision of universal humanity. At the social level, nonconscious affective communication thus bridges Shevites and non-Shevites.

Nonconscious abilities also figure in the lives of the non-Shevite humans of *Darwin's Children*. Especially in the chapter focusing on Mitch Rafelson's work on an archaeological site, intuiting and dreaming emerge as a crucial part of the work of a researcher. In this chapter, Mitch Rafelson searches for the remains of an ancient hunter-gatherer group consisting of both *Homo sapiens* and *Homo erectus* individuals. In the political situation of the storyworld, finding these remains would help to make the case for a peaceful coexistence of *Homo sapiens* and *Homo sapiens novus*, and finding them is thus crucial both for the continued safety of Mitch's own family and for the continued life of the entire species. In this affectively charged situation, Mitch dreams.

> He had dreamed about the bones in the night. He did not know whether artists dreamed their work—or whether detectives dreamed solutions to their cases. But the way he worked was, he often dreamed of the people he found, in their graves or where they had fallen and died.
>
> And sometimes he was right.
>
> Often he was right.
>
> Hell, nine times out of ten, Mitch's dreams turned out to be right—so long as he waited for them to evolve, to ripple through their necessary variations and reach their inevitable conclusion. (*DC*: 351)

Here, the archaeologist taps into the shared senses, instincts, and sociality of all humans, embodied in a dream in which he enacts the movements of the leader of the *Homo erectus* hunter-gatherer group. Eventually he also connects to the *Homo erectus* figure through trance and visions on the field site (*DC*: 362–6). In Mitch's visions, everything falls into place in a great chain of ancestors, different but all essentially human, and the insight about this chain reaches the present through species memory. Both dreams and evolution are figured as predetermined chains of events that "ripple through their necessary variations and reach their inevitable conclusion." Here, nonconscious affective communication bridges the individuals (Mitch and the ancient hunter) across time, as well as the clades of *Homo sapiens* and *Homo erectus*.

Toward the end of the novel, the vision of nonconscious affective communication takes on even more mystical and transcendental qualities, as when three young Shevite women, one of them pregnant, enter into a collective experience of visualizing the deep minds as golden kernels.

> Stella reached down to where LaShawna was, using her palm-touch for guidance. She actually did see something at the bottom of a long, deep well, three somethings, actually, and then four, the baby within her joining. Like four luminous golden kernels of corn, hidden away at the bottom of four separate tunnels of memory and life. (*DC*: 446)

This mystical event is connected to the events centering on the character of Kaye, in which she is overwhelmed by the felt presence of an entity emanating pure love. The experience of being visited by this "caller" is characterized as an epiphany. While the source of the visitation is not traced back to the Christian

God, all textual clues point to an immaterial, all-powerful, all-loving force beyond biology. Given the symbiogenetic theme of the novel, the force might also be traced to the notion of the *Earth system* as a regulator of ecosystemic activity, and its origins in James Lovelock's (2000) *Gaia hypothesis*. In the dramatically heightened moment of death, Kaye's inner monologue takes on the tone of a sermon:

> The memories fall away. We are shaped, but in ways we do not understand. Know that thinking and memory are biology, and biology is what we leave behind. The caller speaks to all of our minds, and they all pray; to all of our minds, from the lowest to the highest, in nature, the caller assures us that there is more, and that is all the caller can do. (*DC*: 455)

At this point of the novel, the "prayer" of all minds including the biological, as an ultimate form of nonconscious affective communication, connects the experiencing individual, and by extension the human species and other biological life-forms, with a divine immaterial force.

As the analysis earlier shows, *Darwin's Children* encourages its readers to consider a conception of cognition that is both more nuanced and more distributed than a conception centered on the waking consciousness of an individual subject. The reiteration of phrases such as "even asleep" in dramatically heightened moments emphasizes this issue as one of the key thematic features of the novel. Such a view of cognition is linked in the novel to systems biology, and more specifically to the *symbiogenetic view of evolution* promoted by microbiologist Lynn Margulis (Margulis and Sagan 2002). The symbiogenetic view emphasizes the role of symbiotic merger in speciation and discards the notion of "individual" organisms and species in favor of a view of "organisms as communities" (Margulis and Sagan 2002: 20).

Bear's poetic interpretation of cognitive and evolutionary theories is fascinating from an enactivist perspective, as it appears to fit well with not just symbiogenesis but also with the harmonious notion of "the deep continuity of life and mind" advanced in an enactivist context by Evan Thompson (2007). Throughout the novel, nonconscious affective communication bridges together living systems of all levels—but, as should be apparent by now, all of those systems are *human*. Nonconscious affective communication serves an instrumental role that strengthens the experience and conception of the human family unit and, by extension, the human species at the top of a hierarchical order of care and meaning, and thus it cannot be said to develop a more-than-human or ecocentric view of the world. Rather, Bear's poetic construction celebrates evolutionary humanism, as the vast timescale of human evolution and the intuitive abilities of individuals are evoked as elements in an awesome cosmic order. Inevitably, after all the "necessary ripples and variations," in the center of that order stands Man. Whereas Margulis and Sagan stress that the "communities" they discuss involve multiple species, most often none of which are human or even animal, Bear's treatment of the model is all about the human—and, as Chu proposes, about the human *as a single species*. Such a treatment collapses both human otherness and nonhuman otherness into panhuman sameness.

2.4.4 The Comforting Promise of the Family of *Homo*

Tom Idema (2019: 97, emphasis in original) has argued that epiphany in the Bear's *Darwin* books is "not merely 'about' evolution—rather, it constitutes an *evolutionary signal*. To be open to what is happening in the world around you means becoming a participant in the making of the future." Thus, for Idema, Kaye's and Mitch's openness to intuitive thinking through dreams and epiphanies is a mark of *evolutionary adaptability*, rewarded by their successful production of offspring. This line of thought leads Idema, who also draws on Margulis and Sagan (2002), to propose that the Darwin novels support "a symbiotic view of life" in which an individual body participates "in a community of others that contribute to its welfare" (Gilbert, Sapp, and Tauber 2012: 333, cited in Idema 2019: 98). He concludes on a profoundly materialist note about intuition and epigenesis.

> This approach to health as constructive participation in "a community of others" is exactly what makes Kay [sic] and Mitch sensitive to calls from the inside, which are actually transferred calls from the outside. Could it be that in times of upheaval, strong stress signals induce epigenetic mechanisms that are accompanied by emotionally intense experiences and imaginative ideas? (Idema 2019: 98; see also Gilbert, Sapp, and Tauber 2012)

I agree with Idema that *Darwin's Radio* and *Darwin's Children* indeed support the kind of interpretation in which Kaye and Mitch "seem to remember their nonhuman origins and move towards a new stage of evolution" (Idema 2019: 98). The novels put forth a symbiogenetic view of evolution and thoroughly reconfigure the role of human cognition in evolutionary processes. The human mind is not viewed so much as a solid result of evolutionary history but as one aspect of a more-than-human network of actors in mid-transformation. Neither the thoughts nor the offspring of Kaye and Mitch are presented as products of human bodies or cultures only. Rather, they emerge from the interaction of human bodies that are already rhizomatically laced with microbiological life and responsive to planetary and populational trends.

However, the radical potential of more-than-human adaptability in *Darwin's Children* is also mapped as part of the cosmic transcendental order of evolutionary humanism that both privileges the human species and sidelines material agency. While Thompson's formulation of the deep continuity of life and mind shows us that the conception of minded/mindful life can be laid out in purely materialist terms, Bear's narrative introduces a transcendental layer to the conception—"there is more," a life beyond memory and biology, manifested in the text as luminous golden kernels. By introducing this aspect, Bear's novel downplays the radical potential of the symbiogenetic conception of mind. If there is a transcendental force that guides and shapes evolutionary and biological forces, material life is ultimately presented as secondary. This is both an antimaterialist and human exceptionalist view of biological life.

Somewhat ironically, the force of the vision of transcendental connection is based on the affective techniques utilized throughout the novel. The descriptions of bodily feelings, including familial connection, touch, warmth, pain, and exhaustion, familiarize my reading body with the fictional characters and help me to tune in to their fictional lives. Moreover, the scenes portraying harrowed parents and hard-working researchers repeatedly amplify my already-existing feelings of carrying a burden of responsibility. Thus, I am also tempted by the novel's promise of a transcendental yet natural unity. That promise offers me a comfortable escape and a temporary relief from grief and burdens. What might a person want more than an experience of unity, a profound sense of being loved by a completely unjudgmental entity? The promise of epiphany is the promise of ultimate comfort and ultimate naturality. Moreover, the unity it offers still centers around the exceptionality of the human species.

Such speciesism is apparent in the novel's dramatic closure, which takes place on the archaeological site of Mitch Rafelson's team. Watching the newly exhumed ancient bones, Stella returns to the protective arms of her human father Mitch, who has heroically found the bones and thus revealed an evolutionary chain that spans from *Homo erectus* to *Homo sapiens novus*. In the human father's arms, Stella thus joins this chain of humans, too. Even if there was a seed of subversion in the first stages of mutant embodiment and mutant sociality, that potential is now brought to a close, as readers are invited to enjoy the warm, familial embrace that affirms universal humanity and erases all uncomfortable differences.

As Sara Ahmed (2004) has argued in her analysis of collective feelings, this kind of pathos involves the construction of borders: the "we" of *Homo* has to stand in contrast to a "them" of some kind. The familial bond, into which the reader is invited to enter, is tight against outsiders: animal, vegetal, mineral, and other nonhuman beings. In Ahmed's (2004: 28) view, "emotions work to create the very distinction between the inside and the outside," both for individual bodies and for collective bodies. In *Darwin's Children*, the narration only invites the reader to form affective alignments between humans of different types—nonhuman life is ultimately subjugated to human life.[22] In this way, Bear's novel exemplifies how speciesism is naturalized through realist characterization and narration.

From this perspective, we could reconsider how the novel uses its readers' attunement to its affective cues for broader purposes. By inviting readers to rehearse their personal and familiar emotions by attuning to the fictional lives of the characters, the novel offers affects of both pain and comfort. Through the narrative, such personal and familial emotions are contextualized as a part of (potentially universally) shared human life. If the resonance between the emotions I feel and the fictional emotions of Mitch and Kaye makes sense to me, it is likely that the extension also makes sense. Thus, I am moved to succumb to the familial pathos of the great reunion of Humans, from *Homo erectus* to *Homo sapiens novus*. In this way, the formal features of the novel play into producing a particular set of ethical possibilities: I am guided to elevate my personal emotion into an exemplary case of universally human emotion. This experiential dynamic is human exceptionalism from start to finish, since it guides my emotions into a narrow template of interhuman sociality.

2.4.5 Why *Darwin's Children* Does Not Afford a Posthumanist Reading

In this section, I have argued that Greg Bear's *Darwin's Children* invites its readers to take part in an affective vision of universal humanity. The novel suggests such a vision both explicitly and through its affective force on receptive readers. This is apparent in the structural similarities between the standard and the mutant perspectives, in the theme of nonconscious affective communication, and ultimately in the storyline of Mitch Rafelson's archaeological quest, which conjoins three different clades of *Homo* in familial unity.

Enacting the embodied reader model, I have adopted the strategy of least resistance. I have intentionally allowed the novel to guide my bodily feelings and emotional patterns, in the hope that this strategy can give rise to insights about the formation of embodied experience in reading. However, my affective reading of *Darwin's Children* is not "natural" in the sense that it would necessarily arise from my biological or evolutionary makeup. Rather, I am guided into adopting a certain *style* of embodied experience, through which the empathetic, socially attuned reading *feels* natural (see Warhol 2003; Braidotti 2013; Noë 2015). A central device in this stylization of experience is narrative form itself: by repeatedly encountering the certain narrative conventions for representing people and environments, I grow to understand these conventions as neutral mirrors of the actual world. Realist characters feel "realistic" because readers have been culturally familiarized with this mode of representing human experience.[23]

As Alva Noë (2015: 51–2) has argued, different conventions and practices afford different *styles of perception*: observing still-life paintings trains us to perceive the world as sets of immobile planes, while playing sports enables a more dynamic and task-oriented style Noë (2015: 51) calls "seeing in the wild." I suggest that the same is true about literature: different kinds of literature train us in different kinds of perception and feeling, thus participating in the formation of our habitual patterns of engaging with our environments.

Exploring the implications of this suggestion is the main task of the rest of this book. In the course of that exploration, some of the experiential patterns that cognitive literary theory presents as simply "mimetic" are unsettled by posthumanist interventions. On the other hand, enactively attending to mutant narratives makes experiential some of the stickier human-centered habits, thus highlighting that theoretical posthumanist reconfigurations of subjectivity do not painlessly give rise to metamorphoses of embodied experience.

In the affective patterns it suggests and upholds, *Darwin's Children* is a remarkably human-centered novel. It affords certain bodily feelings and emotional alignments (the warmth of familial unity, uplifting feelings of universal humanity) while excluding others (e.g., transspecies affection). My analysis of the novel also points to the limits of a more-than-human reading: while some aspects of the novel, such as its engagement with evolutionary theories, do afford posthumanist analyses, its affective patterns do not. As the main aim of this book is to explore the possibility of more-than-human embodied experience, *Darwin's Children* thus needs to be contrasted and compared with readings of stories that involve more defamiliarization and experimentation, and allow for such posthumanist explorations. In the chapters that follow, I foreground how reading the mutant narratives by N. K. Jemisin, Paolo Bacigalupi, and Jeff VanderMeer in a more-than-human manner can develop an awareness of the manipulative aspects of fictional narrative, and give rise to more-than-human modes of experience.

Notes

1 As Elizabeth Grosz (1994: xii) notes, the metaphor of *embodiment* is committed to either a weak or a strong form of dualism between mind and body. Moreover, it implies a *process* of making something ideal or abstract *into* a bodily matter. This book uses *embodied* in phrases that denote such a process, such as *embodied reader*, *embodied subjectivity*, and *embodied estrangement*, as well as in established phrases such as *embodied mind*, *embodied cognition*, *embodied experience*, and *embodied concept*. For all other uses, I prefer the term *bodily*.
2 Since its conception, the Cartesian dualist framework has been challenged by a variety of approaches, from Early Romantics and German Idealists to modern approaches such as psychoanalysis, phenomenology, poststructuralism, ecological psychology, and feminist epistemology. I do not wish to present posthumanist and enactivist critiques as exceptional in this regard. Many of these strains of thought are in active dialogue with the cognitive approaches discussed here, and will be referenced accordingly, but in-depth discussion of any of them is beyond the scope of this book.
3 The second-generation approach to cognition is also referred to as the 4E approach or paradigm. I mostly use "second generation." For differences in usage, see Kukkonen and Caracciolo (2014).
4 Alva Noë (2004, 2015) focuses on action and perception. Other scholars have discussed the enactive dynamics of other cognitive phenomena, such as emotion and feeling (Colombetti and Thompson 2008; Colombetti 2014), and imagination and remembering (Hutto and Myin 2013).
5 For broader overviews of cognitive approaches to literature, see Kukkonen and Caracciolo (2014) and Weik von Mossner (2017a).
6 One clash between these lines of thought stems from their philosophical groundings: cognitive approaches to literature have generally been associated with analytical philosophy, whereas posthumanist thought is associated with continental philosophy.
7 Groundlessness here derives, as does a great part of *The Embodied Mind*, from Buddhist philosophy, and denotes an ontological stance and experiential insight in which "all phenomena are free of any absolute ground" (Varela, Thompson, and Rosch 1992: 144).

8 Braidotti suggests that careful analysis of discursive practices and social imaginaries, and the generation of counter-imaginaries, can help to transform subjectivity. She understands social imaginaries as sources for unconscious identifications, stimulants, or points of reference that "act like magnets that draw the self heavily in certain directions and stimulate the person accordingly … analogous to discursive glue that holds the bits and pieces together, but in a discontinuous and contradictory manner" (Braidotti 2002: 40). By opening up a distance between social imaginaries and one's sense of self, counter-imaginaries can facilitate "processes of resistance to social roles and norms" (Braidotti 2002: 40–1). In the context of this study, we could view mutant narratives and mutant figures as potential counter-imaginaries.

9 According to Warhol (2003: 14), literary criticism and film theory have tended to use the expressive model, and thereby "granted privilege to the idea that every person harbors 'real' feelings, whether consciously or subconsciously expressed, and that literary texts tap into those feelings in more or less legitimate ways." Warhol (2003: 35) further links this claim to the modernist prejudice against popular forms that "so readily and mechanically arouse emotion: it's too easy; it must not be 'authentic'" (see also Section 4.1).

10 For other posthumanist applications of the later work of Maurice Merleau-Ponty, see, for example, Coole (2010) and Connolly (2010).

11 See also Richards (1929) and Ovaska and Kortekallio (2021).

12 Caracciolo (2014a: 394–5) also discusses the study by Kuiken, Miall, and Sikora.

13 In the second-generation approach to literature and cognition, the need for such a praxis has been acknowledged, and it is cultivated with care. Marco Caracciolo, Karin Kukkonen, and Emily T. Troscianko, among others, have presented detailed observations about the particularities of embodied engagement with narratives in both fictional and nonfictional genres, and suggested practical guidelines for embodied reading (see Kukkonen and Caracciolo 2014 for an overview of the second generation). In an earlier version of this text, I have provided a brief critical review of recent work in second-generation cognitive studies. I suggest that second-generation scholars base their readings and theories on phenomenological intuitions that are likely to be based on personal, embodied experience, but they also downplay the situated and first-person aspects of their embodied engagement (Kortekallio 2020a: 69–75).

14 While I see Neimanis's engagement with watery bodies as similar to more-than-human reading in some respects, I do not claim that they would be entirely analogous. I readily admit that water's involvement in cellular regeneration is somewhat different from literature's power to elevate our pulse or affect our perceptions.

15 Elsewhere, I have characterized the willing engagement with such narrative dynamics as *becoming-instrument* (Kortekallio 2019).

16 Critical commentary on Greg Bear's work consists mostly of references to *Blood Music* (1985) in the context of cyberpunk. Scott Bukatman (1993) and N. Katherine Hayles (1999) offer readings of *Blood Music* in relation to the "virtual subject" in postmodern science fiction. Longer analyses of Bear's work are provided by Roger Luckhurst (2007) and Laurel Bollinger (2009, 2010), while Heather Schell (2002) and Tom Idema (2019) focus specifically on the *Darwin* novels. As the primary purpose of my analysis of *Darwin's Children* is to discuss Bear's take on mutant embodiment rather than to enter into a deeper engagement with the author's *ouevre*, such previous analyses are discussed here only minimally.

17 Another major evolutionary-theoretical influence behind the Darwin novels is Stephen Jay Gould's *punctuated equilibrium hypothesis* (see Eldredge and Gould 1972). This hypothesis states that the evolution of species is structured as long periods of stasis punctuated by periods of rapid change, or "leaps in evolution."

18 The scientific coherence of *Darwin's Radio* especially has been commended by biologists (see Goldman 2000; Lynch 2001).

19 Influential works of fiction that convey mutant embodiment by imagining a "next generation" of mutants include Theodore Sturgeon's *More Than Human* (1953), *The X-Men* (1963–), and Salman Rushdie's *Midnight's Children* (1981). Like *Darwin's Children*, these works connect wide-scale mutations with rapid environmental and cultural changes (see also Section 3.1).

20 See *DC*: 182, 206, 242, 248, 250, 251, 263, 285, 288, 327, 387.

21 Such systems are presented as biological in the novel, as they are associated with the microbiological work of Kaye Lang and referred to as "deep minds … [m]inds that talk to each other through chemicals" (*DC*: 58). The novel does not explicitly provide further detail, but the context and the author's epilogue support the interpretation that the immune system is at least one of such minds (see also Idema 2019: 98).

22 The SHEVA retrovirus presents a noteworthy exception: it is definitely of nonhuman origin, its incorporation into the human genome deriving from the shared evolutionary past of all placental mammals. Kaye Lang's research into the retrovirus takes on affective modes, in which she empathetically enacts the perspective of the microbiological entity. However, this quest into the nonhuman world serves the higher goal of asserting the exceptional quality of the human body and mind. Despite its nonhumanness, the retrovirus suffers the same fate as Shevite subversiveness: it is ultimately incorporated into the harmonious community of *Homo*.

23 Furthermore, unnatural narratology has argued that realist narratives, in fact, involve unnatural or outright impossible moves, such as omniscience, and they thus do not hold any special claim to being the most unmediated and accurate style of representation (see Alber, Skov Nielsen, and Richardson 2013).

3

Mutant Figures and Reading Bodies

Having outlined a bodily, experiential, and posthumanist method of reading—*more-than-human reading*—I am faced with the fact that reading is a complex task that cannot be explained through simple comparisons to our everyday interactions with actual people and places. If we consider reading as an event in which both the text and the environment participate, we soon realize that every instance of reading is partly constituted by readers' own experiential backgrounds and current contexts—including the histories of both production and reception of fiction.

One previously expressed critique of the embodied reader model is that the model guides the reader's attention toward a narrowly experienced present moment: one is focused on reading only for affective cues, dismissing things like plot, genre, or intertextuality partially or completely (see Kukkonen 2014). This critique is worth noting: any reading, including my reading of Greg Bear's *Darwin's Children* in the previous chapter, is bound to take place in a network of not only personal contexts but also the material and cultural conditions shared with other human and nonhuman bodies. This means that reading, even when experienced as personal and particular, is historically, socially, and geopolitically situated.

One of the factors contributing to this complex situatedness is *genre*. The particular context of science fiction is both similar to and different from both the literary mainstream and high-brow experimental literatures. Even if genre boundaries have become increasingly blurred during the twenty-first century (see Wolfe 2011; Pettersson 2016: 64–74), the particular conventions of writing, publishing, reading, and discussing in the science fiction context still affect both the texts at hand and their reception. Bo Pettersson (2016) has suggested that the knowledge of the generic context of a work of fiction is ingrained in how the readers interpret its particular way of making sense of reality, that is, *mimesis*:

> Literary representation is not only based on the world and genres authors know and employ but also on what readers consider real in the fictional worlds depicted. Assessing how representation works in literature is fundamental for readers so that they can understand how the real and the fantastic blend in literature. That is, mimesis and genre are often co-determined in interpreting literature: if you do not know the genre, you may misunderstand what is represented and the other way around. (Pettersson 2016: 76–7)

Pettersson's point can be extended beyond representation: as narratives of different genres demand different modes of mimetic sense-making of their readers, it follows that readers of different genres also *participate in different kinds of readerly choreographies*—as they read, their bodily experiences are pushed and pulled by particular generic traditions and figurations, and nuances of those experiences depend on their experiential backgrounds. Encountering a zombie narrative for the very first time may evoke strong bodily feelings, such as disgust or fear, but the lack of genre knowledge probably makes it difficult to experience any sense of *continuity* with other such narratives—whereas when encountering a zombie narrative for the hundredth time, continuity may take the foreground and sensations settle into their established tracks.

Readers of realist and nonrealist texts alike negotiate different narrative strategies, such as allegory or documentary realism, and different levels of fictionality, such as the imaginative recasting of actual places and people. Much of contemporary fiction requires these kinds of readerly skills. Mutant narratives are no different, as they build on shared generic knowledge of mutant figures. In this chapter, I focus on how science fictional *character* invites readers to employ their knowledge of generic contexts and fictionality at the level of embodied experience. Repeated encounters with mutant figures across texts feed into the shared experiential background of science fiction readers, thus guiding how we respond to any new iteration of them. More generally, the dynamic of encountering mutant figures sheds light on how reading participates in the process of *habituation*, that is, of learning and integrating particular forms of feeling, perception, and action.

In Section 3.1, I provide an overview of mutant figures in Anglophone speculative fiction and unravel some aspects of their construction by comparing them to narrative-theoretical models of fictional character. In this process, it becomes questionable whether the term *character* can be meaningfully applied to all of them, and whether character theory can contribute to reading them in the context of embodied cognition and more-than-human experience. This discussion also ties into Pettersson's (2016) notion of the codetermination of mimesis and genre: it appears that some science fictional characters are not designed to be encountered in ways that character theory suggest we should, that is, as representations of humans, but as "pieces of equipment" (Jones 2003: 5) subject to the wider workings of the narrative design. Thus, instead of character-theoretical approaches, I adopt the term *figure* as an option that allows movement away from anthropomorphic modes of reading.

This reconfiguration is needed for a posthumanist understanding of *artificial persons*—human or nearly human bodies and minds that are formed in systemic processes of mutual specification. While all science fictional variations of the theme of artificial persons foreground and defamiliarize human embodiment, narrowing the focus to mutants can orient us toward material entanglements most relevant to more-than-human subjectivity. Due to their entangled nature, mutant figures also show how theories of narrative sense-making, usually limited to the human and the intersubjective, could be modified to better grasp the more-than-human aspects of life and perception.

3.1 Mutant Figures

The mutant embodiment of Greg Bear's Stella, discussed in Chapter 2, is not isolated from other instances of mutant embodiment, fictional as well as actual. These other instances contribute to the experiential background of readers of *Darwin's Children* on various levels of specialization: any reader embedded in the Western cultural context is bound to read the novel in relation to the transmedially franchised mutant superheroes of comic books and blockbuster films, such as *Spider-Man* (since 1962), the *X-Men* (since 1963), and the *Teenage Mutant Ninja Turtles* (since 1984), or the mutants of horror films such as *The Fly* (1958 and 1986) and *The Thing* (1951 and 1982).

However, the genealogy of the mutant figure extends far beyond these most popular instances. The modern mutants of Anglo-American science fiction emerge from a long history of metamorphoses and monstrous/divine figures in both Western and non-Western mythologies. Grotesque imaginary, such as Francois Rabelais's *The Life Gargantua and Pantagruel* (*La vie de Gargantua et de Pantagruel*, c. 1532–64) and Victor Hugo's *The Hunchback of Notre Dame* (*Notre-Dame de Paris*, 1831), and modern-day magical realism—just think of the pig-tailed children of Gabriel García Márquez's *One Hundred Years of Solitude* (*Cien años de soledad*, 1967) and the telepathic witches of Salman Rushdie's *Midnight's Children* (1981)—also contributes to the trope.[1]

Mutant narratives are engaged in imagining species, genetics, and environments, and they do it with all the various strategies and devices of fantasy and speculation. Most iterations of the mutant figure are not overly concerned with fidelity to the actual biological dynamics of genetic mutation: creatures are transformed both before and after their births, in situations ranging from accidents in nuclear power plants to intentional genetic manipulation. As a popular biological term, *mutant* is slightly pejorative, used to indicate freaks of nature whose genetic mutations make them significantly different from their parent organisms. They are often functionally defective, as in the case of albinistic animals, or humans suffering from various genetically derived diseases. Technically, however, mutation is an essential part of sexual reproduction and a driving force of evolution—therefore, all sexually generated creatures are in some sense biological mutants.

Rather than focusing on the technical aspects of their generation, it might be reasonable to characterize mutants by their *relation to the norm of the species* portrayed in the work of fiction. Regardless of technicalities, mutant figures occupy the niche of the freak, the monster, the exception to the rule, the transgression, the ambiguous potentiality that might be realized as either destructive or generative action. In contemporary science fiction, this niche is occupied by not just genetic deviations, but also bioengineered and chemically transformed bodies—as well as by bodies of non-biological origin, such as androids and robots.[2]

My choice of the term *mutant*, instead of the more widely used academic search terms like *posthuman* or *monster*, is motivated by three aspects: the term's historical transformation from a pejorative label into a marker of self-identification, its evocation of the issues of genetic determinism and evolution, and its evocation of painful subjective transformation. Mutation can also function as a figuration for cultural and experiential change. While the terms *posthuman* and *cyborg* usually focus on the technological and societal entanglements of modern human bodies, and *monster* orients us to considering the anxieties and possibilities lurking in the liminal areas of human subjectivity, *mutant* can add to all of these discussions by mobilizing our imagination of biological and ecological change. As the examples in the next sections will demonstrate, mutant figures are stretched between controlled life (*bios*) and radical change (*zoe*), often leaning toward the latter, by describing wild alterity where android/cyborg narratives would present bleak systemic control.[3]

As they incorporate and expand on the dynamic logic of biological mutation, mutant figures can help us navigate within a world that does not consist of sovereign subjects and mute objects but of bodies "inextricably enmeshed in a dense network of relations" (Bennett 2010: 13). Mutant figures point to the effervescence of *form* itself: whatever the current form of the mutant, its next iteration is shaped by circumstances and chance, and therefore it is bound to be something different. This dynamic of continuity and change also thematizes the evolutive logic of narrative experientiality: every instance of reading fiction both draws on our previous experiences and gives rise to new ones.

3.1.1 A Brief History of Mutant Figures

The most prominent feature of mutant figures is abnormal embodiment, in forms ranging from the spectacularly freakish to the invisibly deviant. The spectacularly freakish is tied to particular historical practices in modern show business: as part of the imperial exoticism of the nineteenth century, all kinds of specimens were brought in front of European audiences—strange animals and strange people alike. The figure is inseparable from the scientific investigation of living bodies—as potentially reproducible by technological means, as in Mary Shelley's *Frankenstein* (1818), or as naturally evolving, as in H. G. Wells's *The Time Machine* (1895). The freak shows and natural science exhibitions presented their audiences with a variety of possible forms of animal and human—and served to both confuse and strengthen the boundaries between "normal humanity" and its deviations. Strange bodies were produced as objects for the observing eye of the scientific mind—which was never too far from the voyeuristic or the dominating gaze (see, e.g., Haraway 1992; Grosz 1994). What emerged, quite often, is the understanding of evolution as a linear progression from lower forms to higher. In this conception, the novel idea of evolution was bent to conform to notions deriving from classical and Christian metaphysics. As the unfolding history of mutant stories demonstrates, these notions are still in active circulation.[4]

The stories involving genetic mutation, specifically, emerged during the twentieth century with the development and popularization of ideas in genetics. At this point, the mutant figure is tied to the issues of heredity and generational shift—after the Second World War, stories of mutation in the Western world tend to describe generations of strange children, sometimes leading to new races and breeds of supermen. The Second World War also marks the beginning of the *atomic mutant*, a creature carrying mutations caused by nuclear radiation, a profoundly unnatural creature. A short story by James Blish, "Battle of the Unborn" ([1950]1955), imagines a world infested by atomically mutated humans, and a particularly murderous variation that should, according to the responsible bureau, be either sterilized or segregated on a camp. The object-like aspects of the biologized mutant body are highlighted in a passage that also exemplifies the shift of focus from spectacularly freakish bodies to invisible deviations only accessible with the instruments of science.

> Homo chaos looks like any ordinary human on the outside; but inside, there are easily recognizable signs. No vermiform appendix; a pineal body that shows up coal-black on the X rays, even when the pictures are taken through the foramen magnum; a type of nervous tissue impervious to silver nitrate; Golgi bodies in the brain do not take silver-line stain. And haematological signs: very fast clotting time and sedimentation rate; a high white count with a predominance of young forms that you would call mononucleosis in a normal human. And a few other signs. (Blish [1950]1955: 21)

The objectifying list of descriptions, and the project of classifying mutants by scientific means, is set in a satirical light by the next twist of the plot: the scientist is killed by his mutant colleague, who did indeed look like any ordinary human on the outside. In Blish's narrative, the supposed object of scientific control cannot be contained but escapes its boundaries, taking the place of the human subject in a paranoid turn that also characterizes American post–Second World War monster fiction more generally.[5]

The 1950s stories from American writers are permeated by traces of eugenics and atomic radiation. However, they also carry the hope of an evolutionary leap through a generation of children blessed with the gifts of teleportation, telekinesis, and telepathy, or other special abilities such as great intellect, as in *Children of the Atom* (1953) by Wilmar H. Shiras. In these stories, the rise of the new generation often means the fall of the old. The trope of the superman is utilized and explored extensively. Olaf Stapledon's *Odd John* (1935) is credited to have coined the term *Homo superior*, which has been adopted widely in later mutant stories, including Blish's story.

Sometimes the superman emerges as a group. In Theodore Sturgeon's *More Than Human* (1953), a handful of dysfunctional misfits are joined at an operational level, resulting in a system referred to as a "superorganism" and likened to a radio station with several individual receivers. This "new kind of human being," *Homo Gestalt*, considers human morality as inapplicable to itself.

"Listen," she said passionately, "we're not a group of freaks. We're *Homo Gestalt*, you understand? We're a single entity, a new kind of human being. We weren't invented. We evolved. We're the next step up. We're alone; there are no more like us. We don't live in the kind of world you do, with systems of morals and codes of ethics to guide us. We're living on a desert island with a herd of goats!"

"I'm the goat."

"Yes, yes, you *are*, can't you see? But we were born on this island with no one like us to teach us, tell us how to behave. We can learn from the goats all the things that make a goat a good goat, but that will never change the fact that we're *not* a goat! You can't apply the same set of rules to us as you do to ordinary humans; we're just not the same thing!" (Sturgeon 1953: 211–12)

The atomic mutant stories amplified the exciting tensions of the post–Second World War years: not only has society been drastically transformed by the war, but the very capabilities of human (Anglo-American) culture have been dramatically widened by the invention of nuclear energy and nuclear weapons. At the threshold of this new technology, it appears that a new type of human is also emerging.

While political and technological circumstances have changed from the 1950s, the mutant figures of the twenty-first century still carry this tension of humanity hovering at the edge of the future. Some of the novelty of the tension has worn off, though—as has been apparent at least since the ironic postmodern mutants of the 1980s. This ironic shift in the use of the mutant figure involves a great amount of genre-consciousness. Postmodern variations of the mutant figure are often crafted with a sense of the historical continuum, but earnest narratives of the rise of superior beings are harder to find.

The epitome of the ironic development might be *Teenage Mutant Ninja Turtles*, a parodic comic book concept created by Kevin Eastman and Peter Laird in 1984, which was brought to a wider audience via an action figure production line and a television series. Building on the post–Second World War pulp monsters, contemporaneous superhero comics, and urban legends, the series takes an abomination—the sewer-dwelling turtle transformed by urban chemicals—and turns it into a gang of heroic, identifiable figures. In the same humorous vein, the film *The Toxic Avenger* (1984) features a bullied youngster transformed into a monstrous hulk via exposure to toxic chemicals.

By presenting monstrous bodies as identifiable and sympathetic, these popular iterations of the mutant figure participated in a cultural shift that promoted individualistic variation and flexible identities while acknowledging the hazardous systemic influences of modern consumerist culture. Whereas the atomic mutant was an exceptional, super- or subhuman figure, the *Turtles* and the *Avenger* are offered as widely shareable templates for identification. Monstrosity, they appear to propose, is part of postmodern subjectivity (see also Cohen 1996; Badmington 2004; Hellstrand 2016).

The atomic age tension that links great power with great responsibility, as well as with great challenges in adapting to societal norms, lives on in today's science fiction—perhaps most prominently in Marvel's transmedial *X-Men*, which is arguably the most well-known contemporary iteration of the *Homo superior* trope. The franchise has, since its launch as a comic in 1963, survived two generational shifts by incorporating new themes, such as transsexuality and homosexuality. With the popularity of the *X-Men* films, queer activists have adopted the motto "mutant and proud"[6] as a marker of nonbinary identity. The thematic shift in *X-Men* signals a corresponding shift in the use of the mutant figure: as cultures have grown more sensitive to diversity, strange figures have become acceptable points of identification. This movement has its roots in stories like Sturgeon's, in which the possibility of a *mutant experience* begins to take form. The strange bodies are considered not only as objects of science or thought-experiment, but also as sites of embodied experience, and possibly of experience beyond easy identity-based access.

Articulating both the experientiality and science involved in the lives of mutant bodies posits a remarkable challenge for fiction authors. Octavia E. Butler, in her *Xenogenesis* trilogy (1987–9, also published as the single-volume *Lilith's Brood* in 2000), navigates this challenge by imagining an alien species that intuitively understands and manipulates something that humans can only access through technology: genetic structure. For the Oankali, and for the "constructs" born from crossbreeding Oankali and humans, accessing and manipulating diverse genetic strains is as imperative as breathing and sexual interaction. In *Imago* (1989) Butler articulates this condition in rich descriptions of sensory experience. First-person accounts of characters going through their adolescent and adult transformations evoke the affects of confusion and enlarged sensory perception, while also explaining the metamorphosis in biological and biochemical terms.

> I slipped into my first metamorphosis so quietly that no one noticed. Metamorphoses were not supposed to begin that way. Most people begin with small, obvious, physical changes—the loss of fingers and toes, or the budding of new fingers and toes of a different design.

I wish my experience had been that normal, that safe.

For several days, I changed without attracting attention. Early stages of metamorphosis didn't normally last for days without bringing on deep sleep, but mine did. Tastes, scents, all sensations suddenly became complex, confusing, yet unexpectedly seductive.

I had to relearn everything. River water, for instance: when I swam in it, I noticed that it had two distinctive major flavors—hydrogen and oxygen?—and many minor flavors. I could separate out and savor each one individually. In fact, I couldn't help separating them. But I learned them quickly and accepted them in their new complexity so that only occasional changes in minor flavors demanded my attention.

Our river water at Lo always came to us clouded with sediment. "Rich," the Oankali called it. "Muddy," the Humans said, and filtered it or let the silt settle to the bottom before they drank it. "Just water," we constructs said, and shrugged. We had never known any other water." (Butler 1989: 3)

Compared to the description of mutant bodies in Greg Bear's *Darwin's Children* (discussed in Section 2.3), Butler's narrative blends the biological and the phenomenological in a more nuanced manner. The mode of the passage is experiential from beginning to end, but details of the narrator's physical transformation are woven in. By describing what a "normal" metamorphosis would entail, the passage informs readers that metamorphosis is a common phenomenon in the fictional world. The narrator describes the experience of learning to taste different flavors in river water, speculating about their correlation with chemical structures.

Imago's narrator Jodahs, a Human-Oankali hybrid, is overwhelmed by the instrumental precision with which his body detects the detail of his environment. This sensitivity also applies to his social life: he develops an acute sensitivity for other people's bodily states. What he senses is explained in terms of biochemistry: however, the overall effect of the first person narration is that of exceptional empathy. Jodahs enjoys his connection to others, needs it more than anything: for him, a prolonged solitude can be literally fatal. Throughout the trilogy, Butler develops a model of relational and material subjectivity in which every move made by an individual body connects it to myriad other bodies— both genetically related and environmentally or metabolically relevant.

The flip side of genetic and environmental accidents, the randomness of mutation, is *design*. Biotechnology—selective breeding, genetic engineering, and other modifications to biological creatures—has been the stuff of science fiction since its beginning. Mary Shelley's *Frankenstein* and H. G. Wells's *The Island of Doctor Moreau* (1896) set the ambivalent tone that lives on in the biopunk of today: the ability to use science and technology to modify living beings is presented as both marvelous and terrifying. Biotechnology is intimately connected to the interlinked themes of reproduction and labor. In Lois McMaster Bujold's *Falling Free* (1988), for example, a new breed of four-handed humans is developed in an orbital production plant as workers for industries operating in zero gravity. The first generation of *Homo quadrimanus*, or "quaddies," are property to the corporation, but as they reach adolescence and begin having children of their own, they rise against the corporation in a genuine socialist revolution encouraged and organized by the lead engineer of the production plant. In Peter Watts's *Blindsight* (2006) and *Echopraxia* (2014), the theme of space-faring workers is brought to the twenty-first century as specialized professionals, such as researchers and military experts, are required by their employers to radically extend and amplify their bodily capacities through prostheses and modifications. Watts's narration evokes the posthuman subjectivity of these "bleeding-edgers" through first-person accounts of their technologically enhanced sensory experiences.

The themes of sovereignty and class consciousness are almost always present in stories about artificial people. It is well worth remembering that the word *robot* derives from the Czech word signifying "hard work" or "slavery." The topics of breeding and forced bodily labor also highlight the proximity between artificial people and the other species subjected to human economies: factory-farmed animals, animal test subjects, and the horses and dogs used in sports and certain trades. Rising topics are the use of animal/clone bodies for pharmaceutical purposes, explored recently in Margaret Atwood's *MaddAddam* series (2003–13) and Kazuo Ishiguro's *Never Let Me Go* (2005). The possibility of a synthetic yet autonomous organic life is imagined in Rudy Rucker's *Postsingular* (2007) and *Hylozoic* (2009), as well as in Jeff VanderMeer's *Borne* (2017).[7]

Sometimes, most often in works with transhumanist themes such as Bruce Sterling's *Schismatrix* (1985) or the "Culture" novels of Iain M. Banks, body-modification is presented as voluntary and enjoyable, as part of individualist, late capitalist identity play. Pat Cadigan's short story "The Girl-Thing That Went Out for Sushi" (2012) takes the theme of nonbinary identification from gender to species by portraying space-dwelling people who have chosen to live their lives in various marine-life body designs, that is, they have "gone out for sushi."

I didn't choose octo—back then, surgery wasn't as advanced and nanorectics weren't as commonplace or as programmable, so you got whatever the doctors thought gave you the best chance of a life worth living. I wasn't too happy at first but it's hard to be unhappy in a place this beautiful, especially when you feel so good physically all the time.

It was somewhere between three and four J-years after I turned that people could finally choose what kind of sushi they went out for, but I got no regrets. Any more. I've got it smooth all over.

Only I don't feel too smooth listening to two-steppers chewing the air over things they don't know anything about and puking up words like *abominations, atrocities,* and *sub-human monsters*. One news program even runs clips from the most recent re-make of *The Goddam Island Of Fucking Dr. Moreau*. Like that's holy writ or something. I can't stand more than a few minutes before I take my kribble into my bolthole, close the hatch, and hit sound-proof.

A little while later, Glynis beeps. "You know how 'way back in the extreme dead past, people in the Dirt thought everything in the universe revolved around them?" She pauses but I don't answer. "Then the scope of human knowledge expanded and we all know that was wrong."

"So?" I grunt.

"Not everybody got the memo," she says. (Cadigan 2012: 8–9)

Cadigan's short story evokes many layered meanings attached to mutant bodies: sex correction operations, modifications for life in space, and the conservative prejudice against unusual bodies and identities. Explicitly signaling its genre-consciousness, the narrative refers to *The Island of Dr. Moreau* as a cultural staple of the fear of monstrous others.

In light of the many technosystemic entanglements articulated by these works of fiction, we might consider mutants as a special case of cyborgs: they, too, challenge the boundaries of humanity, and the dichotomies between natural and cultural, biological, and technological. They foreground the interconnectivities and interdependencies of bodies (animate and inanimate) and systems (ecological, social, and technological). Even when they are "freaks of nature," products of genetic accidents rather than technological intervention, mutants are entangled with industrial and postindustrial environments. The *Homo Gestalt* of Theodore Sturgeon's *More Than Human* (1953), for example, form a collective superorganism. The operational structure of the organism is likened to a radio station with four or five individual receivers, and to an all-purpose electric motor. Similarly, Greg Bear's *Darwin's Radio* (1999) and *Darwin's Children* (2003) imagine an epidemic of strange births, connected to a systemic shift in the planetary environment, resulting in an emergence of a new clade, *Homo sapiens novus*. The "radio" in the novel's title refers to the clade's role as a signal from the planetary system. These works of fiction mobilize ideas from systems biology, considering individual mutations as parts of a wider evolutionary and ecosystemic change—which, in both cases, is connected to the effects of human activity in the biosphere. In the fiction of the twentieth and the twenty-first centuries, even the most biological of mutants are linked to the technosphere.

Like cyborgs, mutants thus thematize the coding and programming living bodies—biotechnology, in the broadest sense of the word. However, the mutant figure is not only about humans and their genetic essence, but also about other species and processes: about symbiosis, hybridity, other others, and strange strangers. The mutant shows how human bodies are partly constituted by nonhuman entities, as exemplified by the significance of microbes in Bruce Sterling's *Schismatrix* (1985) and in Joan Slonczewski's *Brain Plague* (2000). Mutant bodies contain strange actors: viruses, bacteria, cancerous growth, genetic material from birds, fish, and mammals—and, as in Octavia E. Butler's fiction, extraterrestrial material.

To sum up, my discussion of mutant figures revolves around the shifting boundaries of human and nonhuman bodies, freakish embodiment and deviant subjectivities, genetics and evolution, and entanglements of both technological and ecological varieties. The science fictional genealogy of mutant figures provides rich soil for new variations of the figure. The genealogy also informs and enriches readerly engagements with mutant figures, old or new. I will now discuss how the experience of encountering mutant figures is related to narratological theories of reading characters.

3.1.2 Mutant Figures and Character Theory

In the previous sections, I have used the term *mutant figures*, not *mutant characters*. This choice is intentional and grounded on the problematic limitations set by the term *character*. While the term suffices in discussions with nonacademic audiences, the specific context of narratology weighs it down with humanist and idealist connotations that would guide my readings to search the fiction for individuality, complex interiority, and embeddedness in primarily social and societal—that is, interhuman—networks of meaning.

Any introduction to character theory will most likely begin with the mimetic statement that characters are "fictional representations of humans" or the structuralist statement that they are "human-like textual constructs." Uri Margolin's

(2007: 66) concise definition balances both aspects: "'character' designates any entity, individual or collective—normally human or human-like—introduced in a work of narrative fiction." What "human or human-like" actually entails is a foundational question in studies of literature and narrative and the core of countless literary analyses. On the other hand, the question is rarely discussed in depth. Postcolonial critics, such as James (2015), have argued that the narratological notion of mimesis assumes a particular kind of reality, and posthumanist critique could well argue that it also assumes a particular kind of human.

Laying the grounds for a posthumanist theory of character, Essi Varis (2019b) argues that both narratologists and lay readers tend to consider characters as mimetic representations of *humans* even when the characters' features would point to nonhuman or purely fantastic directions, as when encountering fictional figures that are introduced as animal, extraterrestrial, or computational. The humanizing tendency is widely shared by readers, as human readers are inclined to find human resonance even in radically antimimetic and/or nonhuman fictional entities. For Varis, this tendency is amplified by the fact that for most people, sociality is limited to interaction with other humans (often much like themselves), and thus

> most of our everyday thinking is filtered through several layers of assumptions about what matters to this specific species ... humans tend to write fiction about humans for human readers, because all these human readers are likely interested in the ways other humans experience their human condition. (Varis 2019b: 3)

This human-centered feedback loop, for both Varis and myself, is the proper context for theorizing fictional characters. It is not that the human-centeredness of fiction is necessarily and permanently the *natural* state for humans—rather, it is the model most consistently amplified by the lived environments of humans concerned with fiction.[8] Lived experience, including the lived experience of fiction, is accumulated through enacting patterns of care and interest (see Colombetti 2014; Maiese 2015), and for most humans who read fiction, human sociality is at the center of these patterns. As has been argued by scholars of the Anthropocene, this situation, particular to rich countries, is an effect of the material organization of energy and matter that separates human consumption from more-than-human production (Salminen and Vadén 2015; LeMenager 2014; Clark 2015). In a hypothetical ecocentric or posthumanist culture, habitual patterns of care and interest would perhaps engage other species and nonhuman materialities more explicitly, and thus the feedback loops would be altered as well.[9]

Not surprisingly, in the humanities the human-centric feedback loop is even more effective than elsewhere. Literary theorists are humanists *par excellence*, as storytelling is generally understood as the most human endeavor there is. This is also the context in which the human-centric and realist notion of mimesis is developed. In most influential narrative theories, mimesis roughly accounts for the recognition of human behavior, emotion, action, and social contexts, and narrativity stands for "mediated human experientiality" (Fludernik 1996: 9, 26). Thus, one dominant idea in narrative theory is that literature represents social life, and that it is encountered and understood with the help of the same cognitive dynamics that are central to understanding the operations of real people. Blakey Vermeule (2010: 7), in her *Why Do We Care About Literary Characters?*, goes particularly far along this path, claiming that "most stories are gossip literature." By "gossip literature," she means "any insightful or exposing tale about other people in which the insight doesn't necessarily put the other people in the best light" (Vermeule 2010: 7). Building on the work of Dorrit Cohn (1999), Vermeule (2010: 14) goes on to argue that gaining social information (even about fictional people) is the main reward of reading fiction, and as a side gain, readers end up practicing their mind-reading skills.[10]

While Vermeule's humanizing approach is not uncritically shared by narratologists at large, as the research tradition is built on the foundations of structuralism and thus tends to consider all elements of narrative (including character, as textual constructs with specific functions), the underlying assumptions guiding theories of character tend to be anthropomorphic (see Jannidis 2012; Polvinen and Sklar 2019. This anthropomorphism not only foregrounds the human subject, but does so in the specific sense of equating human subjectivity with minds, consciousness, and social meaning, thus downplaying the materiality and more-than-human relationality of human bodies.

This anthropomorphic bias is naturalized to the extent that even work that explicitly critiques it can inadvertently support it. Unnatural narratology, for example, has experimented with applying the cognitive reasoning of Fludernik's (1996) natural narratology to works that "radically deconstruct the anthropomorphic narrator, the traditional human character, or real-world notions of time and space" (Alber 2009: 80). While the unnatural approach initially challenges the "mimetic bias" of narrative studies (Alber 2009: 79), it eventually reasserts it by means of inversion: as nonhuman characters are "antimimetic," mimesis "naturally" refers to an imitation of reality in a realist mode (Pettersson 2012) and, more specifically, to the imitation of interhuman sociality (Varis 2019b: 4). On the other hand, in cognitive approaches that focus on the nonhuman and the limits of human cognition, anthropomorphism is viewed as only one possible strategy for representing nonhuman experience (see Bernaerts et al. 2014; Caracciolo 2014a, 2016, 2021; Herman 2019; Pettersson 2016).

For a posthumanist reader, this discussion offers a particular kind of challenge: what kind of fictional beings, actions, and perceptions are recognized as "human"? I propose that what is prereflectively set as "natural" and "familiar" in character theories is the particular experiential realm of modern, Western, humanist, intersubjective sociality. Most theories of character do not account for readerly experiences in which the reader would be comfortable with, to give a few examples, magical thinking (see James 2015; Clark 2015), cybernetic entanglements with technology (see Hayles 2018), or communication with nonhuman entities (see Abram 1996). They only cover the narrow rationalist humanist mode of perceiving reality, which they portray as the "natural" one. Rosemary Jackson, in her 1981 defense of the fantastic imagination, concisely articulates this argument:

> "Character" is itself an ideological concept, produced in the name of a "realistic" representation of an actual, empirically verifiable reality outside the literary text. Realism, as an artistic practice, confirms the dominant ideas of what constitutes this outside reality, by pulling it into place, organizing and framing it through the unities of the text. It presents its practice as a neutral, innocent and natural one, erasing its own artifice and construction of the "real." "Character" is one of the central pivots of this operation. (Jackson 1981: 83)

Herein lies the trouble I have with the term *character*. It asks us to play along in a certain ideological construction of reality, in which reality (both social and material) is "out there," to be accessed and described by both perception and fiction through a mode of realist mimetic referentiality. As Jackson points out, this is not a neutral practice but a naturalizing strategy that constructs a particular mode of perception. Both the concept and the narratological context of *character* are inherently anthropocentric and bound to a naturalized understanding of realism.

The term *figure*, on the other hand, allows me to move these anthropocentric and realist assumptions on one side and focus on something else.[11] My use of the term should not be associated with the structuralist-semiotic usage (Greimas 1973) but rather with the posthumanist feminist practice of *figuration* (Haraway 1992, 1997, 2008; Braidotti 2002, 2013; Bastian 2006; Neimanis 2017;

see Section 2.1).¹² For Haraway (1997: 23) "a figure embodies shared meanings in stories that inhabit their audiences." The notion of stories inhabiting their audiences, rather than vice versa, sits well with the more-than-human mode of reading I develop here. In reading, figures are *incorporated* by readerly bodies. *Figuration*, in my interpretation of Haraway, always includes a context, such as the appearance of the cyborg in both fictional and documentary works drawing on cyberpunk aesthetics, or the entanglement of the lab mouse in the material-semiotic networks of scientific experimentation and animal rights. As such, it is a broader term than *figure*.

Figure connotes three aspects of narrative experientiality that I find particularly interesting: the material force of fictional bodies, that is, the affective and perceptual impact they have on our reading bodies; figures as particular, recurring textual patterns in the whole of the narrative; and figures as habitual patterns of readerly engagement. Thus, *figure* allows me to analyze mutant narratives in ways that develop more-than-human and enactivist perspectives. Moreover, as I explain later in more detail, the term is better suited for analyzing fictional actors who do not evoke impressions of deep and complex psyches. In my readings of N. K. Jemisin's and Paolo Bacigalupi's works in Sections 3.2, 4.1, and 4.2, I will focus primarily on the ways in which mutant narratives invite me to enact the material and bodily movements of mutant figures and thus temporarily reorganize the habitual patterns of my perception, attention, and feeling. This enactive dynamic both amplifies and reconfigures conventional experiential patterns of readerly reception, and that Bacigalupi's fiction, in particular, encourages readers to reflect on their experiential habits of engaging with fictional bodies.

3.1.3 Science Fiction, Realism, and Experientiality

I have now established that *character* is anthropocentric and bound to a naturalized realist understanding of mimesis: the assumption that certain kinds of narratives faithfully represent or at least imitate reality. For many science fiction authors and scholars, fiction is far more integral to the constitution of realities, and even as science fiction evokes lifelike illusions much like realist fiction does, it also foregrounds the process of construction (Mandala 2010; McHale 2010; Roine 2016; Polvinen 2023). No one has experienced faster-than-light travel or encounters with aliens, yet science fiction narrates those experiences for us in ways that make them plausible for the duration of the reading.

As Pettersson (2016: 41–3, 51) demonstrates in his historical account of the concept, the limited understanding of mimesis as "imitation of reality," although drawing on Plato, is quite recent, and the original Aristotelian notion allows for far more flexible relations between actual environments and fictional narratives (see also Kukkonen 2019: 13–15). A wider notion of mimesis calls for a discussion of the strategies narratives use to evoke illusions of reality. Science fiction narratives ask readers to continuously engage with these narrative strategies. They are able to evoke counterfactual worlds precisely because they make use of realist narrative strategies. These include character narration that emphasizes the ordinariness of the character; a view of reality from the perspective of an individual, full of historically insignificant details, and repetition (see Rossi 2012; Pettersson 2016: 67–74). In terms of its form, science fiction is thus often indistinguishable from realist fiction, and readers' identification of it as nonrealist depends on extratextual knowledge.

Following Riikka Rossi (2012), I understand the Barthesian "reality effects" of realism primarily as *cognitive effects* that emerge from encounters with a particular set of narrative strategies. Realism, in Rossi's view, produces a particular kind of faith in the continuity of the storyworld and the experience— the kind of "natural attitude" or nonreflective stance often complicated by phenomenologists.

> The sense of ontological security is a primitive feeling; "basic trust" in the continuity of things and persons is a psychological need of a persistent and recurring kind. It is because of this basic trust we believe that cars will not break down or suddenly leave the street and hit you on your Sunday afternoon walk. The reality effect activated in a literary text could also be seen to activate this "natural" attitude and intuitive belief in the "reality-like" nature of the story. "Walking" through a realist text presupposes a certain non-reflective view. (Rossi 2012: 123; see also Giddens 1990: 97–8)

In the context of *Darwin's Children*, such a "natural attitude" is evoked by character narration, also when the characterization includes "antimimetic" features, most significantly mutant embodiment. As noted in Section 2.3, the plausibility of the teenage mutant Stella is created through realist techniques, and thus she fits perfectly well into the category of realist character. The realist techniques serve to evoke a "character-centered illusion" (Caracciolo 2016) that leads readers to form empathic bonds to the character, as if she were a real person with feelings, thoughts, and aspirations.

The quasi-realist strategies of most science fiction rarely include formal *defamiliarization* in the sense meant by Shklovsky (2012). The defamiliarization typical to science fiction is different from the defamiliarization typical to experimental fiction or poetry. The defamiliarizing elements of science fiction tend to exist on the level of storyworld rather than as formal devices. Thus, the effects of science fictional defamiliarization can be characterized as *diegetic estrangement*, in which the estranging effect lies in the strangeness of the diegetic existent rather than in experimental narrative form (Spiegel 2008). Mutant narratives are a good example of this convention: on the formal level of narration or focalization, there is very little innovation and thus very little of interest for narratologists of the formalist tradition. Yet, the defamiliarizing elements of the storyworld such as strange and improbable bodies make engaging with the narratives quite complex. This dynamic between conventional form and estranging content makes mutant narratives relevant to cognitive approaches to narrative.

Recent work in both science fiction studies and cognitive narratology discusses the dynamic between defamiliarization and naturalization as interdependent. That is, the overall experience of encountering strange worlds "only comes into effect after a successful naturalization [of the novum] has taken place" (Spiegel 2008: 377; see also McHale 2010; Bernaerts et al. 2014; Caracciolo 2016, 2021). In terms of experientiality, the narrative strategies of science fiction depend both on the evocation of real-life experience, or our personal background, and the complex readerly act of encountering and interpreting the defamiliarizing elements of the text. Reading Butler's *Imago*, for example, we recognize the human aspects of mutant embodiment, but also make sense of strange Oankali sensations. It is also important to remember that real-life experience includes the experience of engaging with fictional narratives, worlds, and characters (Mikkonen 2014).[13]

In light of science fiction's complex relations with reality and realism, it is remarkable that science fiction also *resists* realist strategies by drawing on other traditions, such as pulp fiction, fairytale, and action adventure. This is apparent in the mutant figures that do not seem either to meet the implicit requirements of character theory or to evoke plausible reality effects. For instance, this is evident in the mutant youngsters of the *X-Men* franchise, or in the artificial bodies of Paolo Bacigalupi's fiction, discussed in Sections 4.1 and 4.2. Such figures appear to be caricatures rather than fully rendered representations of actual complex persons, predictable in their actions and speech, in a single word deriving from early narratology, "flat" (Forster 1985).

It is important to understand that the flatness of these figures is not a *lack* in characterization but an intentional stylistic feature that has its own affordances. As science fiction author and scholar Gwyneth Jones (2003: 5) has underlined, typical science fiction does not treat characters as ends in themselves but as "pieces of equipment" that serve the purpose of making experiential the societies, technologies, and natural worlds of their imaginary worlds.[14] In some cases, this instrumentality leads to realistically constructed, humanist figures such as Stella—and in others, to the type-based and "flat" characters deriving from pulp fiction and adventure stories, such as Emiko of *The Windup Girl* (see also Mandala 2010; Jannidis 2012). To appreciate what kind of experiences such modes of instrumentality afford to readers, I think it is best to maintain an awareness of fictionality—to encounter a fictional figure as "an artefact, rather than an illusion of reality" (Polvinen 2023: 20).

I claim that all mutant narratives defamiliarize embodied experience and thus have the potential to effect *embodied estrangement*. Whether the defamiliarization happens via disability, superability, gender, race, or nonhumanity, no mutant can be read as a straightforward everyman character. This is what makes the mutant figure a particularly interesting trope for both posthumanist scholars and cognitive narratologists. However, not all narratives featuring mutant figures can be read as *mutant narratives* in the specific sense put forth by this book, as that specific sense requires a certain amount of conflict at the level of narrative strategies too.[15]

As exemplary mutant narratives, I foreground the works of Paolo Bacigalupi and Jeff VanderMeer. They imagine life in transformed societal and ecological conditions, reaching for an understanding and evocative description of those conditions through speculative worldbuilding and defamiliarizing narrative techniques, even if they never quite get there. As in Butler's *Xenogenesis*, their thematic content and their narrative form are in painful conflict: they describe ecological interdependences as crucial to human and nonhuman life, and yet they cannot escape the traditions of human-centered thinking and human-centered narration.

3.2 Bodily Sense-Making and N. K. Jemisin's *The Fifth Season*

In the opening chapter of N. K. Jemisin's science fiction novel *The Fifth Season* (*FS*), readers are invited to imagine a man capable of feeling the vibrations, densities, and textures of physical objects across a distance. He stands on a hill looking over a city, and briefly focuses on a group of women walking in a park.

> The women laugh at something one of them has said, and the sound wafts up to the man on a passing breeze. He closes his eyes and savors the faint tremolo

of their voices, the fainter reverberation of their footsteps like the wingbeats of butterflies against his sessapinae. He can't sess all seven million residents of the city, mind you, he's good, but not that good. Most of them though, yes, they are there. *Here.* He breathes deeply and becomes a fixture of the earth. They tread upon the filaments of his nerves; their voices stir the fine hairs of his skin; their breaths ripple the air he draws into his lungs. They are on him. They are in him. (*FS*: 4, emphasis in original)

The passage draws on readers' understanding of auditory and tactile sensations: hearing the sound of laughter and feeling the wingbeats of butterflies on one's skin. Except it is not the man's skin that feels the reverberations of the women's voices, but his *sessapinae*, a pair of organs situated at the base of one's skull, specialized in sensing vibrations. Jemisin introduces this novel sensory capability, *sessing*, by drawing on other senses more familiar to her readers.

In the passage that follows this description of sensory experience, readers learn that the man—an "orogene" called Alabaster—is not only capable of sensing the vibrations of human bodies and other objects, but also of manipulating said objects. Shortly after Alabaster "becomes a fixture of the earth," he reaches into the bedrock and the magma beneath it, and starts a volcanic event severe enough to destroy both the city of seven million inhabitants and much of the continent on which it is built.

Jemisin's *The Broken Earth* science fiction trilogy, *The Fifth Season* being its first part, describes life on a world characterized by the geological instability of the Earth. On the continent, ironically called the Stillness, the ground can never be trusted. It always vibrates and changes, occasionally rupturing into larger shakes or volcanoes. People have lived on this unstable and broken Earth for millennia, and their societies have completely adapted to the conditions. One part of adaptation has been the "highly unnatural selection" (*FS*, 6) resulting in the evolution of orogenes, who are used as means of controlling the movements of the Earth.

For the purposes of understanding readerly experientiality, we can investigate how Jemisin uses *metaphor* to develop a sense of living in this fictional world. In her broken world, people and minerals take after each other. On the one hand, characters are mentally and emotionally rock-hard. Orogenes are even named after different minerals, such as Alabaster, or Syenite, a name that carries thematically salient meanings: "It forms at the edge of a tectonic plate. With heat and pressure it does not degrade, but instead grows stronger" (*FS*: 331). On the other hand, the geological Earth is a living body, warm and suffering, with volcanic rifts described as wounds: "Magma wells in its wake, fresh and glowing red … This wound will scab over quickly in geologic terms" (*FS*: 7). In the mythology of the storyworld, the Earth is conceived of as an angry father, deranged after losing his only child, the Moon. The bodily feelings arising from the materiality and dynamicity of rock and flesh are central to the experientiality of the narrative, and to the effectiveness of these framing metaphors.

It is an often-stated claim that science fiction tends to literalize metaphors (e.g., Roberts 2005; Stockwell 2000). In Jemisin's work, this technique is utilized in a way that evokes both the somatic responses tied to realist description and the thematic interpretations associated with poetic language. Not only are orogenes mentally and emotionally hardened—at times, their bodies literally turn into stone. Moreover, the physical implications of the literal and metaphoric condition of being "a weapon meant to move mountains" are described in detail throughout the narrative.

> Orogeny is a strange equation. Take movement and warmth and life from your surroundings, amplify it by some indefinable process of concentration or catalysis or semi-predictable chance, push movement and warmth, and death from the earth. Power in, power out. To keep the power in, though, to *not* turn the valley's aquifer into a geyser or shatter the ground into rubble, takes an effort that makes your teeth and the backs of your eyes ache. You walked a long time to try to burn off some of what you took in, but it still brims under your skin as your body grows weary and your feet hurt. You are a weapon meant to move mountains. A mere walk can't take that out of you. (*FS*: 77)

While some of the description is technical, as it pertains to the training of orogenic skills, some of it evokes the experientiality of becoming and acting as a weapon. Literalization complicates the metaphor, as it brings up the material aspects of the orogenes' weapon-like condition—they literally move mountains, and feel the cost of doing so as bodily pain and exhaustion. The weapon-likeness is also literal, to some extent, as the orogenes are designed and instrumentalized for violent purposes. Literalization thus also invites readers to attune to the material aspects of the orogene's condition by enactively imagining them.

3.2.1 Cognitive Metaphor and Corporeal Concepts

Importantly, metaphors afford interpretations that move in both directions. On the one hand, Jemisin makes the geological forces available to the readers' senses by having the fictional bodies of orogenes "take them in." On the other hand, the kinetic forces of lithospheric pressures and temperatures serve to evoke the character-level experientiality of being shaped by the pressures of evolution, societal power, and catastrophes of both personal and environmental kind. In this way, the literalized metaphors of "people are rock" and "rock is alive" function as *cognitive metaphors* that guide readers' overall understanding of the storyworld.

In cognitive linguistics and philosophy of mind, metaphor is understood not as a mere literary trope but as a heuristic pattern or mode of thought (see Lakoff and Johnson 1980, 1999). We understand the functions and characteristics of things based on our understanding of other things. Our understanding of abstract concepts, in particular, is based on our understanding of material things and embodied experiences. The stock examples of cognitive metaphor theory, "life is a journey" and "time is money," exemplify this dynamic: we use a more close-at-hand frame to guide our conceptualization of a more abstract concept such as life or time. "Where do you see yourself in five years' time," asks the job interviewer, suggesting that we project our future life in terms of travel. "The detour cost us 30 minutes," comments a driver, conceptualizing time in terms of money. In the terms of Lakoff and Johnson (1980), we map one *cognitive domain* with the means of another.

Prevalent frame metaphors in *The Fifth Season*, formulated in the style of cognitive metaphor theory, include "people are rock," which can be articulated more precisely as "individuals shaped by evolutionary and societal pressures are rock." Another frame metaphor would be "rock is alive"; more precisely, "the Earth is a living body," and more poetically, "the Earth is an angry father-god." The first set of formulations shows how the subjective conceptual domain is mapped onto the material domain, and the second set shows a mapping done in the reverse direction. The science fiction studies perspective further explains how such metaphors are literalized and elaborated—as evolutionary and societal conditions for creating the rock-like subject, on the one hand, and as a hostile and unstable environment, on the other.

In Brian McHale's (2018: 317) words, speculative fiction "typically proceeds by taking expressions that in most other contexts would be treated as figurative, and constructing or implying worlds in which those expressions make literal sense." The cognitive metaphors "rock is alive" and "Earth is an angry father-god" make literal sense as the dynamic forces of the earth make life risky and difficult for all terrestrial organisms. Despite this literality, the person-likeness (or god-likeness) of Father Earth also maintains its figurative aspect, which is further emphasized by the use of the figure in "dead metaphors," common expletives such as "Earth damn it" (*FS*: 56 *et passim*), "Earth burn it" (*FS*: 69 *et passim*), and "evil Earth" (*FS*: 126 *et passim*).

Such a twofold understanding of metaphoricity is also at the heart of posthumanist feminist figurations, such as the cyborg (Haraway 1997; Bastian 2006). In *The Fifth Season*, the back-and-forth movement between the geological and subjective domains strengthens the understanding of material and causal interdependence between them: readers are invited to grasp the human life on Stillness as something that takes place within geological boundaries, and also see how the geology itself has been affected by human activity.

While the basic logic of cognitive metaphor can be explained through formulaic descriptions, in readerly experience such metaphoricity is entangled with more holistic modes of making sense of human and nonhuman materiality. Such bodily sense-making draws on the wider dynamics of recognition and referentiality. As the orogene in the abovementioned excerpt makes an effort to contain the energy she has drawn from the earth, with "an effort that makes your teeth and the backs of your eyes ache" (*FS*: 77), readers can only understand the passage through a *mimetic* mode of reception. The orogene's fictional body makes sense when we compare it to actual bodies, such as our own. When the orogene walks fast and long to "burn off" some of the kinetic energy of the earth, readers can understand such an experience through their previous experiences of feeling intense emotions, bodily tension, or stress. No reader will have experience of actually internalizing volcanic forces in their body. Jemisin's narrative technique can, however, make them enact an imaginative approximation.

Mimesis connotes a referential relationship between fiction and reality.[16] But since the second-generation cognitive framework sees phenomena like kinetic energy as *experiential* rather than objective properties, the reality in question is necessarily experiential, and a mimetic relationship can only occur if readers already have experience of the worldly things evoked by the narrative. Readers may calculate the kinetic energy contained in the movement and heat issuing from volcanic movements, but their *understanding* of the phenomenon of volcanic activity is still based on their embodied experience with moving, intense, and hot objects (including, perhaps, actual volcanoes). In her work on the phenomenology of movement, and dance in particular, Maxine Sheets-Johnstone anchors this kind of sense-making to our capacity of self-movement. She argues that self-movement, beginning in infancy, gives rise to *corporeal concepts*:

> On the basis of these concepts, we forge fundamental understandings both of ourselves and of the world. We discover opening and closing in the opening and closing of our eyes, mouths, and hands; we discover that certain things go together such as a certain constellation of buccal movements and certain feelings

of warmth—as in the act of nursing; we discover a differential heaviness in lifting our head and lifting our arm and a differential over-all bodily tension in the two movements as well. In making kinetic sense of ourselves, we progressively attain complex conceptual understandings having to do with *containment*, with *consequential relationships*, with *weight*, with *effort*, and with myriad other bodily-anchored happenings and phenomena that in turn anchor our sense of the world and its happenings and phenomena. (Sheets-Johnstone 2011: 118, emphases in original)

In Sheets-Johnstone's line of thought, corporeal concepts begin with moving one's own body, and are only later developed in contact with other bodies and things. Self-movement is also at the base of understanding qualia such as intensity or heat, as we learn about the material qualities of our environments through bodily engagement with them.[17] Sheets-Johnstone's thinking is very close to Lakoff and Johnson's (1999) *embodied concepts*, and to the logic of generalization inherent in it—"certain things go together," as when opening one's mouth gives rise to a general embodied concept of opening.

This kind of anchoring and recognition is not properly metaphorical, at least not in the meaning employed by cognitive metaphor theory, as it does not map meanings across cognitive domains. Rather, it extends meaning within one cognitive domain—material happenings and phenomena, opening of mouths to opening of doors, for example. For enactivist thinkers as well as Sheets-Johnstone, recognition is tied to the skilled actions of animate organisms, and it is discussed in phenomenological terms, as an action performed by the whole living body rather than just by the neurological system. While Sheets-Johnstone's work provides the general phenomenological basis necessary to the consideration of embodied concepts, tying them to our engagements with literature requires theoretical tools specifically tuned to the task.

3.2.2 Bodily Movement, Kinesis, and Kinetics

For Terence Cave (2016), imagination of fictional movement is connected to the capacity for identifying and understanding living organisms. What makes a literary description of someone performing a bodily gesture "come to life" in reading is due to the fact that "the 'imagination of movement' is not some symbolic or figurative effect, operating reflectively: it is a faint but distinct echo in the reader's own motor response system of what it takes in sensorimotor terms to perform a highly specific gesture" (Cave 2016: 29). Cave characterizes this kind of sensorimotor response as *kinesis*, or *motor resonance*, whereas

Guillemette Bolens (2012) prefers the term *kinesic intelligence*. Bolens (2012: 2) also makes a clearer distinction between kinesis and *kinesthesia*: while kinesic responses pertain to the intersubjective sensorimotor understanding of other human bodies, kinesthesia refers simply to motor sensation: one's knowledge of the movements of one's own body.[18] Bolens builds her literary-analytical model on the basis that while kinesthetic sensations cannot be shared, kinesic intelligence is constantly communicated in encounters between people, and between people and artifacts. Bolens's kinesic analysis of literary gestures aims at articulating the combined effect of all the literary means that construct kinesic meaning.

> A person's kinesic style is perceptible in her idiosyncratic movements and the singular way she negotiates social codes and physical constraints, while the kinesic style of a literary work is experienced through its narrative dynamics, which, in relation to the reader's kinesic intelligence, elicit the understanding of bodily events, shaped in language. Kinesic analysis in literature focuses on the exact means—narratological, lexical, syntactic, grammatical, and so forth—used in a text to construct meaning by referring to bodily movement and by triggering sensorimotor perceptual simulations in the reader via linguistic and semantic codes. (Bolens 2012: 28)

Thus, if we analyze the experience of reading *The Fifth Season* in Bolens's terms, we can say that readers' motor response systems *kinesically* echo the orogene's bodily action of walking in a particular way, whereas their understanding of her effort to "burn off" the energy is based on their *kinesthetic* knowledge of experiencing intense bodily feelings while walking. Kinesis and kinesthetics contribute to their understanding of what it could feel like to contain volcanic forces within one's body—a situation that, as such, is not part of any reader's experiential background. In such a way, experiential traces of self-movement and witnessing the movement of others inform the imaginative enacting of strange, even impossible, embodied experience.

Cave (2016: 29, 30) presents the kinesic effects of literature as intersubjective, suggesting that "kinesis should be understood as playing a fundamental role in mind-reading, in the broadest sense of that term," and that motor resonance and mind-reading should be considered as "a single suite of responses [that] affords empathy." Bolens (2012: 10) also explains that kinesic intelligence pertains to "interpersonal gestures and expressive movements [and] implies the possibility of intersubjectivity." Both Cave and Bolens thus present kinesis as a mode for understanding the expressive movements of other humans, and kinesic analysis as an approach for making sense of such expression in literature and art. As such, kinesic analysis would pair well with intersubjective approaches to narrative meaning-making, and particularly well with Yanna Popova's (2015) *participatory sense-making*, in which the reader's enactive construction of meaning is discussed in terms of communicative interaction (see also De Jaegher and di Paolo 2007; Colombetti and Torrance 2009). Given the posthumanist orientation of this book, however, kinesis proves to be too limited.

Cave (2016: 37) allows that "there is no sharp cut-off point between the way animals 'read' each other's movements and the more elaborate performances that humans have developed out of that evolutionary adaptation." Kinesic perception is a social skill not limited to humans, as all kinds of animals are attuned to perceiving the movements and intentions of other animals, and the skill tends to cross species borders. We know this from our shared lives with domesticated cats, dogs, and other animals with familiar styles of kinesic expressiveness. However, neither Cave nor Bolens cover the meaning-making processes that are based on the behavior and feel of nonhuman entities which are remarkably different from human bodies: plants, rocks, machines, rain clouds, or drawn lines, for example.

This restriction has two important implications. First, the concept of kinesis cannot be used to explain affective and meaningful encounters with actual nonhuman entities. Second, kinesic analysis does not reach beyond the mimetic understanding of fictional movement, into perception and meaning arising from the *artifact itself*, for example, from the dynamicity of drawn lines in a graphic narrative, the sensuous feel of words, or the rhythm and pace of narration. Kinesis thus cannot account for the way in which our bodily understanding of the behavior of melting rock or metal informs our understanding of the orogene's bodily feelings, or for the particular affective power of verbs such as "shatter," "burn," or "brim" in the example passage.

If we wish to discuss mutant figures such as Jemisin's orogenes in terms beyond anthropomorphic mimesis, we might use yet another term, couched in a posthumanist understanding of fictional movement. My choice is to appropriate the term *kinetic*—a term Bolens (2012: 10) employs, in contrast to kinesic intelligence, to describe the perception of "aspects of movements that may be objectively measured," and Sheets-Johnstone (2011: 118) employs to refer to one's understanding of one's own body as a material thing. My use of the term carries this distinction between human-like expressive bodies and moving bodies more generally, but allows for perceptual movement over the human–nonhuman boundary. This movement is grounded on previous phenomenological and narratological work.

Nonhuman entities and dynamics appear as meaningful in both traditional and posthumanist phenomenology. Denouncing idealistic aspirations for detached descriptions of consciousness, Maurice Merleau-Ponty (2002: xiv) views humans as "through and through compounded of relationships with the world." Building on Merleau-Ponty's work on language and perception, David Abram (1996) argues that a bodily approach to phenomenology encourages an animist experience of nonhuman bodies as animate, expressive, communicating beings.

> When we attend to our experience not as intangible minds but as sounding, speaking bodies, we begin to sense that we are heard, even listened to, by the numerous other bodies that surround us. Our sensing bodies respond to the eloquence of certain buildings and boulders, to the articulate motions of dragonflies. We find ourselves alive in a listening, speaking world. (Abram 1996: 86)

Abram, following Merleau-Ponty, calls this mode of experience *participatory perception*, which bears a resemblance Yanna Popova's (2015) *participatory sense-making*, but with two significant differences. First, Abram's notion of participation extends from intersubjective sense-making to more-than-human relations; second, Abram does not apply his notion to literary analysis.[19] Abram, writing in the mid-1990s, also does not draw on the enactivist framework but on Merleau-Ponty's phenomenology and anthropological work on indigenous ways of life. Abram's approach is, however, useful to the material-ecocritical argument I am constructing in this chapter, as it provides a bridge between kinesic and kinetic modes of perception.

While responding to the swaying of a tree is distinct from responding to the bending of a human body, the two modes of perceptual meaning-making (kinesic and kinetic) definitely exist on the same continuum. This perceptual continuum goes both ways. I make sense of the movement of the tree through my kinetic understanding of weight, rigidity, and elasticity, familiar to me through my lived history as an embodied being in a more-than-human world, and this kind of kinetic understanding participates in the way I make sense of human movement, such as dance. Likewise, while I certainly perceive human gestures as meaningful and expressive, this kinesic mode of perception also pertains to my understanding of ominously approaching rain clouds, the vigorous growth of bean sprouts, and the gentle swaying of the tree. Whether this kind of perception is a case of animism or anthropomorphization is a topic of its own. For now, we can merely accept that it exists, and that it informs human meaning-making—including the meaning-making processes relevant to the understanding of fictional movement and materiality.[20]

From here, it is not too far-fetched to extend participatory perception into the realm of reading fiction: to perceiving and attuning to the movement of fictional figures and features. The current consensus in cognitive approaches to narrative is that both human and nonhuman characters are experienced through perspective-taking or empathy, even when the nonhumanness of the character would be estranging. This perspectival closeness is considered as anthropomorphic: "The empathetic simulation of the nonhuman character's mind requires projecting partial memories of the reader's own past, embodied experiences onto the nonhuman character, which both presumes and results in some degree of anthropomorphization" (Varis 2019b: 8; see also Bernaerts et al. 2014: 73; Caracciolo 2014b: 123–32).

With my discussion of kinesis and kinetics, I hope to demonstrate that the cognitive dynamic of attuning to fictional figures also involves aspects that can be considered more-than-human, and that we make sense of nonhuman entities in fiction through both anthropomorphization and the kind of participatory perception described by Abram (1996). Part of our human experience is made up of affects, perceptions, and judgments that we share with other animals and even plant life. We share with mammals a preference for warmth over cold, for example; and with green plants, a preference for certain cycles of light and darkness (see Abram 1996; Baluška and Mancuso 2007; Chamovitz 2013). We also recognize material and kinetic affectivity, such as weights and movements. Thus, we don't have full ownership of our human limitations.

Moreover, our experiential background of encountering others is not limited to encountering other humans. We also have experience of encountering nonhuman animals and other entities, and our recognition of their particular forms in fiction is not necessarily anthropomorphic. Laline Paull's *The Bees* (2014), for example, features a heavily anthropomorphized honey bee narrator, but the narrative also evokes affects and images that are characteristically *beelike* and thus not cognizable through anthropomorphic appropriation, such as the descriptions of insect bodies and their neurochemistry. These aspects of narrative sense-making are not necessarily covered by the approaches that focus on storytelling and narrative structure: the recognition of forms and textures is usually not considered central to the narrative-theoretical enterprise. However, I suggest that material sense-making of this kind is a crucial aspect of our overall engagement with literary artifacts: making sense of a plot is not separate from feeling the rhythm and pace of narrative time, and making sense of perspective or character usually involves multimodal enactment of the kinesic style of the fictional entity.

To return once more to *The Fifth Season*, I suggest that the orogenes' bodily materiality can be read as both self-propelled (in the sense of Sheets-Johnstone's phenomenology of self-movement and the notion of kinesis) and more-than-human (in the sense that it shares material properties with nonhuman bodies). I also propose that the thematic interpretation of *The Fifth Season* is dependent on kinesic and kinetic modes of sense-making, and that those modes include more-than-human aspects that can be described in terms of participatory perception. While it is possible to read the furious activity of "Father Earth" or the sensory capabilities of orogenes as purely metaphorical, the intelligibility of such metaphors is based on the embodied and more-than-human aspects of cognition. Furthermore, by fully engaging with the material details of a fictional world as more than a static backdrop to human action, we can begin to articulate the manifold more-than-human dynamics at work in science fictional narratives such as *The Fifth Season*. Thus, through a combination of kinesis/kinetics and the qualities foregrounded in science fiction, we can extend the human exceptionalist work of second-generation cognitive literary theorists, such as Bolens (2012), Popova (2015), and Cave (2016), to more-than-human sense-making processes.

Notes

1 Speculative fiction is also an inherently transmedial genre and influences constantly travel between literature, film, videogames, comics, and other media. While I limit the following overview mostly to science fiction literature, leaving other media completely out of the discussion would be neglectful. I will thus refer to influential works in other media whenever necessary.
2 Often, mutants and androids give rise to strikingly similar themes: evolution and survival in changing environments, living with broken and strange bodies, otherness and social exclusion, the fluid boundaries of humanity, technological power, and systemic complexity. A mutant figure might transgress not only the boundary between human and animal, but also the boundary between human and machine. Biological and biotechnological mutants, however, might bring in more of the environmental themes this book focuses on.

In the comic book semiosphere, the classification of freaks includes not only *mutants* (who have been born with peculiar features or abilities) but also *mutates* (for creatures that are transformed by external effects such as radiation) and *metahumans* (for creatures that attain mutant superpowers after birth). Metahumans come close to the project of consciously altering human bodies, marked by the terms *transhuman* and *posthuman*. One could also consider *parahumans*, *hybrids*, and *khimairas* as belonging to the group of mutants.

3 This is a broad generalization. While android narratives such as *Do Androids Dream of Electric Sheep?* and *A. I.* offer bleak control, so do genetic narratives such as *Gattaca* and *Brave New World*. William Gibson's cyberpunk offers both bleak systemic control and wild alterity.

4 Whereas apes and racialized others were cast in the roles of the lower forms, freaks have always played the role of divergent among proper natural creatures: by their presence, they disturb the natural order, including the idea of a linear evolutionary progress. Biological mutations can be both beneficial and harmful for the life of the individual organism, and their effects do not necessarily conform to either aesthetic or moral ideals. This risky lawlessness gives the mutant figure a demonic quality that affiliates it with tricksters, scapegoats, and other liminal beings.

5 See, for example, *Invasion of the Body Snatchers*, *The Blob*, *Shepford Wives*, and the discussion in Badmington (2004).

6 The phrase is originally coined by the character Charles Xavier but most of all associated to the shape-shifter character Mystique in *X-Men: First Class* (2011).

7 These themes are discussed in Section 4.2 in connection to Paolo Bacigalupi's novel *The Windup Girl* (2009).

8 Polvinen and Sklar (2019) argue that "particular metaphorical structures of anthropomorphism, naturalization and belief" also dominate the language and approaches used in discussions of literature, whether in homes, schools, or voluntary reading groups. They point out that there is little popular vocabulary by which to describe one's engagement with the synthetic aspects of narratives, and suggest that cognitive literary theory can play a role in providing that vocabulary. See also Polvinen (2016, 2017).

9 For such hypothetical cultures in speculative fiction, see, for example, Ursula K. Le Guin's *Always Coming Home* (1985) or Kim Stanley Robinson's *Mars* trilogy (1992–6).

10 The humanizing stance is also common in empirical studies on narrative and empathy (see, e.g., Hakemulder, 2000; Kidd and Castano, 2013; for a critique, see Keen 2007) and rhetorical ethics (see, e.g., Nussbaum 1990; Sklar 2013).

11 Unlike most narratologists, I do not make a strict difference between character and first-person narrator. In the phenomenology of reading, different techniques of narration—free indirect discourse, variable focalization, and first-person narration—can give rise to the imaginative modeling of fictional people in one's readerly experience. While it is difficult to make generalizations about all

narrative techniques and modes, it is safe to assume that all of the abovementioned techniques can bring about the experience of encountering fictional figures that resemble actual bodies or people (and also used to confuse or counteract this effect). This is what matters most for the purposes of this book.

12 It should be noted, however, that especially in her earlier work, Haraway (1992) draws on the semiotic theory of Greimas, which is not quite as disembodied as the structuralist tradition would suggest (see Bertetti 2017).

13 Despite his thorough conceptual reevaluation of cognitive estrangement, Spiegel (2008) is not particularly interested in the readerly aspects of the phenomenon. After identifying the estranging strategies of science fictional storytelling as "diegetic estrangement," he labels the effect on the audience as "just estrangement" (Spiegel 2008: 376). This choice leaves ample room for further phenomenological and descriptive characterizations of estranging effects, on which I will focus later.

14 Jones's analysis pays no attention to the many science fiction narratives in which perspective is itself part of this imaginative worldbuilding—the New Wave of the 1960s, cyberpunk fiction of the 1980s, and many contemporary works developing nonbinary perspectives such as Pat Cadigan's "The Girl-Thing That Went Out for Sushi" (2012) discussed earlier.

15 Of recent speculative fiction, Margaret Atwood's *Maddaddam* series (2003–13) and Kazuo Ishiguro's *Never Let Me Go* (2005) are not in fact mutant narratives in spite of their involvement with themes of animal rights and biotechnology. They engage in speculative worldbuilding, but only to the extent that is necessary for criticizing current societies and ideologies, that is, they do not strive to describe alternative modes of life and experience. On the other hand, Rudy Rucker's *Postsingular* (2007) and *Hylozoic* (2009) might be applicable. Rucker's work might even be characterized as new materialist fiction, as it foregrounds the vitality inherent in matter itself.

16 In narratological discussions that draw on James Phelan's (1989) tripartite model of character, the mimetic function is usually discussed in terms of the similarities between fictional minds and actual minds. What counts as "mind" in this context is typically defined through intersubjective and self-reflective modes of thought, emotion, and perception. The kind of bodily and material awareness I am interested in is rarely addressed outside the second-generation cognitive framework.

17 See critique of the "Mary in the black and white room" thought experiment in Sheets-Johnstone (2011: 141–9).

18 Kinesthetic knowledge can be either conscious or unconscious, depending on the moment (Bolens 2012: 2; Cave 2016: 40).

19 Abram makes the radical claim that in a modern society the animist tendencies of human perception have been harnessed into the act of symbolic sense-making— primarily reading. While I appreciate the stimulus of Abram's vision of the alphabet as a system of magical symbols, this aspect of his thinking does not pair well with

the enactive framework that this book advances. The enactive approach does not concentrate on the symbolic level of textual signs, but on the experiential level of making sense of narratives.

20 While the scope of this book does not allow venturing into the specifics of the perceptual abilities of plants, it should be noted that such abilities exist—and thus we can assume that plants, too, respond to each other and other worldly things through some kind of somatic and bio-chemical dynamics (see, e.g., Baluška and Mancuso 2007; Chamovitz 2013). My line of argument, while placing human life in the larger realm of nonhuman perceptions and responses, stays with the perceptions and responses of human bodies as they engage with literature—but through the notion of kinetics, I will broaden the understanding of these perceptions beyond the intersubjective.

4

Readerly Choreographies and Paolo Bacigalupi's Climate Fiction

The reading process involves many different aspects that can be called more-than-human, and practicing one's readerly sensitivities to those aspects can help us better describe their shapes and textures. Theoretical considerations and apparatuses can help amplify the bodily experientiality of narratives and thereby turn the reading process toward the material and more-than-human dynamics of experience. One way of understanding this is through *readerly choreographies*, or genre-typical patterns of bodily feelings evoked in reading (see also Kortekallio 2022).

When considering readerly choreographies, Paolo Bacigalupi's climate fiction provides an interesting case study for a number of reasons. First, it engages with the themes of biological evolution, biotechnology, and societal change at the time of climate change, as well as with personal change in this wider context. Second, it both employs and reconfigures the traditions of science fictional characterization. Bacigalupi utilizes time-worn stock types of popular fiction, from artificial girls and cyborg gunmen to cunning oriental merchants. His work thematically connects the technique of type-based characterization to the context of cultural stereotyping and social construction of identity. Third, Bacigalupi's fiction is highly affective in its frequent descriptions of material events, strange bodies, violence, and action, and this affectivity affords a demonstration of what more-than-human reading can do in terms of embodied experience. Bacigalupi's human characters tend to be as objectified and instrumentalized as cattle or genetically modified corn, and the affective patterns of *being instrumentalized* resonate in embodied experience in disturbing and even destructive ways.

The dynamic of kinesic and kinetic sense-making is also at play in Paolo Bacigalupi's work, of which I will focus on the short story "The People of Sand and Slag" (2004) and on the novel *The Windup Girl* (2009). In contrast to what has come before, I will argue that the mimetic recognition at play in readerly imagination is sometimes entwined with a *recognition of artifice*—the reflective understanding of fiction as a form of affective technology that takes hold of readers' cognitive tendencies and twists them to its own purposes. This reflective understanding is tied to the entangled notions of artifice and artistry: works of fiction are deliberately artificial compositions of elements, and while many forms of fiction may hide this artifice (realist novels being a paradigmatic example), I argue that science fiction foregrounds it (see also Varis 2019b; Polvinen 2023). Sustained engagement with the technological aspects of science fiction can develop this recognition of the artifice into an embodied and intuitive mode of experience.[1]

In reading "The People of Sand and Slag," I extend my kinesic and kinetic analysis from reading individual figures to the wider dynamics of *figuration* (Haraway 1992, 2008; Neimanis 2017) and *readerly choreography*. These are ways in which fictional figures and figurations invite readers to reflectively enact whole kinesic and kinetic styles that are thematically relevant (cf. Noë 2015; Kukkonen 2019). In my analysis of Bacigalupi's novel *The Windup Girl*, I demonstrate how a mutant narrative can thematize and instrumentalize figurations associated with stock types of genre fiction, and make experiential the exploitation and instrumentalization inherent in the novel's particular context of capitalist biotechnology.

4.1 Moving with the Figures of Bacigalupi's "The People of Sand and Slag"

Paolo Bacigalupi's short story, "The People of Sand and Slag" ("PPS"), is set in a techno-industrial milieu. The main figures rising from that milieu include three "tactical defense responders" that guard industrial mining grounds from intruders—usually by killing or "slagging" them on the spot—and one dog that intrudes. The story is told in sensory language that evokes forceful cutting and slicing, starting from the introductory action scene where the security team in a flying vehicle rides over lakes and mountains of mining waste. "Ahead, the ragged cutscape of mined mountains stretched to the horizon. We dipped again into mist and skimmed low over another catchment lake, leaving choppy wake in the thick golden waters ("PPS": 50).

The cutting and slicing of this odd terrain sets the tone of the narrative, anticipating the cutting and slicing of animate figures that follows later on in the story. The flying passage mimics the thrill of an action film or a first-person shooter video game, thereby producing a generic frame for reading. The setting evokes the genre-typical figure of the hypermasculinized action hero, complete with associated kinesic, kinetic, and affective style and plot expectations.[2] A team of problem solvers is on a mission, having fun while at it. Their hardened bodies are equipped with overtly fantastic techno-gear ("TS-101 and slashbangs," "impact exoskeleton," "bandoleers of surgepacks," "PPS": 49) and routine protocols for typical scenarios. The figures and the premise all play into reading the story in the context of action adventure or masculine cyberpunk, and into seeking the familiar affective pleasures of corporeal excitement and identification with a heroically capable, technologically augmented body (see also Tidwell 2011: 97). This reading strategy is, however, soon turned toward a new direction.

"The People of Sand and Slag" employs metaphorical figures and kinesic/kinetic effects. The main figures of the short story serve as metaphorical caricatures, their kinesic styles echoing the harshness of their surroundings and their geopolitical and economic situation. However, the complexity of the storyworld complicates the reading of simple genre-typical figures. Even though the overall effect Bacigalupi's text achieves is distinctly technological and military, the goal of the mission in the initial scene is not set up as patriotic or humanitarian: the fantastically equipped team of experts is set off by the "monotonous slopes" ("PPS": 51) of the industrial wasteland they are guarding while ripping up its face. Despite their heroic air, they are complacent components in a techno-industrial machinery, programmed for nonchalantly violent border-control and bonus-hunting. One of the explicit motivations of the team's actions is saving up for the new "Immersive Response," a virtual reality gaming platform on which they play war games.

Ending the introductory scene, the figures plummet from their vehicle into the ground, smashing their exoskeletons and limbs into pieces. This is portrayed as standard procedure, with no emphasis on the demolition of their bodies. They rise from the ground and instantly heal. From this point onward, it becomes exceedingly clear that the narrated bodies are as technological as their vehicle and equipment, designed from scratch to be regenerative and truly omnivorous: their diet consists primarily of the ubiquitous toxin-saturated mud and sand. One of them even explicitly declares: "We can eat anything. We're the top of the food chain" ("PPS": 55). In the grim future of the story, the "food chain" is rather short, as there are practically no unmodified organisms left alive. Humans have completely adapted themselves to a drastically impoverished ecosystem that seems to consist entirely of ore, oil, the hi-tech gadgets manufactured from them, and the posthumans themselves.

The posthumans appear to be content in their niche. In addition to playing "Immersive Response" games, they are in the habit of cutting and piercing their invulnerable bodies with trendy packs of blades and spikes. The presentation of these habitual practices modulates the initial action hero schema in a superhuman or inhuman direction, and suggests that the narrated bodies are part and product of a particular ecosystem.

"The People of Sand and Slag" generates a diverse array of bodily feelings, ranging from the thrill of the initial scene to awe, disgust, and sensory numbing. Once again, these bodily feelings can be described as kinesic and kinetic echoes of bodily responses to actual material surroundings. However, in this section, in addition to evoking kinesic and kinetic echoes, the short story thematizes the very dynamic of kinesic and kinetic imagination, and the way habitual patterns of bodily response participate in the formation of embodied subjectivity. It does so by using both familiarizing and defamiliarizing techniques.

4.1.1 Readerly Choreographies and Figurations

The story draws attention to repeated actions: playing a game, eating sand and mud, casual modification of bodies, routinely checking the premises of the mine, and routinely "slagging" living creatures with the naturalized assumption that they are expendable. The routinized quality of such actions is communicated through simple statements with no emphasis: "We ate sand for dinner" ("PPS": 53); "After dinner, we sat around and sharpened Lisa's skin" ("PPS": 54). This is presented in a scene portraying a familiarized, even domestic night at the home base: "It was comforting to hear those machines cruising back and forth all day. Just you and the bots and the profits, and if nothing got bombed while you were on duty, there was always a nice bonus" ("PPS": 54). For the protagonist, the rumble of industrial machinery is the sound of home.

The everyday frame of the strange actions of the posthuman figures serves a twofold purpose: with its plain and matter-of-fact style and conventional narrative form, it invites readers to participate in the atmosphere of domestic routine. With its strange contents, however, it defamiliarizes that routine and leads readers to wonder how it is possible for the characters to experience such a life as natural. While readers are invited to adopt the position of a posthuman figure tranquilly eating sand for dinner, no human alive can do so without feeling estrangement.

What makes this estrangement particularly *embodied* is that the narrative is bound by the experiential sphere of a posthuman figure. The narrative form invites identification with the numb and routinized figures, but a regular human body resists it. In such a dynamic, the close connection of bodily feeling and emotion becomes salient. As the conceptual tool of *readerly choreography* is tuned to describing the affective patterns, kinetic portrayals (Colombetti 2014), and kinesic styles (Bolens 2012) that particular fictional bodies afford to readers, it can help us unravel the experiential tangle of enacting the bodily actions of posthuman figures.

As explained in Section 2.2, *readerly choreography* aims to capture the sense of what it feels like to enactively attend to the bodily experientiality of a narrative as it unfolds, with a focus on reading singular fictional figures within their generic and environmental contexts (see also Kortekallio 2022). While *readerly choreography* might also pertain to the experience of engagements with particular narratives and the kinesic styles of particular characters, I have coined the concept to better grasp the iterative experiences of engaging with genre-typical feeling and action, such as the excitement and pleasure of reading action adventure stories or the anticipatory dread that fills horror film screenings. "The People of Sand and Slag" is exceptional in the way it varies the familiar figurations of popular cyberpunk action, exaggerating the toughness and physical capabilities of stereotypical, technologically enhanced action heroes. This goes on until it becomes difficult for readers to continue to perform the habituated experiential moves of excitement, action-derived pleasure, and identification with the heroic protagonist. In other words, "The People of Sand and Slag" estranges the readerly choreography of popular cyberpunk action. As I will show later, the short story further amplifies my estrangement by evoking bodily feelings of disgust and anger.

Similar estrangement happens in engagements with many works of recent speculative fiction, such as the popular film series *Hunger Games*, the television series *Westworld* or *Altered Carbon*, and in action film and television more generally. Such fictions in various media tend to aestheticize violent acts and present human bodies as dispensable fodder for violence, taking this instrumental affectivity to such extremes that the viewers are bound to object. *Westworld* and *Altered Carbon*, in a tradition that has been circulating at least since the cyberpunk wave of the 1980s, also imagine bodies as temporary, exchangeable vessels for disembodied minds (see Hayles 1999; Vint 2006). In the logic of the storyworld, human bodies are included in the category of natural resources, to be shaped and modified into more interesting and fashionable products, in this case, hypermasculinized action figures. Staying with this logic of instrumentalization and the narrative strategies that encourage readerly resistance to instrumentalization opens the way to a posthumanist ethical reading of "The People of Sand and Slag."

4.1.2 Responding to a "Dead Dog Story"

Bacigalupi's short stories are particularly direct in their display of fictionality and thus effective in inviting a reflective mode of reading. "The People of Sand and Slag" points attention to its affective devices and thus thematizes the dynamic of kinesic and kinetic imagination. This is already apparent in feeling with the bodily action of the posthumans, but interaction with nonhuman elements—a dog and the soil—takes readerly awareness even further.

As a counterpoint to the superhuman quality of its protagonists, the story provides an icon of vulnerability: a stray dog. The dog is miraculously found where the "enemy" was supposed to be, trespassing in the midst of the tailings mounds and catchment lakes of the mining area. The protagonists do not first identify the creature as a dog: they take it to be an unsuccessful "bio-job," a bioengineered creature similar to their programmable sentinel centaurs. In her analysis of the "The People of Sand and Slag," Christy Tidwell (2011: 103–4) notes how it matters that the animal is specifically a dog, not a rat or a pigeon for instance: "Not only is it 'man's best friend' and therefore an inherently sympathetic creature to many human readers, but it is repeatedly described as a thing unto itself, not created simply for entertainment or service." For most readers, a dog is an animal that is not exploited or instrumentalized, and thus it stands in clear contrast to the "bio-jobs." In Tidwell's reading, the dog represents the inherent value of life, nonhuman and human alike.

The dog is thus offered to the readers as a sympathetic agent. The narrative holds the dog's fate in the air as the protagonists debate whether they should destroy it, eat it, sell it, or keep it. When they decide to keep it, the tension eases only to be increased again as the posthumans realize what hard work caring for a vulnerable animal is. For them, breaking a bone or losing a limb may be inconvenient if unplanned, and aesthetically pleasurable if planned. In this mindset, the dog appears to be poorly designed and thus not fit for living. They end up roasting it on a spit and eating it.

With the dilemma of what to do with the dog, the story extrapolates from the incessant metabolic, regenerative, and habitual processes of the posthuman bodies into their ethical capabilities. In the logic of the narrative, the posthuman subjectivities of the protagonists are enacted in repeated patterns of bodily action. In effect, the sum of their enhanced abilities is presented as a lack. As the posthuman figures are not partial to the repeated pattern of fearing hunger, pain, disability, and death, they have not developed the ability to assume the same pattern in others. In fact, they cannot comprehend a reality where such fears are present. Despite or due to being invincible, the posthuman body is constrained by the practices of self-preservation and exploitation, and therefore it cannot connect to others. To highlight this, the narrative presents the posthumans "experimenting with vulnerability," as Lisa, the only female figure in the crew, asks her fellows to amputate her arms and legs. As she lies on a beach, a torso already sprouting tiny new limbs, she looks at the dog and reflects: "This is as close as I'll ever get to it" ("PPS": 65).

This is where the narrative turns readers toward its own kinesic and kinetic effects, and to the readerly choreography that usually results in feelings of sympathy or empathy toward the characters. The actions of the posthumans are fantastically exaggerated: every move they make entails either unintentional or intentional violence toward other living creatures or toward earth itself. By presenting the figures performing actions that would make a normal human reader feel pain, anguish, disgust, or fear—and evoking those feelings as echoes at least in the reading body—the narrative highlights the fact that these figures are incapable of such feelings. The dog figure widens the readers' emotional distance to the posthuman figures: they are guided to feel sympathy toward the dog's suffering and wonder about the callousness of the posthuman figures. Thus a gulf opens between the feeling body of the human reader and the fictional, insensate body of the posthuman.

Donna Haraway has often foregrounded science fiction as a particularly fruitful site for exercising the bodily skills of reading and thinking. Haraway uses the acronym "SF" to refer to several overlapping phenomena: science fiction, science fact, speculative feminism, and speculative fabulation. In "The Promises of Monsters" (1992), Haraway refers to science fiction in two contexts: as a site for exploring alternative worlds and as a reading strategy. She invites readers to loosen their cognitive ties to normative conceptions of (social) reality and think "under the sign of SF": the "science fictional, speculative factual, SF place" becomes a conceptual location in which monstrous others can become visible (Haraway 1992: 295). In reading John Varley's novella *Press Enter*, Haraway also refers to the "anti-elitist reading conventions of SF popular cultures" as a potent method for political action:

> SF conventions invite—or at least permit more readily than do the academically propagated, respectful consumption protocols for literature—rewriting as one

reads. The books are cheap; they don't stay in print long; why not rewrite them as one goes? Most of the SF I like motivates me to engage actively with images, plots, figures, devices, linguistic moves, in short, with worlds, not so much to make them come out "right," as to make them move "differently." These worlds motivate me to test their virtue, to see if their articulations work—and what they work for. Because SF makes identification with a principal character, comfort within the patently constructed world, or a relaxed attitude toward language, especially risky reading strategies, the reader is likely to be more generous and more suspicious—both generous and suspicious, exactly the receptive posture I seek in political semiosis generally. (Haraway 1992: 326)

Haraway describes the receptive posture of an SF reader in robustly corporeal turns of phrases—the SF "motivates [her] to engage actively" and to make the stories "move." In this model of reception, the reader is both conscious of the fictionality and artifice involved in the experience of engaging with an SF narrative ("suspicious" of it) and able to "test their virtue" by generously accepting the experiential affordances it provides.

"The People of Sand and Slag" is exactly the kind of SF that invites a "generous and suspicious" receptive posture. Sympathetically engaging with the posthuman perspective of these action figures, going along with the readerly choreography it suggests, I am encouraged to feel the pleasure of good design: the rush of the vehicle, and the cut of the blades on the posthuman skin. This pleasure extends to enjoying the design of the story itself: its skillful manipulation of genre tropes, its vivid language, and its grim imagery. The artifactuality of this fiction is foregrounded as a source of brutal aesthetic enjoyment. As Abigail Nussbaum (2008) has pointed out in her review of *Pump Six and Other Stories*, "The People of Sand and Slag" is blatantly a "dead dog" story: a machine that uses the cheapest tricks in the writers' technical manual, and does not even try to hide it. Nussbaum's response, like my own, brings forth the story as an aesthetic and affective object, to be compared to other such objects.

Even at the beginning of the narrative, the double take effected by the incredible landing crash of the posthumans invites me to doubt the affective powers of style and form: the power of vivid language and first-person perspective to persuade me to adopt the implicit attitudes embedded in them. However, the exaggeration also draws attention to the artifice at play in generating affect, and gives rise not only to a double consciousness but also an enactive double vision of fiction (Polvinen 2017, 2023). In other words, I feel the affect, yet I also notice how it is achieved through narrative techniques. To rephrase this in Haraway's terms: I become suspicious of the narrative exactly because I generously engage with its "images, plots, figures, devices, linguistic moves, in short, with worlds."

In reading the story, attention also takes hold of the technologies presented in the story—weapons, vehicles, videogames, and biotechnology. All technological production in the story follows the same logic of dividing the world into matter, which is considered only as a reified resource, and human reason, which shapes matter. As it manipulates the living flesh of its readers, the narrative itself can be experienced as a technological apparatus—and thus its readers are aligned with matter, the object of violence and utilization. While reading, I am affected by the story, sliced and turned and polluted by it, as the hills are sliced and turned and polluted by industrial machinery. As I go through the feelings of thrill, awe, pleasure, distress, and disgust, I end up enacting a wasteland-like state: the narrative exploits my tendencies for feeling with the narrative elements and adds insult to injury by doing it with clichés such as the chase scene and the dead dog.

However, unlike the posthumans of Bacigalupi's narrative but almost certainly like most of his other readers, I am a feeling critter with *response-ability* (see Haraway 2008: 19–27, 71). I am able to respond with anger and reflection, and object to the exploitative dynamic the narrative spins out. I do not want to be treated as inert matter, neither as a reader nor as a living body. Nor do I wish this kind of treatment for other living bodies or Earth systems. When I object to the affront of this dead dog story, I am also inclined, by the force of the narrative itself, to direct my critical gaze toward industrialized production of technological devices and action hero narratives.

4.1.3 Dancing with Affective Devices

In reading ecological science fiction such as Bacigalupi's "The People of Sand and Slag," awareness of the synthetic aspects of fiction comes to cultivate awareness of the synthetic aspects of embodiment and the production of bodies in a technocapitalist society. The narrative presents its own affects as material forces that rouse certain receptive postures—generosity, pleasure-seeking, moral distress, suspicion, and self-reflection—and, through kinesic and kinetic experientiality, forms an analogical link between textual affectivity and the material-semiotic production of such entities as strip mines, video games, and invincible bodies. In this manner, the short story develops in its readers a material-discursive conception of narratives and other meaning-generating apparatuses.

The fictional world of "The People of Sand and Slag" is a caricature of a society permeated by war and industry. Both stories take issue with the advancements of biotechnology and pharmaceutical drugs by presenting a rift between the individual benefits of certain treatments—invulnerability and picture-perfect physical appearance—and the societal harm they can do. Bacigalupi's stories thus articulate class consciousness as well as environmental concern, tying them together in the individual fates of their artifactual figures.

Arriving at a systemic understanding can occur in a number of ways, top-down thematic analysis included, but in my view the narratives themselves invite one to begin from the kinesic, kinetic, and affective responses described earlier. As an enactive reader, I have moved from kinesic, kinetic, and affective responses toward constructing thematic interpretations. This movement activates my experiential background of reading science fiction.

In this mode of reception, fictional figures are primarily encountered as affective devices, that is, artifacts that, in their motions and feelings, recreate types familiar from literary and cultural traditions (see Caracciolo 2014c; Warhol 2003: 24). Enacting typical motions and feelings in reading the text, in turn, recreates the habitual kinesic, kinetic, and affective patterns of response tied to these cultural forms: their readerly choreographies. On the level of motor response and affective attunement, readers live through (or enact) the readerly choreographies specific to, for example, the rebellious robot or the teenage mutant. During personal histories of reading, such choreographies are enacted countless times, and thus they stay relevant to and active in the embodied experience of readers. This *enactive performativity* plays a part in the constitution of embodied subjectivities, as theorized by feminist critics (Butler 1990; Warhol 2003). I propose that literary analysis can take hold of this dynamic in an intentional, methodological manner, engaging with fiction through more-than-human reading.

In Bacigalupi's stories, there is no such thing as a natural human being—every figure is produced in specific material-discursive processes. However, there is a certain nostalgia for natural humanity. Beneath the posthuman themes, Bacigalupi is a remarkably humanist writer: he writes about the advances of biotechnology and medicine in order to portray how humans lose their humanity. This chapter is very much about staying in that uneasy position: about being both critical of and sympathetic to humanism, and about attaching personhood and emotion to puppet-like fictional constructs even when we know they are tools. As Haraway has repeatedly stated, the crucial time and place for critical inquiries is in the middle of a crisis: she urges us to stay with the trouble. In this spirit, I seek to learn from these puppets.

4.2 Instrumentality and Materiality in Bacigalupi's *The Windup Girl*

> Out on the streets, she tries to blend into the daylight street activity. Mizumi-sensei trained her to walk in certain ways, to accent and make beautiful the stutter motion of her body. But if Emiko is very careful, and fights her nature and training—if she wears *pha sin*, and does not swing her arms—she almost passes. (*WG*: 149)

In *The Windup Girl* (*WG*), Bacigalupi creates yet another creature constrained by her production history and social status. Emiko is an artificial person, genetically engineered to be an optimal servant, "pillow companion, secretary, translator and observer" (*WG*: 146). However, Emiko has been designed for environments particular to Japanese business life—formal meetings, rooms with climate control, and courteous companionship—not for the tropical heat of Bangkok. She is also permanently marked as artificial with a genetic tweak that forces her to move in mechanical "stutter-stop" jerks and twitches. This gives her a particular style of movement, accentuated by her formal training as a "fine courtesan." Hiding this distinctive style in her new, hostile environment requires her to take up certain techniques of the body—a local style of dress and restricted movement (she moves with deliberate slowness and does not swing her arms, as this would cause her body to display its characteristic jerks and twitches).

Besides producing a particular bodily aesthetic, this modification is a means of societal control—as the "New People" are easy to recognize as artificial, they cannot blend into the social circles of "natural" people. With the New People, Bacigalupi creates an artificial slave class that illustrates the thematic tensions of his future society: the dramatic global transition to ecosystems constituted only by human-created species, the ubiquity of capitalist exploitation of human and nonhuman resources, and the desperate need to protect whatever is still considered natural.

Removed from her Japanese niche and brought to the tropical city of Bangkok, Emiko has lost her bearings altogether: the climate is too harsh on her body and the culture too harsh for her education. Moreover, the protectionist agenda of the Thai nation will not tolerate her gene-modified foreignness. After being discarded by her former owner, she is classified as "invasive species"—much like genetically modified rice and corn, produced by multinational agribusiness corporations that threaten to destroy the few remaining domestic grains cultivated by Thai farmers. This cultural status constrains Emiko's movements as much as her genetics do. She must be very careful not to betray her abnormal nature, as doing so would lead to her destruction. In the day-to-day realism of the novel, this condition is portrayed through Emiko's act of constraining the jerks and twitches of her body: if she practices continuous control, she "almost passes" (*WG*: 149).[3]

Reading descriptions of Emiko's movements, I feel a nervous tension in my muscles. I become aware of my posture, of the ways I cross my legs and move my hand to turn the page, and of the potential audience watching my body. This tense awareness is amplified by other tensions at play in the novel: the personal worries of other characters, the societal instability, and above all the anxious anticipation of the promised monsoons. The monsoons pose both a promise and a threat: they might both ease the heat-stricken exhaustion pestering the city and break the great dike that protects the city from the risen sea level. Through kinesically attuning to Emiko's careful movements, I get to participate in this complex material-political situation in which the whole society is, so to speak, on its toes.

Crucially for the reading experience, this participation is primarily due to *affective* rather than *emotional* engagement with the character. Emiko is forcefully present as a set of affective descriptions of bodily movements and feelings, but the character is too flat and type-based to inspire what Caracciolo (2016) calls "character-centered illusion." Hence, I fail to interpret her as a fully-fledged fictional person, deserving of empathy or sympathy. Curiously enough, the flatness of the figure does not prevent me from feeling pangs of anguish and pain when reading scenes in which Emiko is violently abused, or from feeling pleasure and elation at the rare scenes in which she enjoys flowing water or freedom of movement.

In this section, I discuss the dynamics of this apparently conflicted mode of engagement through kinesic and kinetic analysis. Discussing bodily feelings at the level of kinesic and kinetic resonance provides detail to the analysis of bodily reading and helps to negotiate the boundaries between affective and emotional responses to fictional events. Kinesic reading also brings out differences between the kinesic affordances available to different kinds of readerly bodies. A female body, responding to a fictional female body, draws from a certain kind of experiential background not necessarily available for bodies of other genders. While this difference is not absolute or based on "natural" sexual binaries, it emerges in a way that demands to be acknowledged when reading the stereotypically gendered figure of Emiko.

This gendered experience is, however, only one way of reading the novel. Kinetic analysis in a new materialist vein can develop gendered, human-centered experience into a more-than-human one. Kinetically attuning to the material aspects of fictional nonhuman beings plays a crucial part in this exercise.

4.2.1 Exploitation of the Artificial Woman

Emiko is introduced as an iteration of an old pulp fiction type: the artificial woman, an object of sexual objectification, often figured as a puppet, an automaton, or a doll. Her first appearance in the novel is in a bar scene in which she is subjected to severe sexual abuse, which is described as an everyday occurrence. The narration of the scene, focalized through Emiko, is a mixture of violent affective cues and contextualizing reflection.

> Emiko moans again as her body betrays her. She cries out. Arches. Her body performs just as it was designed—just as the scientists with their test tubes intended. She cannot control it no matter how much she despises it. She comes.
>
> The audience roars approval, laughing at the bizarre convulsions that orgasm wrings from her DNA. (*WG*: 55)

This passage figures Emiko's body both as an object that "betrays her" and "performs," and a subjective condition in which she "cries out," "arches," and "comes." This duality of embodied experience is central to the novel as a whole, and it serves to highlight the instrumental nature of the artificial woman. It is made very clear that the audience or the woman abusing her on the stage do not view Emiko as a person, but a "piece of genetic trash … a toy for them to play with, to break even" (*WG*: 53). Through both objectification and the aesthetics of mechanical jerks and convulsions, the character drawn in the scene calls up visual memories of countless previous iterations of the artificial woman, from Maria of *Metropolis* (1927) (display of jerking movements) to Pris of *Blade Runner* (1982) (doll-like appearance) and Ava of *Ex Machina* (2014) (being on display as a sexual object), and countless encounters with dramatized sexual violence.

Scott Selisker (2015) has noted that, in its treatment of the GMO theme, *The Windup Girl* "weds the effects of genetic modification to a logic of programmability … the novel treats genetics like a program that might allow or compel the body to do anything that a computer program might allow a computer to do" (Selisker 2015: 508). Selisker especially points out how the depiction of Emiko draws on the visual aesthetics of the human automaton, complete with its puppet-like, mechanical style of movement. In embodied reading experience, the involuntary jerks of Emiko's body underline the genetically determined aspects of her behavior.

From the start, Emiko's identity is narrated as conflicted between pride in her training at the Japanese "creche" and shameful anger at the mechanically sexual aspects of her engineered body. The training, the acculturation and the elegance, is what she loses at moments of panic and humiliation. In these moments, Emiko resembles not the masterpiece of Japanese techno-cultural ingenuity that she believes herself to be, but "nothing but a silly marionette creature, all stutter-stop motion—herky-jerky *heechy-keechy*" and "nothing but a wind-up" (*WG*: 54, emphasis in the original)—a mechanical toy, possibly even a broken one. Importantly, these insults are meted out in a chapter focalized by Emiko herself, forming the base for a narrative of self-loathing and callous self-objectification. Emiko is aware that she has been created for the purpose of serving as a versatile, sophisticated assistant, and the narration implies that her current use as a simple puppet is a mockery of that purpose.

This conflation of the genetic and the programmatic also gives rise to the theme of "nature versus nurture" in the novel—Emiko is depicted as constrained by both her genetic design and her behaviorist training, and readers are left to wonder which influence dominates her actions. The conflict of these two influences is also present in the male perspective on Emiko. When succumbing to the spell of Emiko's sexual attractiveness, Anderson Lake ponders whether his reaction is the result of Emiko's successful design.

> Does her eagerness to serve come from some portion of canine DNA that makes her always assume that natural people outrank her for pack loyalty? Or is it simply the training that she has spoken of? (*WG*: 262)

This basic paranoia about the possible mechanistic nature of erotic desire is at the heart of artificial-woman narratives. The "schizoid android" theme has been identified as one of the characteristic features in Philip K. Dick's influential work (Hayles 1999: 168–91). Rudy Rucker, in his early cyberpunk novel *Software* (1982), has captured the core of this patriarchal paranoia most lucidly:

> The sex was nice, but confusing. The whole situation kept going di-polar on Sta-Hi. One instant Misty would seem like a lovely warm girl who'd survived a terrible injury, like a lost puppy to be stroked, a lonely woman to be husbanded. But then he'd start thinking of the wires behind her eyes, and he'd be screwing a machine, an inanimate object, a public toilet. Just like with any other woman for him, really. (Rucker 1982: 83)

By creating such a time-worn iteration of the type of the artificial woman, Bacigalupi calls up a generic frame of reading the novel. The choice of figure is both cynical and transparent, allowing Bacigalupi to manipulate the affective responses of his audience without getting very deep into the ethical questions of exploitation or gendered violence. This artificiality is highlighted when Anderson Lake's wonders "if she were a real person if he would feel more incensed at the abuse she suffers." If Emiko were a real person and not a fictional figure, would we still willingly and complacently read about her suffering? I do not think that this is a question most actual readers of the novel would spontaneously pose. Awareness of the novel's fictional status and narrative strategies is built into the style and logic of the novel in such an explicit way that it seems unlikely that anyone would mistake Emiko for (a depiction of) a real person. This does not, however, mean that readers would be unaffected by the stimulation provided by the presentation of the figure. On the contrary, the entertaining force of *The Windup Girl* is largely due to the corporeal thrills it affords.

In fact, the novel latches on to its readers' capacities for feeling the thrills, making them aware of its own affective strategies and thus inviting them to reflect on the systemic production of affect. It shares this strategy of estrangement with the short story "The People of Sand and Slag." In a reading oriented toward bodily engagement, the combination of affective style and type-based characterization translates as a peculiar feeling of *being played* by the narrative (see Polvinen 2012). Reading about puppets, I feel that I temporarily adopt the postures, gestures, and submissive attitude of one. Accepting this puppetry is a starting point for an analysis of the novel's gendered structures of feeling and the readerly choreography it offers.

4.2.2 Kinesic Description as an Instrumentalizing Technique

As discussed earlier, Emiko is introduced to readers in a scene in which she is sexually abused on the stage of a bar. Scott Selisker (2015) discusses the scene, arguing that by depicting a callously watching, objectifying audience, Bacigalupi redirects readers' feelings of disgust from the genetically modified organism (Emiko) to the exploitative interaction effected in the act of watching (Selisker 2015: 512). While Selisker offers a reading of the objectifying gaze, a complete mapping of the scene's affective force would include other senses besides vision. An analysis more attuned to touch and kinesthesia results in a different kind of interpretation of the scene's affects. From a feminist perspective, it is also important to account for the experientiality of Emiko's female body, in all of its stereotypical artificiality, and for the meanings emerging in a reading done by a reader grown into female modes of embodiment.

The scene is focalized through Emiko's feeling body, and it recounts the experiential details of her sexual humiliation, from the splash of cold water on her nipples to the forced arching of her backbone in the hands of her dominator, and to simultaneously feeling the restricting grip of the bar clients' hands on her ankles and wrists and the dominator's manipulation of her genitals. She "writhes, her body shaking and jerking, twitching in the ways that windups do" (*WG*: 55), and eventually climaxes, in what is described as "bizarre convulsions" (*WG*: 55).

Reading such descriptions in a mode attuned to kinesic and kinetic resonance necessarily evokes mixed feelings, which are also somewhat dependent on the reader's previous experience with both sexual acts and pornographic descriptions. Bacigalupi has primed the scene by describing the suffocating heat of the bar, and the unbearable perfection of Emiko's oiled skin, "soft like butter when a man touches her" (*WG*: 51). The action of sexual abuse is punctuated by references to liquid running down this perfect, too-hot skin. While the passage does not read as purely pornographic—mostly due to the prominence of the distancing and contextualizing commentary from Emiko's perspective—it does contain sexually arousing affects that play into the complex response.

The jerking and twitching of Emiko's body is construed by the narrative as estranging, as something an onlooker would watch as one would "an insect under a magnifying glass: fascinated, and yet also repulsed" (*WG*: 53). Emiko also detaches herself from these movements, in an act of forceful disgust at her own body. As mentioned earlier, this style of movement is familiar from earlier encounters with the artificial woman. In the classic genre film *Metropolis* (1927), it is precisely the mechanical, jerking dance of the feminine robot that drives the watching crowd of men into a frenzy. Still, from an experiential perspective, it is easy to relate to some amount of involuntary nervous muscular spasming during a sexual act. The reflexive jerking movements can be connected to the more forced attempts at achieving climax and to the repetitive manipulation of erogenic zones. I would thus read the depiction of Emiko's "inhuman" movements as an exaggerating caricature of the mechanical—perhaps stereotypically female—aspects of human sexuality. By depicting these aspects as strange and unnatural—not only to the audience, but to Emiko as well—Bacigalupi repeats the act of severing the sexual female body from the experiencing mind. On the other hand, the defamiliarization of the sexual body makes it more available to conscious analytical contemplation.

The recognition of the bodily experientiality of sexual movement does not necessarily lead into a naturalizing reading of the scene. Rather, recognizing the dynamic helps one to also recognize the acts of fictional construction involved. Bacigalupi's narrative plays with the experiential affectivity of sexual bodies and uses this affective force to increase readers' involvement in the fictional events of the novel. While the abuse of the artificial woman does not necessarily evoke sympathetic or empathetic reactions from all actual readers, it is bound to evoke at least some kind of affective reaction due to its kinesic and kinetic power. Perhaps the abuse only serves as entertainment of the "lower faculties" of the senses, while the reader's analytic mind is already busy situating the scene into the larger plot and thematic unfolding of the novel. Perhaps this analytic reader understands the abuse as the motivation for the character's later acts of vengeance. These cognitive processes of detached deduction are not, however, separate from the kinesic recognition of bodily movements. Rather, I suggest that kinesic and kinetic recognition is integral to the interpretive process.

After a series of passages highlighting the many limitations to Emiko's agency, she begins to find capabilities of her own. These capabilities all circulate around Emiko's desire for freedom—the dream of a village of New People, up North, and the means of getting there. On a kinesic level, this desire is realized most forcefully in the two scenes in the novel in which Emiko moves fast. The first one begins with walking in a crowd, practicing control, on a mission to find transport to the North. She feels the people on the street watch her suspiciously, and panic starts to rise in her. As portrayed through inner monologue, she deliberately convinces herself to slow down her movements.

> Too fast. Slow down. You have time. Not so much as you would like, but still, enough to ask questions. Slowly. Patiently. Do not betray yourself. Do not overheat.
>
> Her palms are wet with sweat, the only part of her body that ever really feels cool. She keeps them open wide like fans, trying to absorb comfort. (*WG*: 149–50)

The passage underscores both the social and the material limitations of Emiko's condition. In kinesic reading, the controlled slowness of Emiko's movements takes central stage. She cannot move freely, fearing that she is found out as a windup, and she cannot move fast, fearing that her body overheats. Soon, in escaping an assaulter, both of these fears are dispersed:

> She plunges into the street, not caring that she shows herself as a windup, not caring that in running she will burn up and die. She runs, determined only to

escape the demon behind her. She will burn, but she will not die passive like some pig led to slaughter.

She flies down the street, dodging pyramids of durian and hurdling over coiled hemp ropes. This suicidal flight is pointless, yet she will not stop. She shoves aside a gaijin haggling over burlap sacks of local U-Tex rice. He jerks away, crying out in alarm as she flashes past. (*WG*: 155)

Kinesically attuning to Emiko's movements, I feel exhilarated by this sudden explosion of energy after all the constraints and wariness. The motion verbs in the passage—"plunges," "flies," "dodges," "hurdles," and "flashes"—evoke a sense of muscular power being rapidly exerted. In this instance, the materiality of the body is emphasized in such extent that the kinesic and kinetic modes of understanding bleed into each other: Emiko's body reads not just as human, but as material in a more *physical* sense. The use of power in contact with other material bodies on the street directly translates into a basic form of energy: heat. Being unable to sweat, Emiko's body has no way of getting rid of excess heat, caused both by the surrounding heat of the dry-season day and by her own exertion. After running into a passer-by and falling down, she finds her limit and collapses "drunken, overwhelmed by the furnace heat within her," "burning up" (*WG*: 1556).

In the other scene featuring a fast-moving Emiko, she is figured as a full-blown action hero. The narration takes time to focus on Emiko's visual perception and reflections in a style reminiscent of slow-motion frames in action films—in which the hero(ine) is fast enough to dodge bullets.

The white shirts are running for her—running full bore—and yet somehow, strangely, they suddenly seem slow. Slow as honey on a cold day ....

The white shirts mouths open to shout again. Their spring guns rise, seeking her. Emiko watches their slit barrels zero in on her. Wonders absently if perhaps she is actually the slow one. If gravity itself will be too slow.

The wind gusts around her, beckoning. The spirits of the air tug at her, blow the black net of her hair across her eyes. She pushes it aside. Smiles calmly at the white shirts—still running, still pointing their spring guns—and steps backward into open air. The white shirt's eyes widen. Their guns glint red. Disks spit toward her. One, two, three ... she counts them as they fly ... four, five –

Gravity yanks her down. The men and their projectiles disappear. She smashes into the balcony. (*WG*: 284–5)

Reading these scenes, I enact a particular readerly choreography. The swiftness and fluency of action, combined with the exciting situation, works to alert my senses in a pleasurable way. I enjoy Emiko's control over the situation. However, despite the seeming simplicity of the pleasurable experience, there is also a great amount of habituation and mediation at play in enjoying this scene. The scene evokes bodily memories and schemas of the countless times I have settled on a seat or a sofa to watch an action film, comfortable and motionless while stimulated with vivid effects. I recognize the chase-and-escape scene as a staple of action adventure, and the act of jumping from the rooftop as a familiar motif in such scenes. The short descriptive sentences of Bacigalupi's narration mimic the kinesic styles and fast cuts familiarized by cinematic action, and thus activate the particular experiential background supposedly shared by Bacigalupi's readers.

In comparison to the experientiality of "The People of Sand and Slag," the defamiliarizing techniques of *The Windup Girl* are less drastic. Readers are invited to enact the thrill of the action and the capability of the fictional figure, which largely stay within the conventions of action adventure in terms of their affective intensity. Emiko may move faster than bullets, and she may burn from exhausting herself, but these are staple effects. Rather than searching for estrangement in our kinesic and kinetic responses to the individual fictional body, we can consider Emiko as a *mutant figure*, that is, as a pattern in the larger network of readerly experience.

4.2.3 Making Sense of Artificial Women: Essential Categories or Monsters?

A figure such as Emiko that both thematically and formally repeats familiar patterns that derive from a long lineage of artificial women invites a reading that considers her as a "thing" rather than as a fictional person (see Oulanne 2021). We do not *need* to search for psychological depth or uniqueness in order to make sense of her, as even her existential reflections are iterations of routinized patterns of presenting particular kinds of angst. Readers also do not *need* to fall under a character-centered illusion in order to be affected by such a thing-like figure. On the contrary, Emiko's foregrounded fictionality opens up possibilities for interpretations that build on the power of fictional figures to move readers in corporeal ways. The abovementioned kinesic and kinetic analyses describe some aspects of this power, but they do not engage the cognitive dissonance between mimetic response (feeling with the figures like they were actual persons) and awareness of fictionality (knowing that the feeling itself is an effect of narrative strategies). While this kind of cognitive dissonance can occur in engagement with many kinds of figures and narratives, cognitive literary studies have suggested that narratives featuring artificial people—robots, androids, living dolls, and so forth—are particularly effective in evoking feelings of unresolvable ambiguity in readers.

Lisa Zunshine (2008; see also Jannidis 2004: 185-95) has argued that this kind of cognitive dissonance is inevitable, as human minds are hardwired for perceiving everything in certain essential categories: natural kinds (i.e., living beings), artifacts, and substances. Natural kinds, such as people, plants, and animals, have inner essences, whereas artifacts perform functions. In Zunshine's (2008: 8-9) examples, a skunk painted to look like a zebra is still perceived as a skunk, that is, it retains its "skunkness"; but a cup with the bottom sawed off loses its function as a cup and becomes perceived as something else, perhaps a bracelet or a cookie cutter. In Zunshine's humanist model of cognition, these categories are mutually contradictory, as one cannot perceive a given entity as both an artifact and a natural kind.

Zunshine (2008: 8) further stresses that cognitive essentialism does not result from culture or upbringing, as it has been found even in three-year-old children. Zunshine attributes the fascination we feel when encountering fictional cyborgs and robots to the way they disturb our categorizing processes. Not knowing whether to interpret the figures as inanimate objects or living beings, we hover between the options. In her mind, we remain "perennially titillated by robots, cyborgs, and androids because they are brought into the world with a defined 'function'—as artifacts usually are—and then rebel against or outgrow that function by seeming to acquire a complex world of human feelings and emotions" (Zunshine 2008: 19).

Even though Zunshine's argument is grounded on sound neuropsychological research, I do not find it entirely convincing. In particular, her evolutionary-psychological claim that habituation or analysis "will not change the cognitive architecture that underlies essentialism" seems too limited (Zunshine 2008: 22). From a phenomenological standpoint, it is possible to perceive entities as simultaneously living and object-like, and to habituate oneself to such a mode of perception. From an enactivist standpoint, it seems rather deterministic to assume that just because human *brains* default to particular kinds of categorizations, human *minds* or *experience* were radically resistant to change. While it is true that evolution is slow, and plausible that modern human brains share their neurological structure with prehistoric humans—a structure "that evolved to deal with natural kinds and artifacts but not with artifacts that look and act like natural kinds" (Zunshine 2008: 53)—what matters most for an enactivist response is that humans, understood as whole organisms, are capable of remarkable learning and change. It seems not only plausible but probable that perceptive habits and styles gradually change due to accumulated experience. Perceiving a given entity as both living and artificial does not seem all that impossible.[4]

The claim about the naturality of essential categorization seems to fall apart even when presented with the well-documented existence of animist perception: an animist would quite easily perceive rocks or cars as animate beings, and particular animals as messages to be attended to, that is, artifacts with a purpose (see Abram 1996). But even modern Western habits of perception and the context of reading fictional figures show the limitations of Zunshine's model. The experience of enacting the readerly choreography of Bacigalupi's Emiko points to a more fluid conception of life and artifice.

As a formal pattern in a fictional narrative, Emiko is the product of the transmedial and global genre of contemporary science fiction and of the consumerist logic of popular culture. On a diegetic level, she is a product of an industrial system that modifies human genetic material according to commercial purposes, and sells the cultivated and trained bodies to the service of companies and individuals. The language used around Emiko also frames her as a high-tech product. Emiko's former owner often describes her as "optimal," but, as Emiko bitterly reflects, she is "not optimal enough for a return ticket" back to Japan (*WG*: 283), as she can be discarded and replaced with a newer model. She is described in terms of programming and product development, and at her lowest point referred to as a mechanical "marionette creature" and "a wind-up toy" (*WG*: 54). In light of Zunshine's categories, Emiko reads both as artificial and as living.

However, the boundary between the artificial and the living is not quite as solid as Zunshine suggests. This is apparent in how the figure of the artificial woman, especially in the context of genetic engineering, also points to the long history of *breeding*, or *artificial selection of inheritable traits*.[5] Emiko can be aligned with pure-bred dogs or horses, carefully cultivated for both aesthetic and functional purposes. The fact that she suffers from the "poor design" of the pores in her skin serves to remind readers of the dysfunctions brought on by extensive breeding, such as the breathing problems of short-nosed dogs and cats. The emphasis on Emiko's embodied experience of overheating evokes in readers a bodily feeling of suffocating anxiety—a feeling that could also be easily attributed to dysfunctional dogs and cats. The figure thus combines, in readerly experience, features of living bodies (feeling and suffering) and artificial constructs (function and purpose).

As the example of pure-bred animals shows, hybrid creatures are a familiar part of modern environments, and they thus inform our encounters with fictional hybrid figures. However, we should not consider fictional figures simply through the cognitive psychology of encountering actual living beings and artifacts. The recognition of the basic nature of cognitive categories is without a doubt useful for understanding the default operations of human minds, but a model that uses those categories to explain our complex, skilful engagement with fictional figures seems too straightforward.

As I have already argued, following Merja Polvinen (2023; see Section 4.1), engagement with fictional figures necessarily involves an awareness of fictionality. This also applies when we make sense of fictional bodies through kinesic and kinetic intelligence. All fictional figures, not just those that are explicitly artificial, constantly challenge us to acknowledge their ontological ambiguity. They are not living creatures but artificial constructs made of words, and yet we cannot help but respond to them like we would to living creatures. What makes explicitly artificial figures interesting for cognitive literary studies is that they invite us to pause and reflect on our responses to that ambiguity.

Consider how Zunshine describes the experience of encountering fictional figures. She explains that when encountering a fictional entity that fits a particular essential category, identified unambiguously as either a living being or an artifact, readers "go on and on in an agreeable feedback loop"—but when the entity turns counterontological, the loop "comes to a screeching halt" (Zunshine 2008: 65).

> When we encounter a fictional character whose ontology seems to pull us in two different directions, we intuitively grapple for the ways to restore at least one of our broken feedback loops (for we cannot restore both) and to resolve the cognitive ambiguity by conceptualizing that hybrid as either a living being or an artifact. (Zunshine 2008: 79)

I propose that the same dynamic could be said to pertain to reading all fictional characters, and the "breaking" of feedback loops would also happen at moments of metafictional awareness, that is, when a narrator or a character points to their ontological status as a fictional construct. Choosing to ignore the fictional entities' fictionality and read them like "real people" is one popular way of resolving ambiguity. However, certain kinds of narratives and reading habits can develop other styles of responses, including styles in which readers stay with the ambiguity, even enjoy it. Polvinen (2023) has explored such responses at length in the contexts of both metafiction and speculative fiction, and Essi Varis

(2019a) has suggested that readers of speculative fiction are particularly prone to adopt an ambiguity-embracing style of response.

Building on recent work in cognitive narratology, Varis (2019a) has argued that the most fitting analogue for fictional characters is not the human, but *Frankenstein's monster*. In Varis's "monster analogy," fictional characters are always artificial, made of recycled parts, yet they prompt us to engage them in sympathetic and empathetic ways despite our better knowledge: "creatureness in itself can be characterized as monstrous, a cognitively threatening and fascinating aberration" (Varis 2019a: 69). We *know* they are not really alive, yet we engage them in the same anthropomorphizing mode of interpretation we use for engaging with living beings. The arguments Zunshine makes about the perennial fascination of hybrid characters could—as Varis does—be applied to all fictional characters.

Crucially for my argument, Varis's model accepts the ambiguity of fictional characters as an integral part of reading experience: "There is no need to decide whether they should be considered as skillfully crafted plot mechanisms or as startlingly relatable mock-humans because they are, by definition, both" (Varis 2019a: 74). This self-reflective perspective on the activity of reading supports the enactivist-posthumanist view of literary engagements that this book advances. The realm of fiction constantly participates in our lived experience, and readers routinely negotiate many different levels of fictionality in their everyday encounters not just with fictional characters but with figures in media and advertisement.

However, unlike most characters, mutant figures constantly remind readers of their ambiguous nature. "The People of Sand and Slag" and *The Windup Girl* are such powerful stories because they foreground the artificiality of fictional figures. Genetically engineered figures are particularly strange, as they tick all the boxes on the list, fitting both categories: they are both *natural* (breathing, eating, feeling) and *artificial* (designed, constrained, augmented). Moreover, through the affective style of Bacigalupi's writing, as readers we feel the impact of these fictional bodies as perspiration on our skin and tension in our muscles. Nevertheless, we also accept them as fictional constructions that add to a long lineage of figures and caricatures. We are invited to shift between perceiving hybrid figures as artifacts and as people, and even to keep the apparently contradictory views active simultaneously (see Polvinen 2023). This cognitive trick transcends not only the distinction between artifacts and living things (as presented by Zunshine), but also the distinction between the synthetic and the mimetic in fictional character (as presented by Phelan 1989).

Seeing both sides of this divide is a *skill* we can learn through reading mutant figures. Learning this skill is based on the cognitive default settings of categorization. We do tend to conceive of artifacts in terms of their functions and living things in terms of their essences. Yet, as Zunshine herself demonstrates in her readings of golems and *Great Expectations*, writers exploit this tendency and manipulate our minds into thinking beyond it. We can learn to hold categorization at bay and realize that sometimes (quite often) things are both artificial and alive.

From a new materialist perspective, the artificiality of Emiko also aligns her with other genetically modified organisms that inhabit Bacigalupi's postnatural storyworld. This alignment helps us understand Emiko as an affective device in the wider context of Bacigalupi's narrative. Reading kinetically, I attune not only to the materiality of human bodies, but also to the materialities of nonhuman bodies and forces. The muscular tensions I feel when reading descriptions of weather-related bodily feelings, for example, are also present when I read descriptions of animals working and springs being wound up (see Kortekallio 2020b).

This attunement to nonhuman materialities affords a broader new materialist reading of *The Windup Girl*. Bacigalupi's work has previously been analyzed from posthumanist and new materialist perspectives (Tidwell 2011; Idema 2019). Developing those perspectives further can enrich our thinking of how an artificial, gendered figure might align with various nonhuman figures and forces.

4.2.4 The Material Agency of a Fictional Fruit

Networks of biological species (some natural, most human-made), corporations, and political systems make up much of the experiential texture of *The Windup Girl*'s storyworld. The novel begins with an encounter with a newly reengineered fruit, *ngaw* or rambootan:

> Not a single one of these furry fruits should exist; he might as well be hefting a sack of trilobites. If his guess about the *ngaw's* origin is correct, it represents a return from extinction as shocking as if a Tyrannosaurus were stalking down Thanon Sukhumvit. But then, the same is true of the potatoes and tomatoes and chiles that fill the market, all piled in such splendid abundance, an array of fecund nightshades that no one has seen in generations. In this drowning city, all things seem possible. (*WG*: 5)

The passage, narrated from the perspective of the agribusiness agent Anderson Lake, details a startling spread of strange species: trilobites, ngaw, Tyrannosaurus, potatoes, tomatoes, and chiles. Setting the nutritional plants in direct comparison with the creatures mostly known in fossil form is an efficient way of describing the situation in this imaginary Bangkok: most of these plant species have indeed been as definitely extinct as trilobites and dinosaurs, but now they have returned. The mood evoked by the narrative perspective is a mixture of exhilaration and wonder. Lake buys two kilos of the sweet furry fruit, not bothering to haggle.

Reading a story that begins with defamiliarizing basic staples of the contemporary diet, readers cannot make too many assumptions about the storyworld. Contrary to the majority of far-future science fiction that only mentions agriculture in passing, *The Windup Girl* takes it as its main focus.[6] In the novel, seed stocks are the most valuable treasure any nation or corporation can harbor. Usually only the corporate seeds can survive the disease epidemics and pests ("cibiscosis," "blister rust," "ivory beetles") that attack both crops and the health of humans. However, Lake's "guess about the *ngaw's* origin" is that it has been reengineered by secretive "gene hackers," whose genius makes Thailand one of the rare nations that can cultivate noncorporate food stocks. Genetic engineering is thus characterized as both the reason and the cure for the tangle of extinction, poor soils, and impervious strains of plant diseases—whether one is for or against it, "it is the ocean they all swim in. The very medium of life" (*WG*: 69).

In this biotechnological risk society, most opt to stay with the safe, patented food brands engineered by the transnational megacorporations, such as U-Tex rice, SoyPRO, and TotalNutrient Wheat. Eating, in this fictional Bangkok, is thus always an act that involves caution and a particular awareness to the origins of the food. The narrative often makes this point by focusing on particular instances of people responding to food items. When the expatriate business people have their first taste of the *ngaw*, they are first wary of the fruit, suspecting it might be tainted with blister rust. Lake assures them that the "lady who sold them … [h]ad the certificates" and that they are "cleaner than U-Tex" (*WG*: 129). Tasting the fruit that has now been labelled as safe to eat, Lake's associates' "eyes widen," and "smiles appear" (*WG*: 129). One of them "chews thoughtfully" (*WG*: 129) and reminisces about another fruit, the lychee, that he once tasted. Not only does the *ngaw* stir up bodily responses and memories, but it also makes the group speculate about its possible origin, viability, and commercial value. Lake's search for the gene hacker responsible for creating the fruit spans the entirety of the novel.

The fruit thus appears as a motif in a specific assemblage that is simultaneously material, ecological, commercial, and political. Its capacity to evoke activity in other bodies is what Bennett (2010: 3) would call "thing-power," or "the vitality intrinsic to materiality," which is independent of human subjectivity yet accessed through "a certain anticipatory readiness ... a perceptual style open to the appearance of thing-power" (Bennett 2010: 5). Bennett, drawing on Bruno Latour and Greimasian structuralism, would call such a fictional fruit an *actant*, whereas I will limit myself to the more conventional literary-theoretical terms *motif* and *device*.[7]

Drawing on new materialist thinkers such as Bennett and Karen Barad, as well as on biosemiotics and actor-network theory, proponents of material ecocriticism suggest that matter itself can be considered a text: "a site of narrativity, a storied matter, embodying its own narratives in the minds of human agents and in the very structure of its own self-constructive forces" (Iovino and Oppermann 2012: 83). The idea is rooted in conceptions of matter as *material-semiotic* or *material-discursive*: that is, formed in processes of meaning-making that take place between material actors. I agree, in principle, that a posthumanist theorization should find ways to discuss meaning in terms that do not confine it to human interaction. However, I would not quite so readily describe material meaning-making in terms of narrative. In deference to enactivist thought, I maintain instead that material activity on all levels *generates meanings* in the basic sense of creating difference and value (see especially Thompson 2007).

Discussing material agency in terms of narrative poses several problems, which I will not address here at length. My critique here is mostly cognitive. Not only does narrativization rely on the cognitive processes of memory and prediction (which scientific consensus currently associates mostly with human cognizers), but, perhaps more importantly, it appears to be tied to the interpretive traditions of human cultures—whatever causal and relational patterns humans find in the dynamics of matter, those patterns are, by necessity, already the result of cognitive selection and interpretation (see also Hayles 2018). Understanding the liveliness of forests or microbes as "stories" is an interpretive act—perhaps useful, but also misleading.

Pieter Vermeulen (2019: 102) makes a similar critique, suggesting that instead of storytelling, *writing* might provide "a more revealing model" for material agency. Human actions, especially in the Anthropocene, leave tangible and irrevocable traces in the Earth, in its geology and ecology, in a process that Vermeulen calls *inscription*—and the Earth itself inscribes meaning onto living matter. For Vermeulen (2020: 102–3), the task of the Anthropocene-oriented scholar would be to read such inscriptions—interpret them in all-too-human, albeit technologically augmented ways.

While Iovino's and Oppermann's textualizing articulation mostly makes sense to theorists well versed in poststructuralist approaches, they also propose that a new materialist approach to reading can "focus attention on bodily experiences and bodily practices (where 'body' refers not only to the human body but to the concrete entanglements of plural 'natures,' in both human and more-than-human realms)" (Iovino and Oppermann 2012: 76). I find this reconfiguration of bodily practices the most generative proposal made by material ecocriticism, and Vermeulen's idea of inscription helps us narrow the focus on the traces left on bodies by different material agencies.

Through impressing themselves upon writers, nonhuman beings push through texts written by humans, their impressive (or inscriptive) force amplified or otherwise filtered by the text.[8] In Iovino and Oppermann's readings, such nonhuman agency is often traced from anthropomorphizing descriptions of nonhuman elements, for example, rivers and seas.[9] In *The Windup Girl*, however, nonhuman entities are not described in terms that would imply anthropomorphism or intentionality. Rather, human entities in the novel come to resemble nonhuman constructs in the ways they are produced and used. This situation opens up to new materialist analyses of material agency that do not require intentionality on the part of the nonhuman.

In light of the kinetic analyses practiced above, the fictional fruit *ngaw* affects readers in ways that are analogous to the affects of fictional human bodies: it is a bundle of affective and sensory cues that draws on and participates in readers' embodied experience in several modalities. Reading descriptions of fictional fruit, readers can experience gustatory and kinetic traces of sweetness, acidity, juiciness, and viscosity, or even the complex mix of sensations characteristic of the *ngaw* itself, if they happen to be familiar with it. They can enact the experience of manipulating the fruit, putting it into their mouths and chewing, "spit[ting] the fat pit into [their] palm," and "examin[ing] the black seed, wet with [their] saliva" (*WG*: 132). As the fictional fruit organizes around and within itself an assemblage of various human and nonhuman forces, readers can recognize similar assemblages in their lived material and political realities. By such a bundle of cues, the fictional fruit gains material agency.

From the beginning of the novel, food is also evoked as a matter of temporal continuities of generations, crops, evolution, extinction, and de-extinction. Thus it participates in the portrayal of a specific moment of future history and bridges it to the contemporary readers' empirical moment. As Lake searches for the history of *ngaw* from Expansion-era nonfiction books, the temporal relation is brought to the foreground: in the book he sees pictures of obese tourists shopping for fruit on a market. Lake's irritation of "the waste, the arrogance, the absurd wealth" (*WG*: 93) of the past—the present day of the novel's publication—is readily available to readers. The people of the past are, on the same page, explicitly called "fat, self-contented fools" whom the focalizer would like to toss of his balcony "the way they undoubtedly tossed aside fruit that was even the slightest bit bruised" (*WG*: 93).

Through the temporal estrangement of being addressed accusingly by a fictional inhabitant of the future world, readers are bound to view the present world as defamiliarized. Even if most of the potatoes, tomatoes, and fruit we eat today are not genetically modified in the strict sense, they are definitely engineered through artificial selection and brought to the market via specialized procedures of trade and logistics. Through the simple act of describing the current situation from a fictional future standpoint, *The Windup Girl* can make readers more aware of their dependence on actual networks of food production. Whether they would align with the focalizer and consider this dependency as "foolish confidence" is of course another matter.

In the instance of my first-person reading experience, the novel guides how I perceive my reading and eating body. Buying lunch in a Kurdish restaurant in Helsinki—rice, with a sauce of tomatoes, potatoes, and chiles, nightshades of perhaps Polish or Spanish origin—and eating it, I am haunted by the fictional equivalents of the foodstuffs, along with their economic and political entanglements. I recognize my eating body as an agent in global networks of food production, logistics, and marketing. I am, quite literally, constructed by these networks, as they enable both the renewal of my tissues and the continuity of my vital processes. Moreover, specific foodstuffs affect my dispositions, moods, and capabilities in different ways. Food, understood literally rather than as a symbol or metaphor, can be conceived of as "an actant in an agentic assemblage that includes among its members my metabolism, cognition, and moral sensibility" (Bennett 2010: 51).[10] This awareness of material networks amounts to an altered orientation: I pay more attention to the networks and their particular dynamics. With enough rehearsing, this attention might become habitual and affect my actions within the networks.

4.2.5 Against Niche and Nature

The ecological notion of *niche* is central to the affective structures of Bacigalupi's fictional world, as it is adapted for the use of political ideology. The notion serves a function within a particular constellation of nature and culture, as it is understood as the natural, unalienable habitat of a particular species—a natural boundary that should not be transgressed. Any transgressions are, in an idiom coined in the novel by the conservationist Christian sect called Grahamites, "against Niche and Nature," and genetically modified organisms are transgressive by default. This puts the genetically modified bodies of *ngaw* and Emiko in a perilous situation.

In *The Windup Girl*, the Environment Ministry of Thailand is determined to protect the integrity of the Thai country from invaders. In this protective effort, environmental conservation is entangled with economic, political, and spiritual concerns, as the ministry officers disinfect contaminated fish farms and burn contraband stocks of products ranging from grain to electronic appliances and luxury clothing. The boundaries of the nation are cared for with exquisite hygiene. Anything deemed "against Niche and Nature" is a target of righteous disgust and hatred. Genetically modified humans are only allowed in the country after the purchase of severely restricted import permits. Without a permit, a "New Person" (the Japanese idiom), or "windup" (pejorative colloquialism), is treated according to the rules designed for invasive species. And, as the Thais do not consider genetically modified organisms to have souls, the life of one bears no karmic cost on the killer.

While guarding their nation from the foreign agribusiness invaders, the Thai also cultivate a rigid system of moralistic rules of acceptable and non-acceptable life. In denying access to genetically modified seed, they also close their eyes from the development of the life around them: the Thai soil, transformed by the joint disasters of climate change, industrial agriculture, and plant disease epidemics, already bears strange fruit. Anonymous "gene hackers" create new and resurrected strains of vegetal life, including the *ngaw* that figures throughout the novel; the experimental nearly invisible domestic cat, "cheshire," has gone feral and transformed the local ecosystems; and New People mingle with natural humans, despite the demands of niche thinkers. As Emiko herself puts it, the Thais and the Grahamites are both "focused on their Noah's ark, after the flood has already happened" (*WG*: 165). The disastrous mixing of the natural and the artificial has already happened, in agriculture and human populations alike.

While this kind of transgression of categories is familiar from cyborg narratives, *The Windup Girl* is exceptional in the way it portrays genetic engineering as ubiquitous in all sectors of society. The novel's focus on genetically modified organisms of all kinds, including but not limited to humans, serves to align the artificial woman with other artificial life-forms. While genetically engineered humans in fiction have sometimes been employed as stand-ins for factory-farmed or genetically engineered animals,[11] the alignment with the kinds of foodstuffs already in circulation—grains, fruit, and vegetables—is a rarer contribution to the genre.

When witnessing the nearly invisible movements of the cheshires, Emiko notes to Lake: "Just think if they had made New People first" (*WG*: 164). In his own mind, Lake narrates Emiko's supposed thoughts on the matter: before the lesson learned from the rapid growth of the cheshire population, New People might have not been made sterile nor marked with physically obvious characteristics. They might have been the next step in human evolution. "Instead, [Emiko] is a genetic dead end. Doomed to a single life cycle, just like SoyPRO and TotalNutrient Wheat" (*WG*: 164).

Later twists of the plot shed ironic light on Lake's musings, as the novel eventually presents the advance of genetically engineered life-forms as an inevitable development. The apparent sterility of corporate life-forms, both New People and the genetically modified grains they are explicitly aligned with, can be bypassed by the efforts of gene hackers: at the end of the novel, new life emerges from a strand of Emiko's hair.

The bioengineered life of Bacigalupi's fiction challenges the conceptual dichotomy between natural species and human culture. Bacigalupi's portrayals of genetically modified bodies are steeped deep in ecological and political entanglements. Readers are oriented toward thinking about the networks of production, marketing, distribution, and regulation that shape every encounter with a technological body in a late capitalist system, whether the body is a potato, cultivated to perfection through centuries of artificial selection and a decade or two of genetic engineering, or an athlete, born and bred within high-technological medical and nutritional networks. The flood *has* already happened, and Bacigalupi's novel enables us to attune to it with more sophisticated senses and devices. It invites readers to corporeally engage with matters of patented life, induced sterility, and the precariousness of life in a risky environment. It also helps us counteract what botanists Elizabeth Schussler and James Wandersee have called "plant blindness": our tendency to notice plant life only as a background for human and animal life, rather than as significant in itself (see Allen 2003). Focusing on the material alignments the figure affords does not erase its problematic status as a gendered stereotype, but it does enable some mental moves that would be ruled out by a rigidly human-centered approach.

In Bacigalupi's postnatural narrative, Emiko is left outside human civilization, to live in its ruins and participate in the slow evolution of a new ecology. In this resolution, she does not fill the role of the woman in a rebuilding narrative, mothering children for the continuation of human race in a purely human effort. Rather, she is conflicted like the character Lilith of Octavia E. Butler's *Dawn*, a functional part of a system in which the illusion of sovereignty is impossible. She may well serve as a mother to future children, but in the genetic sense rather than the familial—her children, like Lilith's, will be "mixed" by an expert, and she might not be the one to parent them. In this role as well as in her role in the revolution plotline, Emiko is more a construct than a subject, a material node of activity in a more-than-human assemblage. As in Haraway's (2016) "Camille Stories," fertility and reproduction are not individual but collective matters. In *The Windup Girl*, however, the world is not freed of the shadow of the patriarch—the gene hacker Gibbons still holds an inordinate amount of power over the reproduction of human, animal, and plant bodies.

It is precisely this conflict that makes *The Windup Girl* a mutant narrative. With its vibrant materiality, it evokes in its readers a corporeal sense of more-than-human entanglement, and thus reaches toward an ecological understanding of more-than-human ethics. Yet it is caught up in the human-centered and sexist conventions of both the science fiction genre and of fossil modernity more generally. Attuning to the novel's violent figuration of a gendered stereotype reproduces gendered bodily feelings connected to reification and exploitation, but critical reflection and a new materialist interpretation of those feelings can help to nourish the growth of ecological subjectivity. The novel contains seeds for change—but they are only fertile after repeated technological-theoretical interventions. That is, they call for critical reading.

4.2.6 How to Appreciate Painful Affects

In this chapter, I have discussed the fiction of Paolo Bacigalupi through more-than-human reading and readerly choreography. In order to focus on the bodily and material aspects of the narratives, I have intentionally ruled out the concept of *fictional character*, choosing instead to discuss fictional bodies in terms of *figures*. The notion of figure has also enabled discussion of individual figures as iterations of genre-specific types. I have presented an approach to reading that does not center on mimesis on the level of purely human sociality.

I have argued that kinesic and kinetic intelligence pertain to the thematic interpretation of mutant narratives, and that Bacigalupi's narratives in particular thematize the dynamic of bodily responses to fictional figures. Imaginatively enacting the movements and bodily feelings of the posthuman and mutant figures of "The People of Sand and Slag" and *The Windup Girl*, I am guided to both accept their kinesic styles and, through its defamiliarizing exaggeration of painful affects, *resist* such an easy identification. In this process, I become aware of the narratives as *affective technologies* that make use of my capability for bodily and affective response: my *response-ability*.

I consider Bacigalupi's stories as mutant narratives in that they reach for posthumanist or ecological modes of storytelling and experience, but still struggle with the traditions of both realist narration and the science fiction genre. In my readings, this struggle is lodged in the complex affectivity of the central fictional figures. The posthuman and postnatural figures of "The People of Sand and Slag" invite readers to enjoy the heroically capable bodies and their actions, and yet the story defamiliarizes this pleasure by taking the consequences of postnatural embodiment to their extreme logical conclusions. *The Windup Girl*, on the other hand, mobilizes the type of the artificial woman in ways that serve to reinforce the binary separations between male and female, mind and body, and the particular figuration of women as objects. Kinesically attuning to the sexual violence and instrumentalization performed in the novel is a painful and derogatory experience: as a more-than-human reader, I feel that I am also used and violated by the novel. Yet the narrative also disturbs any binaries by evoking alignments between the artificial female body and other genetically modified life-forms, and by thematizing the experience of being instrumentalized. Bacigalupi's narrative encourages me to reflect on the painful and shameful feelings particular to the trope of the artificial woman, and broaden them to pertain to the wider exploitation of other life-forms. In this way, *The Windup Girl* calls for bodily reading that is *performative* in that it actively generates meanings, rather than *receptive*, as in simply reading for pleasure.

In an interview (Prendergast 2010), Bacigalupi admits that the painful affectivity of his stories is an intentional strategy: "The stories are designed to hurt," and the pain is meant to drive home his ecological agenda. With this statement, Bacigalupi also presents a challenge to literary critics and scholars: the design of his stories *requires* readers to both feel the pain and work with it. I suggest that the method of more-than-human reading, and the particular analytical notions of kinesis, kinetics, and readerly choreography, provide ways for literary scholars to do just that: to engage with fictional narratives in enactive ways that can give rise to new interpretations about gendered performativity and power, ecological interdependence, and more-than-human relationalities.

Posthumanist feminist approaches, and new materialism in particular, help to make sense of how fictional figures participate in the material construction of my embodied experience. As affective devices, fictional figures are activated in the ways in which I move my body, in the ways I respond to touch and rain, and in the way I read other fictional figures: in short, in *readerly choreographies*. *The Windup Girl*, as a whole, and Emiko, as a particular pattern within that whole, participate in my lived experience and amplify certain features in it.

In this chapter, I have discussed *estrangement* only minimally, as a cognitive dynamic that forms part of the experience of reading mutant figures. It is, however, essential to both reading mutant narratives and developing posthumanist modes of experience, and thus it deserves more elaboration. The next chapter discusses how estrangement functions in the context of New Weird fiction, and develops the notion of *embodied estrangement*.

Notes

1 While this line of argument could be made with regard to other elements of fiction, I will continue discussing fictional figures and fictional movement in particular. See Roine (2016) and Polvinen (2016, 2017) on fictional worlds and Varis (2019a, 2019b) on fictional characters in graphic narratives.
2 For theoretical models on how cognitive categories, schemas, prototypes, and stereotypes might function in reading (genre) literature, see Culpeper (2002) and Hogan (2003). While these theories draw on cognitive theories that are too disembodied and computational for the purposes of this book, they nevertheless have significant explanatory power.
3 The theme of "passing for human" is typical to cyborg and android narratives, as analyzed by Koistinen (2015) and Hellstrand (2016). Fictional cyborgs and androids often wish to be integrated into human society, to be treated as ordinary human beings despite their apparent differences (e.g., *A. I.*, *Blade Runner*, or the cylons in the 2004 adaptation of *Battlestar Galactica*). Bacigalupi's Emiko thus employs themes that are relevant primarily to cyborg and android narratives.
4 Zunshine (2008: 55) does not claim that there are ontological essences, only that "the quirks of our cognitive architecture" have evolved to perceive such essences. For discussion about cognitive plasticity and perceptual change, see Section 2.1.
5 Other influential crossings of the topic of genetic manipulation and the type of the artificial woman can be found, for instance, from Theodore Sturgeon's *Venus Plus X* (1960), Bruce Sterling's *Schismatrix* (1985), Nicole Griffith's *Ammonite* (1992), and Johanna Sinisalo's *Core of the Sun* (2016).
6 Notable exceptions to the rule include Kim Stanley Robinson's *Mars* trilogy (1992–6) and other terraforming fiction, and N. K. Jemisin's *Broken Earth* trilogy (2015–17).

7. *Actant*, in Latour's and Bennett's reformulation of Greimas, is a way for describing the activity of nonhuman things (that are usually themselves assemblages of other things): "something that acts or to which activity is granted by others. It implies no special motivation of human individual actors, nor of humans in general" (Latour 1996, quoted in Bennett 2010: 9; see also Greimas 1973).
8. An evolutionary psychologist might add that the rivers and seas do not only impress themselves on writers, or human individuals, but on generations of humans, and that through this environmental pressure, the rivers and seas (and other nonhuman entities) become cultural objects that are recycled in texts. As I will discuss in more depth in Chapter 6, this is how nonhuman elements can also participate in the lived experience of readers.
9. The authors stress that anthropomorphism does not necessarily imply anthropocentrism, but can function instead as "narrative expedient intended to stress the agentic power of matter and the horizontality of its elements" and "reveal similarities and symmetries between the human and the nonhuman" (Iovino and Oppermann 2012: 82; see also Bennett 2010: 99; Bernaerts et al. 2014; Pettersson 2016; Herman 2019).
10. Jane Bennett discusses both the empirically studied cognitive-affective effects of omega-3 fatty acids and the experiential comments on eating provided by Friedrich Nietzsche and Henry David Thoreau (Bennett 2010: 39–51).
11. For example, Margaret Atwood's *Oryx and Crake* (2003) and Kazuo Ishiguro's *Never Let Me Go* (2005).

5

Embodied Estrangement and Jeff VanderMeer's *The Southern Reach*

In an essay on anthologizing *The Weird*, Jeff VanderMeer (2014d) describes his experience of being haunted and colonized by the stories he reads. Acquiring and editing the stories for the anthology required him to dig deep into both the fiction and the lives of authors—to become "a detective trying to solve an inexplicable case" (VanderMeer 2014d). The fiction, the lives of authors, and the editorial process began to overlap and intermingle, feeding into the thinking and writing of the editor/author.

In another essay, "Hauntings in the Anthropocene," VanderMeer (2016) describes his experience of being affected by a major ecological catastrophe. In April 2010, the Deepwater Horizon oil drilling rig exploded, spilling 4.9 million barrels of oil in the Gulf of Mexico. VanderMeer, a Florida resident, was haunted by this event, to the extent that the expanding shape of the oil spill emerged in his dreams—but in an inverted form, as a natural area that grows over human settlements and obliterates all infrastructure and technology. This dream image found literary expression in the novel *Annihilation*, published in 2014 as the first part of VanderMeer's trilogy of New Weird novels, *The Southern Reach*.[1]

In his essays, VanderMeer describes a particular experience of literary creation that emerges from an accumulation of influences, or, "the mulch, the thick substrate, that at some point manifests in one's own stories" VanderMeer (2014d). This experience of strange emergence is at the core of this chapter. The term *uncanny* illuminates one aspect of it, yet it is more than a simple response to the almost-familiar: VanderMeer describes it in dynamic terms, as an aspiration "to be true to the underpinnings of the world, and the struggle to understand that world. This impulse is tempered by the recognition that we can never know all of it, or even most of it—and that this seeming lack is not a failing but a strength" (VanderMeer 2014d). In this chapter, I strive to describe this kind of ongoing, seeking estrangement in the dynamic terms put forward by enactivist theory.

Building on the theoretical work laid out in the introduction of this book, I suggest that *embodied estrangement* can describe certain material strategies of estrangement found in VanderMeer's *The Southern Reach* and in other works of science fiction. Among other things, VanderMeer's use of embodied estrangement affords counteracting the philosophical paralysis of *cognitivist nihilism* (Varela, Thompson, and Rosch 1992). Such a countermove builds on readers' experiential background in encountering horror fiction tropes, and partly depends on their capability for enacting fictional movement in a kinesic mode.

Carefully articulating the cognitive processes of encountering the unknown can help us better appreciate the meaning-making effort of VanderMeer and other writers and readers of strange fiction. I have previously argued that the affective experience of *being impressed* by both nonhuman and textual actors is a crucial component of this process (Kortekallio 2019). Here, I want to further explore how the estranging experiences of more-than-human entanglement, figured as being *impressed, haunted, permeated*, or otherwise affected by either fictional narratives or the nonhuman environment, can be articulated in terms of bodily and more-than-human sense-making. In the following sections, I will focus particularly on bodily feelings of *hovering at the edge of an abyss* and *being haunted*. I argue that by evoking these bodily feelings, *The Southern Reach* trilogy can amplify readers' experiences of epistemic uncertainty when facing nonhuman unknowability.

5.1 Weird Strategies of Estrangement

In the case of Jeff VanderMeer's *The Southern Reach*, embodied estrangement is largely a matter of genre—or rather, a formidable tangle of different genres and styles. The trilogy has most commonly been received as "ecologically minded Weird fiction" or "eco-horror," while traces of the American naturalist tradition and Kafkaesque surrealism have also been detected.[2] Idema (2019) considers *The Southern Reach* in terms of LeMenager's (2017) "genre trouble":

> VanderMeer conjoins topoi from different literary traditions to represent nature disrupted: Germanic and Greek mythology (the enchanted forest, Leviathans); Gothic, fantasy, and (New) Weird (the human threatened by supernatural forces

from inside and outside); modernism (reflections on the nature of experience and consciousness, the relation between self and other); postmodernism (the questioning of reality and truth); biological science fiction (cancerous growth, infection, mutation); and detective (inexplicable murders, excess of irreconcilable information). (Idema 2019: 105)

Even if VanderMeer's repertoire contains a broad range of styles and influences, the context of Weird fiction may provide the richest potential for interpretation. The potential arises not only from the stylistic features typical to the Weird tradition, but also from the notion of *weird* as a particular kind of affect or atmosphere.[3]

Weird fiction, as well as the contemporary movement of the New Weird, is often characterized by its evocation of a sense of dread, awe, or terror (Miéville 2009; VanderMeer 2008). Traditional Weird fiction, stemming from the 1920s and 1930s work of H. P. Lovecraft and others, is differentiated from other horror fiction in that the horror element is of cosmic rather than mundane nature (see Joshi 1990; Robertson 2018) and from Golden Age science fiction in its mistrust in the scientific enterprise (see Carroll 2015). The tradition of cosmic horror can "be regarded as a heroic but doomed attempt [at communicating] the incommunicable" (Stableford 2007: 71), and as an antihumanist realization of the limitations of human perception and knowledge of the horrifyingly vast and strange cosmos (Robertson 2018: 23–8; Faassen and Vermeulen 2019). The New Weird of the twenty-first century, however, moves beyond horror and epistemic despair by weaving them into descriptions of mundane life. Gry Ulstein (2017) distinguishes between the Old and the New Weird by pointing out that they convey monstrosity in different ways:

> Crudely put, traditional weird fiction, closely tied to Lovecraft, is all about encounters with, and subsequent escapes from, inconceivable monsters whose mere existence drives people mad (Cthulhu). The new weird has adopted the cosmic horror of the old weird, but typically approaches it in different ways; often it is more about researching, articulating, and *embracing* the monster rather than escaping it. (Ulstein 2017: 75, emphasis in original)

In New Weird texts, this tendency for "embracing the monster rather than escaping it" often manifests as an intentional literalism of fantastic and science fictional elements. This insistence on a "real-world" feel is also foregrounded by the definition by Ann and Jeff VanderMeer, in an introduction to the anthology that has helped shape the genre. They claim that New Weird often chooses "realistic, complex real-world models as the jumping off point for creation of settings that may combine elements of both science fiction and fantasy," and that it is "acutely aware of the modern world, even if in disguise, but not always overtly political" (Ann and Jeff VanderMeer 2008: xvi).

In an interview with VanderMeer, one of the more canonized New Weird authors, China Miéville, shoots down critical attempts to read his strange stories as allegorical (VanderMeer 2011: 58). The New Weird, he argues, anchors itself to empirical reality while acknowledging the perceptual limitations of encountering that reality, that is, committing to "the weirdness of the real." In doing so, the New Weird not only recirculates certain horror tropes (e.g., encountering monsters beyond one's perceptual abilities) but also recontextualizes them as belonging to everyday reality. VanderMeer, too, admits to a mimetic intention of sorts, identifying as one of the motivations behind *The Southern Reach* "an attempt at conveying the truth that the world is stranger than we recognize, that we understand less of it than our brains trick us into believing" (Mendelsund 2014).

This should not, however, be understood as reduction of the weird into any world of objective "facts," as the weird (as a mode rather than a genre) is characterized by particular affects and effects. Mark Fisher (2016: 15, emphasis in original) detects the weird by "a sense of *wrongness*: a weird entity or object is so strange that it makes us feel that it should not exist, or at least it should not exist here." According to Ann and Jeff VanderMeer (2011: xiv), the weird "is as much a sensation as a mode of writing," and it makes people resort to explanations such as "I know it when I feel it." The notion of *weird* as a mode or a sensation blurs the stylistic lines between the Old and the New Weird and provides opportunities for new inquiries. So how do works of the Old and the New Weird mobilize weird affects and sensations? How does this weirdness warp themes and narrative structures, and how is it entangled with various genre tropes?

In VanderMeer's fiction, weirdness peers out of social interaction and biological life. His Veniss cycle (a number of short stories mostly published in the 1990s and the novel *Veniss Underground*, 2003) and Ambergris novels (*City of Saints and Madmen*, 2002; *Shriek: An Afterword*, 2006; *Finch*, 2009) are all set in fantastic worlds full of human, animal, vegetal, machinic, and fungal life in complex metatextual entanglements that defy the very notion of "setting" (Robertson 2018). After the baroque density and experimental textuality of VanderMeer's earlier work, *The Southern Reach* trilogy seems almost mundane at a first glance. The fictional world appears to be modeled on the empirical world, in a comparatively realist and coherent mode. The characters have mundane jobs, relationships, and personal interests—they are researchers and investigators, psychologists, and lighthouse keepers. The root of the trilogy's strangeness lies not in a wildly fantastic fictional world but in the tension between what appears to be normal, modern human life and the inexplicable weirdness that contaminates it from all directions. For Faassen and Vermeulen (2019), this tension is also a way of addressing the "ineluctable anthropocentrism" of human subjectivity, as *The Southern Reach* trilogy "inscribes itself into the long lineage of weird writers who have struggled with the human's fatally anthropocentric and pathetically anthropomorphizing drives." For posthumanism, then, the Weird becomes relevant because its persistent focus on affect is inseparable from the thematic tension between the human and the nonhuman.

In the first novel of the trilogy, *Annihilation (Ann)*, weirdness reaches readers through a strange, detached narrator. The novel is written in the form of a field journal of an unnamed biologist of an expedition team. The team, sent by a clandestine government facility, the Southern Reach, explores an area, simply called "Area X," which has been transformed by an unknown Event. All humans and their technology have vanished, leaving behind only what returnees from previous expeditions characterize as "pristine wilderness" (*Ann*: 55 *et passim*). Area X will not yield to scientific investigation: it permeates and contaminates the investigators, transmuting their sense of reality and self. Yet the interpretation offered by the novel, through the biologist narrator, is materialist, pragmatic, and scientific: Area X is presented as a transitional ecosystem inhabited by organisms that transgress human understanding, and the only way of making sense of the area is to continue exploring it.

Due to its focus on exploring the limits of human experience and perception, Weird fiction is exceptionally suited to effect embodied estrangement in readers. I also see embodied estrangement as a strategic effect that is made possible by the narrative techniques of VanderMeer's trilogy. This strategic effect partially overlaps with what Timothy Morton (2007: 63) has called *ecomimesis*, a rhetorical device by which one attempts to "undo habitual distinctions between nature and ourselves." Ecomimesis is a matter of experience rather than argument: "If we could not merely figure out but actually *experience* the fact that we were embedded in our world, then we would be less likely to destroy it" (Morton 2007: 63–4, emphasis in original).

Previous studies have also argued that the New Weird in particular can take advantage of "fiction's prerogative to assert rather than argue" (Prendergast 2017: 337) and experiment with "ways to move beyond cosmic fear" (Ulstein 2017: 75). The conceptual work done in the New Weird movement itself can help us to gain a better grasp of the experiential and narrative dynamics of embodied estrangement. In *The Southern Reach*, VanderMeer takes on the challenge of introducing imperceptible environmental processes into human experience. The mystery of Area X is constructed as a puzzle for both characters and readers, and the themes of knowing and not-knowing emerge on every page of the trilogy.

The Southern Reach often reverses conventional subject–object dynamics, nonhuman entities look (or seem to look) at humans, and humans feel their gaze. Particularly interesting in this setup is how the notion of strange entities "peering through things" blends into more tactile and visceral notions of being "contaminated" by said strange entities and phenomena (among them, the beauty of nature). Tied into the structure of sensory modalities, the blending also effects a shift from one cognitive metaphor to another: from *seeing as epistemic control* to *feeling as partial knowing*. In VanderMeer's trilogy, the latter is presented in highly ambivalent terms, as both painful and truthful.

Reading *The Southern Reach* in a more-than-human mode, I hope to amplify the kind of experience that goes, even if just slightly, beyond what is considered real in a human-centered culture. In fact, I propose that this kind of amplification of more-than-human experientiality can function as a form of posthumanist critique.

5.1.1 Destabilizing Human Mastery

As articulated by cognitive literary theorist Karin Kukkonen (2014, 2019), reading involves the constant readjusting of one's expectations and interpretative models as the narrative unfolds, a kind of "predictive processing." Such an understanding of the reading process emerges from a wider embodied and enactivist understanding of cognition. In the classic articulation of *The Embodied Mind* (Varela, Thompson, and Rosch 1992: 241 *et passim*), the basic dynamic of enactive cognition is figured as "laying down a path in walking." This is a process that is metaphysically "groundless," as it cannot be traced back to a stable foundation in either a pregiven world or a permanent self. Such a lack of foundations is one of the central findings of cognitive science.[4] Varela, Thompson, and Rosch (1992: 200) claim that a realization of this view of the self as phenomenal or operational leads to a "sense of vertigo" in which we need to "delve deeper."

I suggest that VanderMeer's fiction provides readers a chance to delve deeper into groundlessness, in terms of both theme and readerly experience. Previous research has discussed the horrific and monstrous affects of *The Southern Reach* in the context of the ongoing ecological catastrophe, arguing that the trilogy can provide models for moving beyond the fear of the unknowable (Prendergast 2017; Ulstein 2017) and "allows the reader to eventually experience radical alterity as something other than merely destructive" (Idema 2019: 31). Idema also connects radical systemic and perceptual uncertainty to ecological systems themselves, arguing that VanderMeer's fiction can experientially simulate ecological interaction. Discussing these claims from an embodied experiential perspective can unravel how Weird fiction braids embodied cognition into material ecologies.

While the stated aim of *The Embodied Mind* is to guide Western science and philosophy out of the nihilist anxiety evoked by the realization of groundlessness, here it is more important to *stay with* that anxiety and figure out how it is articulated and evoked in VanderMeer's fiction. In this context, the bodily feelings tied to nihilism are entangled with nonhuman monstrosities, which include the nonconscious aspects of human embodiment. If human selves are "transparent models" (Metzinger 2003: 1) and human bodies are "spaceships for bacteria" (Bear 2003: 376), then groundlessness definitely sounds like something human cultures should learn to accept. VanderMeer's fiction is committed to decentralizing the human subject "within a universe that clearly sees us as simple atoms like everything else" (VanderMeer 2016), developing a mode of ecological existence that has been called "dark ecology" (Morton 2013, 2016) or "weird ecology" (Tompkins 2014).

First, let us turn an analytic eye toward the treatment of *observation* in *Annihilation*. In the novel, the biologist-narrator's scientifically trained attention is tuned toward nonhuman ecosystems—plant and animal life in the transitional zones between saltwater marshes and freshwater forests— rather than interhuman relationships. References to the research team's social relations are often unemotional and nondescriptive, and the team members are only identified by their professional functions: the biologist, the psychologist, the anthropologist, and the surveyor. Such reduction of individuals into their functions is explained as part of the protocol of the Southern Reach institution— stripping the expedition members of their personal details is supposed to protect them from the effects of Area X.

As Siobhan Carroll (2016) shows in her analysis of the explorer figure in recent works of Weird and New Weird fiction, selfless restraint is at the heart of the idealized expedition. Expeditions, in Carroll's historically informed reading, combine scientific and imperialist agendas and also pave the way for capitalist appropriations of the "as-yet uncommodified natural landscape" (Carroll 2016: 72; see also Moore 2015). As part of such operations and especially in narratives of such operations, the individual explorer ideally functions as a "vanguard of civilization" (Carroll 2016: 72), which includes being capable of self-mastery and detached observation even at the face of terror.

Annihilation sets such explorer characters into ironic light, as any such capabilities of self-mastery are undermined from the beginning. Nonhuman animals help to destabilize notions of human mastery. The narrator reports several instances of being seen by the strange animals of Area X in ways that do not fit her conception of how animals usually see humans. These creatures, however realistic their portrayal, appear too conscious for comfort.

The first encounter of this kind is with a pair of otters, occurring on the first day of the expedition observing the biological life of the area. The strangeness of the otters is evoked in a brief flash in the middle of a passage that describes the biologist's other observations. She feels that the otters can see her watching them—and that "things were not quite what they seemed, and [she] had to fight against the sensation because it could overwhelm [her] scientific objectivity" (*Ann*: 30). She recalls experiencing the same feeling before.

The encounter with the otters momentarily disrupts the reliability of scientifically trained observation. As the passage also reveals that the biologist is accustomed to "fighting" strange sensations, rationality emerges as a means of resistance at the face of the fantastic and the unknowable. In the pages that follow, observation and other research tasks are contextualized as a way to calm the nerves of the explorers (*Ann*: 31). After nightfall, hearing a strange cry from the marshes, the explorers shout back to it "confident that eventually we would photograph it, document its behavior, tag it, and assign it a place in the taxonomy of living things" (*Ann*: 31).

Throughout the novel, rational scientific observation gives way to moments of *being observed in return*. Nonhuman critters also take on performative roles, giving the impression of camouflage and pretense. Moments like this occur often enough in *Annihilation* that one critic has called it the "uncanny sense that there is always a pretense performed by the natural" (Uhall 2016). This sense of performativity emphasizes the unknowability of Area X, and the limits of scientific objectivity. In resisting the status of objects, the nonhuman entities of Area X disturb the whole foundation of the explorers' mission of epistemically or institutionally controlling the area.

Nonhuman entities also enter the bodies of human observers and actively transform their perceptions and feelings. Very soon during the expedition, the biologist enters an underground construction (which she perceives as a tower while others refer to it as a tunnel) and becomes contaminated by strange fungal spores. The contamination makes her more sensitive to the nonhuman life of Area X and alters her perception while making her feel physically stronger. Among other alterations, she begins to perceive the walls of the underground tower as breathing and flesh-like.

The contamination also makes the biologist impervious to the hypnotic suggestion practiced by the psychologist of the expedition group. From the training period on, the purpose of the suggestion has been to instill in the group a specific model of perception. The model affirms the subjectivity of the expedition members as distinctive, certain, and separate from the environment. The environment, and the underground tower in particular, is asserted as a lifeless artifact.

After being contaminated, the biologist is forced to realize the artificiality of this model of the environment—but instead of finding a "truthful" or "natural" way of perceiving, she is equipped with another model that is equally artificial, namely the spore-induced perspective where everything appears excessively alive. As a result, there is no way she can trust her own senses. The spore contamination and the organizational training both operate as parts of her perception, but she does not consider either of them "true." As the contamination progresses, she feels oppressed by the vividness of her impressions of the wilderness and cheated by the inhuman strength of her body: "The brightness in my chest continued to sculpt me as I walked, and ... I believed I could have run a marathon. I did not trust that feeling. I felt, in so many ways, that I was being lied to" (*Ann*: 93).

Science fiction and fantasy are full of narratives about (often horrifying) assimilations and mergers with other entities. This dynamic of self-destruction is dominant in many of the so-called zone novels, such as the Strugatsky brothers' *Roadside Picnic* (1972, also known as *Stalker*), Stanislaw Lem's *Solaris* (1961), and the apocalyptic novels of J. G. Ballard such as *The Drowned World* (1962), *The Burning World* (1964), and *The Crystal World* (1966). In these narratives, the protagonists generally meet their doom in the maddening and/or lethal ordeals of strange environments. However, like some of the more recent post-catastrophic audiovisual narratives, such as *Fallout* (1997–18), *Lost* (2004–10), or *Fringe* (2008–13), *The Southern Reach* does something different. Area X is well beyond the scope of human minds, definitely hostile to humans and destructive to the fixed ideas they have of themselves, but this destruction implies *transformation* rather than *the end of the world*. But what sets *Annihilation* apart even from the rest of post-catastrophical narratives is that the biologist successfully *resists* the merger with the strange entity of Area X.

As Elvia Wilk (2019, emphasis in original) points out, the "new nature" of Area X cannot be rationally explained by the biologist. Rather, it "constitutes its own form of knowledge, an embodied knowledge *rooted* in place." The novel arrives at such an embodied knowledge both by destabilizing rationality and by amplifying the bodily feelings of more-than-human experience. The narrative routinely evokes hesitation and suspicion by providing multiple speculations on a given observation or feeling (e.g., *Ann*: 18), referring to the relative ignorance of the narrator at the time of experience compared to the time of writing (e.g., *Ann*: 24, 55), and describing failures in understanding (e.g., *Ann*: 141). The observational methods and attitudes of the biologist fail her one by one: she cannot remain objective, her microscope does not register some of the obviously alien cells in her samples, and all the pre-expedition conditioning and training given at the Southern Reach facility proves irrelevant to the task. Along with the possibility of epistemic control, the biologist loses her sense of mission.

As rational observation loses its grip of the world, the bodily feelings of more-than-human experience creep in. The "brightness" the biologist is contaminated with reconfigures her moods and perceptions, and she can no longer deny what her senses tell her, namely that the animal life of Area X *regards her* as she does them. Prendergast (2017) has noted that *Annihilation* presents animals as ethical subjects, but in my mind, the novel does far more than that: it presents a coevolutive understanding of a world in which the human subject is not alone in the world but continuously observed, infected, and transformed by nonhuman presences. Human and nonhuman bodies exist in feedback loops of mutual specification. In addition to presenting such a more-than-human understanding, however, *Annihilation* also acknowledges human resistance to it, and the limits of human ability to understand the nonhuman.

In the act of resisting, the biologist performs a reluctant transformation that the readers can also enact. In this bodily process, which we can begin to understand through the notion of readerly choreography, the certainty of rational knowledge about both selves and environments is gradually annihilated. In the next section, we will face this monstrous event.

5.2 From Cognitivist Nihilism to Ecological Monstrosity

The New Weird makes use of the genre conventions of both science fiction and horror, and by doing so can nudge our habitual patterns of readerly engagement into new directions. In this section, I build on George J. Sieg's (2009) work on the experientiality of horror to demonstrate how *The Southern Reach* mobilizes and reconfigures the corporeal model of the Lovecraftian "Gnostic victim." Attending to the embodied experience of reading shows that it does so through the evocation of particular gestures and motions.

Staging an encounter between the biologist-protagonist and the nonhuman unknowable, *Annihilation* presents a detailed choreography of existential and epistemic uncertainty. The biologist has arrived on a rocky coast at the end of a drunken and disoriented evening, and there she encounters a disorienting critter.

> What I found when I finally stood there, hands on bent knees, peering down into that tidal pool, was a rare species of colossal starfish, six-armed, larger than a saucepan, that bled a dark gold color into the still water as if it were on fire. Most of us professionals eschewed its scientific name for the more apt "destroyer of worlds." … I had never seen a destroyer of worlds before, even in an aquarium, and it was so unexpected that I forgot about the slippery rock and, shifting my balance, almost fell, steadying myself with one arm propped against the edge of the tidal pool.
>
> But the longer I stared at it, the less comprehensible the creature became. The more it became something alien to me, the more I had a sense that I knew nothing at all—about nature, about ecosystems. There was something about my mood and its dark glow that eclipsed sense, that made me see this creature, which had indeed been assigned a place in the taxonomy—catalogued, studied, and described—irreducible down to any of that. And if I kept looking, I knew that ultimately I would have to admit I knew less than nothing about myself as well, whether that was a lie or the truth.
>
> When I finally wrenched my gaze from the starfish and stood again, I could not tell where the sky met the sea, whether I faced the water or the shore. I was completely adrift, and dislocated, and all I had to navigate by in that moment was the glowing beacon below me. (*Ann*: 174–5)[5]

The passage makes it easy for readers to enact the location, posture, and movements of the narrator's body. We read her as standing, "hands on bent knees, peering down into that tidal pool" (*Ann*: 174). In the pool, she sees an impressive starfish. This encounter catches her by surprise and we read her as shifting her balance and almost falling, ending up awkwardly perched against the edge of the pool.

As we follow the biologist's location, posture, and movements, we can also enact the bodily feelings and cognitive trajectories woven into the narration. The perceptual and kinesic action in the passage is inseparable from the cognitive-affective unfolding of the experiential world. Seeing, the primary means of epistemic control, turns into futile staring that yields no result: "the longer I stared at it, the less comprehensible the creature became." The strangeness of the starfish grows to encompass nature and ecosystems, and "something in [the biologist's] mood and in its dark glow" makes the starfish seem irreducible to scientific knowledge. The kinesic action in the passage further emphasizes this failure in understanding. The biologist fails to keep her balance, and she fails to make sense of the starfish.

In the last sentences of the passage, perception, emotion, and sense-making come together in a global sense of disorientation that is mapped in spatial terms: the biologist is "completely adrift, and dislocated." This fictional experience conveys the disorientation of not just a skull-bound mind, but an entire embodied organism.

In the pages that immediately follow, the biologist recounts "a similar experience at a thousand times the magnitude" (*Ann*: 175): the encounter with the Crawler, the monster that writes the spore-emitting words on the wall of the underground tower. This encounter involves a psychedelic confusion of sensory impressions, starting with a blue-green light that overwhelms her sense of vision (*Ann*: 176). The biologist hears an "unearthly noise [that] had a texture and a weight, and with it came a burning smell, as of late fall leaves or like some vast and distant engine close to overheating" (*Ann*: 176). In her retrospective commentary of this description, the biologist admits that the particularities might be produced in the act of remembering: "It is difficult to tell what blanks my mind might be filling in just to remove the weight of so many unknowns" (*Ann*: 176). In this way, the narrative leaves a door open to the irreducible mystery of the perceptual event while simultaneously providing very detailed and rich description.

Like the encounter with the starfish, the encounter with the monster brings the biologist to the limits of her perceptual and cognitive abilities. In her perception, the shape of the monster keeps changing, evoking optical illusions and impossible sensations. This perceptual uncertainty leaves her in an all-encompassing feeling of existential insecurity that we might as well identify as *groundlessness*. The motif of staring without comprehension, combined with a loss of balance, is repeated. The luminous starfish of the biologist's imagination grows in size, its rough surface blending with the surface of the coastal rock, and sends its light to join the light of the night sky. The biologist is left in between these two incomprehensible entities, permeated by light: "I was teetering on its rough, luminous surface, staring up at the night sky again, while the light of it flowed up and through me" (*Ann*: 178).

Reading through these fictional situations, I am prompted to enact uncomfortable bodily feelings of losing full vision and balance. While the detail of description provides plenty of other sensory cues, some of them beautiful (blue-green light) and some frightening (burning smell—overheating engine), the sensorimotor feelings form the base notes of the affective dynamic of the reading event. The abundant detail adds complexity to the basic bodily feeling of *failing to maintain sensorimotor control*. As sensorimotor control is precisely the bodily ability that, in enactivist theory and phenomenology of the body more broadly, maintains our sense of a stable self, the bodily feeling of losing that control serves to temporarily undermine coherent subjectivity itself (see Sheets-Johnstone 2011; Thompson 2014: 334). Evoking the destabilization of the lived body is thus an effective way for articulating failures in other kinds of control—for example, epistemological or existential.

5.2.1 Cognitivist Nihilism and the Gnostic Victim

The encounters with the starfish and the monster form a sublime scene, beginning with the mundane observations of the biologist but growing beyond them into cosmic existential dread. For a moment, it seems that the novel has turned from the materialist treatment of everyday weirdness into an older style of Weird and horror fiction—the protagonist finds the limits of her comprehension, and is forced to stay there, succumbing to madness. It seems there is no option other than a final fall into the abyss—a nihilism, or annihilation of the perceiving rational subject. A closer look at both the textual detail of the fictional encounters and the notion of nihilism, however, shows that this would be a hasty conclusion.

The Embodied Mind defines nihilism in Nietzschean terms: "The nihilistic predicament is the situation in which we know that our most cherished values are untenable, and yet we seem incapable of giving them up" (Varela, Thompson, and Rosch 1992: 128). They connect this predicament specifically to the cognitivist attachment to consciousness and free will. *Cognitivist nihilism* thus involves both the realization that cognitive science does not support the existence of an central, conscious, masterful self, and the persistent inability to think of human experience without such a notion.[6] *The Embodied Mind* claims that cognitivist nihilism is incapable of coming to terms with the *groundlessness* at the heart of both Western science and subjective experience. Enactive cognition, in contrast, is metaphysically "groundless," as it cannot be traced back to a stable foundation in either a pregiven world or a permanent self. Using robustly corporeal terms, Varela, Thompson, and Rosch claim that a realization of this view

> initially results in a sense of vertigo due to the collapse of what we had supposed to be sure and stable foundations. But rather than sweeping this sense of groundlessness under the rug by once again pitching the internal and the external against each other—we need to delve deeper into this sense of groundlessness and follow through all of its implications, philosophically and experientially. (Varela, Thompson, and Rosch 1992: 200)

As discussed earlier, the "sense of groundlessness" as a bodily feeling figures prominently in VanderMeer's *Annihilation*. Moments of characters losing their balance occur at thematically crucial moments also in the other parts of the trilogy, *Authority* and *Acceptance*. VanderMeer's fiction thus provides opportunities for "following through" the implications of groundlessness in terms of both theme and readerly experience. As such, it enables moving beyond nihilism.

Cognitivist nihilism becomes more tangible when we bring in the tradition of Weird fiction, and H. P. Lovecraft in particular. George J. Sieg (2009: 34) argues that Lovecraftian horror emerges particularly from the experience of the victim's perception and reason being violated. Lovecraft's characters are "stripped down to being bare instruments of perception—impaled by an intrusive, inescapably bizarre alien otherness." Sieg locates this kind of "Gnostic horror," found in classic vampire fiction and the *Exorcist* films alike, in the perspective of the victim rather than in the presence or characteristics of the monster. The victim, whether the virginal heroine ravished by demonic forces or the pure-minded scientist driven mad by eldritch horrors, needs to be "innocent, *as regards the horror*" (Sieg 2009: 34, emphasis in original). In Sieg's analysis, the innocence of Lovecraftian victims is tied to their position as rational, sane, white, and Aryan subjects forced to encounter a world of reason-defying miscegenated monstrosities.[7] The Gnostic victim thus suggests the cognitivist nihilist readerly choreography of hovering at the edge of the unknowable, helplessly staring into the monstrous abyss. As readers enact the bodily feelings that such a fictional situation evokes (perhaps including vertigo, an empty feeling in the stomach, and a weakening or loss of balance), they also rehearse cognitive and affective patterns bundled with the bodily feelings. This example shows us how readerly choreography unfolds as enactment of patterned fictional feeling and movement, and how it draws on readers' habitual knowledge of genre-typical figures.

Going back to the text of *Annihilation*, we can ask whether the encounter of the biologist and the monster fits into the dualist horror schema, characterized earlier as cognitivist nihilism and embodied in the Gnostic victim. We already saw how the scene destabilizes sensorimotor control and the reliability of perception. However, it seems to map rationality and subjectivity in a way that differs from the cognitivist nihilist pattern. The biologist continues to observe the monster even when her sight fails her, focusing at first on reports from her other senses (*Ann*: 176). Even when those reports appear confusing and potentially misleading, as she admits that her mind might be filling in the blanks, the narration retains a calmness detached from the perceptual confusion.

Moreover, the biologist rationally recognizes that the monster is an *organism* with strange but partially comprehensible abilities, and thus contextualizes the monster as part of the ecosystem of Area X. In this ecological mode of thought and experience, she accepts the unknowability of the monster. Thus, even when limited rationality might be necessary for the coherence or continuity of her subjectivity, total epistemic control is not, and she does not succumb to madness. In this regard, the figure of the biologist differs from the tradition of Gnostic victims.

Sieg (2009: 53–4) concludes that for Lovecraft, "there was no solution or escape from the horror, as becoming the monster through deliberate identification is hardly an option for the extreme reductionist. For him, life is a conceptual nightmare with only the void of an empty consciousness as contrast." But Sieg's analysis inadvertently provides a conceptual way out of horror: relinquishing purity and becoming monstrous. As Ulstein's (2017) and Prendergast's (2017) analyses suggest, this is exactly what happens in *Annihilation*. As Ulstein puts it, the trilogy presents the monstrous as "a potentially emancipatory catalyst for starting to think in weird terms" (Ulstein 2017: 94).[8]

The weird can, in case of the biologist, also be interpreted in ecological terms. Even before entering Area X, she is open to the notion of ecological interdependence—in fact, she cannot figure herself outside of such relationality. She figures herself as an expression of her environments. This anti-individualism marks her as not "innocent, as regards the horror," as a proper Gnostic victim would be. In a move that finalizes the readerly choreography of resisting cognitivist nihilism, she closes her eyes and turns away from the monster.

This move—literal to the nonconscious system of readerly response, literal and figural to a conscious critical mind—reconfigures the trope of the Gnostic victim. As the biologist turns away from the edge of madness, readers may performatively enact the movement and accept, on the level of nonconscious kinesic response at least, the cognitive reorientation entailed in it. The move now exists as a possible response to encountering monstrosity. The turn can by no means be read as a victory of the masterful human subject, as the monster still forces the biologist through an excruciating near-death experience, and after leaving the underground tower, she is gradually transformed into something nonhuman. But even after all this, there is no complete annihilation of the perceiving subject: the biologist endures "beyond the endurable" (*Ann*: 182). The narrative maintains a pragmatic, reporting tone, and the biologist goes on living and exploring an area that supports monstrous beings as part of its common ecology. The latter parts of the trilogy take this trajectory further, with *Acceptance* in particular focusing on life in a strange and dangerous ecosystem.

5.2.2 Accepting Monstrosity

In Haraway's terms, the biologist's turn away from the edge of madness marks a decision to *stay with the trouble*. After this turn, at the climax of *Annihilation*, the trilogy goes on to explore the messy and painful business of living with monstrous creatures, with the biologist eventually becoming monstrous herself. By the end of *Annihilation* we lose sight of her, as she disappears into Area X. She resurfaces in the last book of the trilogy, *Acceptance* (*Acc*), to be seen through the eyes of her doppelgänger, Ghost Bird (a figure I discuss in more detail in a later section).

By the end of the trilogy, the biologist has become a mountain of moss-covered flesh, many-eyed and glorious—strange, but definitely perceived as a material and biological *organism* by the other characters and especially by her doppelgänger. The monster is described in multisensory terms, as carrying a briny and herbal smell and emanating a sound resembling the wind and the sea. It is described as muscular and wide, covered with dried seaweed and barnacles. During the descriptive passage of Ghost Bird's encounter with this organism, the affective tone shifts from an initial fear and awe to something like curiosity and respect.

> Nothing monstrous existed here—only beauty, only the glory of good design, of intricate planning, from the lungs that allowed this creature to live on land or at sea, to the huge gill slits hinted at along the sides, shut tightly now, but which would open to breathe deeply of seawater when the biologist once again headed for the ocean. All of those eyes, all of those temporary tidal pools, the pockmarks and the ridges, the thick, sturdy quality of the skin. An animal, an

organism that had never existed before or that might belong to an alien ecology. (*Acc*: 196)

Performing a great feat of mental flexibility, Ghost Bird recognizes the organismic in the monstrous and accepts it as belonging to her world. The scene echoes an earlier recognition: the biologist's encounter with the Crawler in the underground tower. While both the Crawler and the biologist-as-monster are recognized as parts of the ecology of the area, the ecology itself is still "alien."

The respect performed in this passage both does and does not depend on readerly feelings of familiarity. On the one hand, the organism is described in appreciative terms that connect it to the familiar realms of animal and machine (good design, intricate planning). On the other hand, the sum of description still amounts to an irreducibly strange entity that defies known categories, except, perhaps the category of the organism. Imaginatively enacting Ghost Bird's experience of these monstrous organisms defamiliarizes readerly notions of what it is to perceive natural organisms, and thus it entails embodied estrangement.[9]

The alternative to cognitivist nihilism, as presented in *Acceptance*, is not a harmonious return to nature. Certain passages of the biologist's account of her life in Area X are certainly romantic, such as her comment that she has become so attuned to the messages of animal and vegetal life, whether natural or unnatural, that she no longer wishes to consume any of that life (*Acc*: 177). However, her attunement is jarred and her daily routines perverse. For decades, she postpones her transformation into monstrous form by inflicting pain on herself (*Acc*: 179–80). Still, in the hope that allowing that transformation to happen will open up new vistas of knowledge, she eventually gives in (*Acc*: 180).

As the monstrous is presented as something beyond human experience and language, the trilogy offers no first-person perspective on the transformation. Following the biologist thus brings the embodied reader to another limit—not of reason and mastery, but of human forms of experience and narrative. Tracing the movements of her fictional body will not bring us any closer to more-than-human experience. It is thus time to move on to the wider weirdness of the trilogy and consider the experiential dynamics arising in the more-than-human reading of it.

5.2.3 Control, on the Edge

The protagonist and focalizing perspective of *Authority* (*Aut*) resembles the biologist in one central kinesic aspect: he is often seen teetering on various edges. In his recurring dreams he stands at the edge of a cliff, staring at miles of still water and the behemoths within, "conveying such a sense of power that he can feel the havoc of their passage even from so far above" (*Aut*: 3). Such views beckon the dreamer into hours of silent fascination. The weight of this silence is only accentuated by the "whispers echoing up to him" (*Aut*: 3).

The protagonist, ironically self-named "Control," performs cognitivist nihilism in complex gestures. His social status is unstable, as he is portrayed as a tool for willful authoritative figures (federal intelligence agents for mother and grandfather, and several loci of power at the Southern Reach headquarters) and as being constantly on the verge of losing his professional credibility as a governmental agent (the job as the acting director of the Southern Reach facility is described as his last chance). Moreover, his thoughts and perceptions are always tinged with moments of profound epistemic uncertainty. In addition to the recurring dream that opens the novel, Control is haunted by glimpses of disturbing images and associations, such as a water stain in the ceiling resembling "variously an ear and a giant subaqueous eye staring down" (*Aut*: 91) and a recurrent smell of rotting honey that he interprets as the scent of a cleaning product used in the Southern Reach facility. The physical environment disturbs him by always being something other than it seems—an experience in which both the continuity of the environment and the stability of the experiencing self are called to question.

In reading experience, Control's hauntings evoke a bodily feeling of a *strange presence*, as if something was hovering just beyond the edge of my visual field. The exploration of this phenomenological periphery is also what *The Southern Reach*, as a whole, affords to readers. This experience is thoroughly *weird*, in the specific sense that the narrative constantly evokes the sense of being on an edge, of almost perceiving something unperceivable. This *something* includes not only the monsters of Control's dreams, but also the nonconscious aspects of cognition: habitual patterns, the influence of authority figures, and the gravitational pull of specific places and people. It becomes very clear that Control is guided by forces beyond his consciousness and beyond what is explicitly explained by the narrative. Curiously, however, the border zone between the conscious and the nonconscious is quite wide, and even manageable to some extent.

As the novel progresses, Control becomes acutely aware of the borders of his subconscious pressing in on his conscious mind. Thus he nurtures his hunches and intuitions. The novel maps Control's mental state in very specific spatial terms: he is constantly on the edge of a cliff, between a secure foothold and the vastness of the sea, teetering on a position that is both *compromised* and *a compromise*. This position is reflected even in the actual diegetic placement of the character in a town "close to the sea but not on the coast" (*Aut*: 68), a choice on Control's part that is assigned to intuition and rationalized: "The fact was, the Southern Reach knew so little about Area X, even after three decades, that an irrational precaution might not be unreasonable" (*Aut*: 68–9).

Through Control's perspective, the novel negotiates the boundary between conscious and subconscious thought. Control maintains a careful relationship with his intuitions and with the behemoths of the subconscious. Such an attitude is contextualized in the text as a survival strategy: when rational inquiries fail to make sense of Area X, instinct might prove a useful ally to the conscious rational mind.

This view is supported by later scenes. For instance, the "superstition" expressed by researchers at the Southern Reach facility is framed as a reaction to the incomprehensible circumstances, as the superstition "wasn't even unreasonable, really. How many invisible, abstract incantations ruled the world beyond the Southern Reach?" (*Aut*: 105). Thus, negotiation between the conscious and the subconscious is a theme that extends from the personal story of Control into the larger story of scientific inquiry and human control over nature, where nature takes the role of the subconscious, and real-world monsters from Area X step in to accompany the dream-image behemoths.

Whatever the "invisible, abstract incantations ruling the world" are thought to be, they have the effect of debilitating the researchers' rational faculties and morale. In contrast to *Annihilation*, and reiterating the motif of porous boundaries, *Authority* focuses on Area X's cognitive effects at the area's periphery rather than at its center. Area X works within the facility through the weird items brought back by the expedition teams, including journals, videos, an immortal plant, and the words seen by the biologist on the wall of the tower and reproduced by the former director of Southern Reach on the wall of a closet adjacent to her office. Due to the weirdness of such items that with their presence ridicule the very notions of *border* and *quarantine*, the researchers are, as the narrative puts it, "mutated under their skin" (*Aut*: 68). *Authority* proceeds to slowly reveal these mutations from the perspective of Control, eventually revealing how he too has transformed. The narrative arc of Control's story leads him to a real-world reckoning with his nightmares: in the end, he not only travels to the coast and sails along it in a small fishing boat, but literally jumps into the kind of abyss described in the introductory scene.

This central motif and narrative device of border-crossing in *Authority* could be termed *haunting*. The conscious narrative perspective of Control is haunted by echoes and ghosts of the nonconscious. Even if this psychoanalytical model is not uniquely *weird*, weirdness arises from how the narrative repeats the motif of haunting in the level of fictional environments. Area X itself, not just the characters' perceptions of it, is presented as a locus of material agency that actively transforms both the nonhuman environment and the people involved in researching it. This agential environment fits Wilk's (2019) definition of the weird as "an element or zone or experience that is not completely explainable according to our current structures for categorizing the world." By building on the long tradition of haunted areas in horror fiction, VanderMeer thus conveys a conception of more-than-human agency.

This conception is not just a disembodied idea, but a *cognitive ecology* (Cave 2016), available to the bodily sensibility of readers as a lived environment of sorts. Through its focus on the psyche of a human protagonist, *Authority* makes this posthumanist experience of agency accessible also to readers who are habituated to more humanist models of agency and meaning. The notion of haunting also helps us understand the more-than-human affectivity of literature. As mentioned in the introduction to this chapter, VanderMeer (2014d, 2016) has described his writing process in terms of being haunted by nonhuman things and events, such as the Deepwater Horizon oil spill, as well as by literature, such as the works included in the *New Weird* anthology.

For readers familiar with *Annihilation*, Control's dreams and intuitions bring up a bodily sense of recognition. We recognize the particular muscular tensions of standing on an edge of a body of water, about to fall in, and might remember the scenes in which the biologist stares into an overgrown swimming pool, or a tidal pool. The dream-image behemoths call up memories of fictional encounters with strange animals and the Crawler, memories bundled with the affects of dread, awe, fascination, and sheer material impressiveness or *thing-power* (Bennett 2010). In this way, the story of Control contributes to the longer-term affective and kinetic experientiality of the trilogy, which slowly dissolves the certainty of a self-contained human subjectivity through evocations of partial and vague memories and associations. Neither the characters nor the readers are ever fully *there*—rather, bits and pieces of them take shape through hauntings and hunches, or emerge as fleeting stirrings in the landscape.

VanderMeer's characters also follow genre-typical patterns. Despite his approach to characterization, which draws on psychological realism where Paolo Bacigalupi's approach does not, the characters of *The Southern Reach* are just as instrumental as Emiko of *The Windup Girl* is. Thus, they too become meaningful only in the context of genre traditions. The biologist, as demonstrated previously, moves with a lineage of other figures—Gnostic victims and scientists exploring strange areas and meeting their fates. In encountering the monster and in becoming one, her movements, gestures, and feelings follow the trajectories created by others before her. As she recreates this traditional pattern with new variations, the figure offers readers a chance to enact the bodily feelings of turning away from the edge of an abyss, thus effecting a slight change in their habitual readerly choreography.

Such patterns of expectation and response are not limited to a figure's lineage within a genre. Intuitively if not necessarily consciously, readers will also compare and contrast the corporeal and thematic aspects of figures within the trilogy. As readers move and feel with a figure such as the biologist, they imaginatively adopt her style of movement, feeling, and perception, which subtly shapes their sensitivity to following encounters with other characters, as well as their expectations of plot events (see also Kukkonen 2014, 2019). Already familiar with the biologist's struggle to maintain epistemic control over Area X, and her eventual surrender, they might expect similar turns from Control's story, too. In part, Control fills those expectations, but he does so through a very different pattern of response. He reiterates and variates the nervous twitches of Kafka's K, the looping logic of metaphysical detectives, and the futile resistance of Gnostic victims. As the analysis earlier demonstrates, his character is built onto the rigid, even if leaky, binaries of the conscious and the subconscious, self and other, Human and Nature, and thus the trajectory of his transformation also follows a different pattern, meandering through obsessions with control, meaning, and language.

Both everyday perception and the figurative work of fiction involve continuous reenactment of previously occurred perceptions and experiences, echoes of gestures and bodily feelings, half-remembered memories and half-formed ideas, and everything else that constitutes an *experiential background* (Caracciolo 2014c). While all reading experiences necessarily activate the experiential backgrounds of readers, *The Southern Reach* makes use of readerly experiences of partial and vague recognition in ways that dissolve the certainty of a self-contained human individual.

5.2.4 Contamination by Experiential Motifs

The Southern Reach iterates and variates certain particular experiential motifs that are perceptual and linguistic. Perceptual alterations that are linked with contamination by Area X are repeated, with slight variations, throughout the trilogy. Such experiential motifs include a feeling of personal strength and stamina (*Ann*: 93, 151; *Acc*: 321), smelling "rotting honey" (*Ann*: 24, 25; *Aut*: 20, 87, 108, 163; *Acc*: 255, 279), a feeling of there being a "second skin" (*Acc*: 158, 185, 197),[10] as well as other bodily feelings of pressures, presences, and enhanced senses. *Authority* and *Acceptance* also circulate fragments of dialogue that readers will remember from *Annihilation*, such as the hypnotic suggestion "paralysis is not a cogent analysis" (*Ann*: 27; *Aut*: 184, 233; *Acc*: 75) and "is there something in the corner of your eye that you cannot get out?" (e.g., *Aut*: 229; *Acc*: 81, 98; see also *Acc*: 94). Some of these fragments are linked to the mind-control techniques used by the Southern Reach agency. Thus, the repeated motifs serve to remind readers that while the focalizing characters' perceptions and utterances might seem personal to them, they are in fact constituted, to an unknown extent, by outside forces. In an interview, VanderMeer has himself identified this technique and its estranging effect on readers:

> You have a sense of processes going on beneath the skin, behind the walls. Dialogue can even accentuate this idea—in *Authority*, for example, in the hallways of the Southern Reach stray fragments of speech from *Annihilation* linger, a kind of displaced residue that the main character can't identify but the reader can. (Mendelsund 2014)

As VanderMeer notes, the emerging sense is of processes "going on beneath the skin, behind the walls," that is, on the far side of various boundaries, hidden from direct perception. Replying to VanderMeer, the interviewer Peter Mendelsund (2014) refers to the fragments of dialogue as "splinters of dialogue [that] were echoing around the Southern Reach," thereby evoking a memory of the ominous splinter that, in *Acceptance*, pierces Saul Evans' skin and leads to the transformation of both Evans himself and the whole area (*Acc*: 25).

Between the two of them, VanderMeer and Mendelsund seem to suggest that language itself can function as a contaminating agent, entering readers and changing how they think and feel, with or without them being conscious of the influence. While VanderMeer and Mendelsund only discuss dialogue, I propose that the dynamic of contamination also unfolds through textual motifs that have to do with sensory, kinesic, and kinetic experience, such as smelling rotting honey, the uncanny sense of bodily strength, and standing on the edge of a body of water. The scent of honey in particular is repeated in a way that is accessible to readers, but not to the focalizing characters. The scent is mentioned in the narrative accounts of both Control (in *Authority*) and Saul Evans (in *Acceptance*), but the characters do not connect it to the contamination. Control explains the scent through assuming it arises from a cleaning product used in the Southern Reach facility, and Saul Evans experiences it only briefly in a scene at a bar, and interprets it as coming from the bar kitchen (*Aut*: 87; *Acc*: 255, 279). In encountering these experiential motifs, readers, for their part, recognize both the experiences and their connection to contamination.

Due to this recognition and the perspective provided by knowing the storyworld, readers are then likely to doubt the interpretative abilities of both Control and Saul Evans, judging their reasoning as flawed and biased. This, in turn, serves to relativize their reliability as sources of experiential knowledge, as the reader is bound to interpret their perceptions as altered by either the Southern Reach organization or Area X.

Importantly, this is a sense-making process that pertains particularly to reading fiction. While one could argue that instinctual warnings and paranoid feelings, *hauntings* in brief, might play a part in making sense of one's actual environments, I would not claim that such sense-making and the readerly cognition I discuss here would be *analogous*. This point is also made by Karin Kukkonen (2019: 19, emphasis in original), who notes that in everyday contexts, sensory flow is "largely unstructured," while the literary text "can be understood as a *designed* sensory flow that guides these adjustments of our predictions in particular ways."

Hauntings experienced while reading fiction are thus likely to be linked to textual patterns that are, to some extent, intentional on the part of the author. VanderMeer's essays and interviews show us that he is very aware of the potential effects his authorial choices have on readers. By such choices, readers are invited to repeatedly return to the borders of their perception and consciousness, to consider whether there is something in the corner of their eye or behind their back, and to familiarize themselves with an uncertainty of this kind. Reading such fiction could thus be considered as engagement with affective technology, especially in cases where the reader attends to both the textual design and their affective and emotional responses (see also Polvinen 2016, 2017, 2023).

5.2.5 The Solid Presence of a Ghost

The Southern Reach not only draws on the dynamic of partial recognition, but also thematizes it by presenting a *doppelgänger* of the biologist, Ghost Bird. This mutant figure first appears in *Authority* as a counterpart and challenge for Control, and she also acts as a focalizing character in *Acceptance*. Ghost Bird affords yet another opportunity for discussing fictional figures as affective devices. What is particular to this case is that rather than functioning as a defamiliarizing device, Ghost Bird *familiarizes* certain aspects of mutant experience, including a sympathetic attunement to monstrous organisms and an acceptance of the condition of "brightness." In the context of *The Southern Reach*, the strangest thing about Ghost Bird is her pragmatic attitude toward Area X.

Ghost Bird is sometimes interpreted as nonhuman due to her origin as a creation of Area X (Ulstein 2017; Idema 2019; Faassen and Vermeulen 2019). Ulstein (2017: 87) notes how the trilogy makes a transition from the perspective of the biologist to the "acutely nonhuman, extraterrestrial" perspective of Ghost Bird. In Ulstein's reading, the latter becomes

> the ultimate emissary of Area X and most important mediator of VanderMeer, taking on the viewpoint of the nonhuman and offering this viewpoint to the reader. The reader has already been prepared for this transition in focalization by the sensitivity for the nonhuman perspective in the biologist. (Ulstein 2017: 87)

If we follow Ulstein's reading, it appears that Ghost Bird is a key figure for a posthumanist reading, and a narrative device that draws on the readers' familiarity with the biologist. While I agree with Ulstein and others about the importance of the character, I find it difficult to read Ghost Bird as primarily *nonhuman*. Her perceptions and concerns are constructed in ways that follow the traditions of depicting human minds, and for all relevant purposes, the bodily experientiality that arises from reading her body is not particularly estranging. While she is compared to other monstrous creations of Area X, she is also deemed "a viable mistake—a mutation" (*Acc*: 185). Of Area X's creations, she is also the only one which is explored through a focalizing perspective. Thus, rather than reading Ghost Bird as a nonhuman character, I would read her as a *mutant figure*, that is, a figure that somewhat awkwardly negotiates the boundaries of the human and the nonhuman. Like Carroll (2016: 77), I place Ghost Bird in the realm of the more-than-human zone of "ecological uncanny."[11] The more-than-human aspects of Ghost Bird take shape in contrast to other characters, most importantly the biologist and Control.

As Ulstein also notes, understanding Ghost Bird largely depends on recognizing earlier events in the trilogy. In *Acceptance* especially, Ghost Bird recirculates the thoughts and motions of the biologist: she walks the paths of Area X, and descends the steps of the underground tower to encounter the Crawler. She has access to the memories of the biologist, but knows herself to be a different individual with her own experiences (*Acc*: 36). For readers, Ghost

Bird's ruminations and actions present a chance to both reenact and reassess the actions of the biologist.

As Ghost Bird emerges as an individual character, readers are also invited to enter "spirals of might-have-beens" and compare her thoughts and actions to those of the biologist. By her name and inexplicable emergence from Area X, Ghost Bird can also be interpreted as a materialized ghost of the biologist. This is also how the author views the character, telling an interviewer that *Acceptance* is "filled with ghosts" (Mendelsund 2014). However, the relative independence of Ghost Bird makes this interpretation *weird*, if not altogether implausible: for a ghost, she is remarkably lively. She is described as a solid and steady presence, strong and protective whereas the biologist was often shaken and always antisocial (e.g., *Acc*: 192, 239). In terms of readerly choreographies, reading Ghost Bird affords bodily echoes of steady gazes (e.g., *Acc*: 82), purposeful walking, and even powerful rowing, which is described in kinesthetic detail (*Acc*: 112). In *Annihilation*, the biologist is described as "self-contained." However, in the specific sense that links sensorimotor coherence and focus with a clarity of common sense, this term applies even more to her doppelgänger. In this way, the figure of Ghost Bird inverts the logic of haunting: after encountering the doppelgänger, the original is bound to feel somewhat insubstantial and disjointed, a creature not quite connected to the material world.

Through Ghost Bird's perspective, Control's humanness is ridiculed as a neurotic grasping to a long-lost order, exemplified and enlarged in Southern Reach research of Area X. Through Control's perspective, Ghost Bird appears as recklessly aloof, unconcerned with the human world and their own survival, and focused instead on unimportant matters such as the flight of birds (*Acc*: 82). What Control perceives as "the real world" is his former lifeworld of careers, institutional conspiracies, and systematic investigation—all that is opposed to idealized Nature. The "unnatural" agency of Area X—its resistance to technology and systematic investigation, the strange creatures it produces, the pervasive sense of being *regarded* by it—demolishes the binary categorization of Nature and Culture, thereby depriving Control of the distance his professional and personal identity is built upon. Control conceives of this demolition as the work of a unified intentional agency, or a *conspiracy*.

Ridiculing these thoughts, Ghost Bird's perspective constructs Control as an unstable person to be protected from knowledge that might shatter his fragile sanity, and a person blind to nonhuman expressivity, for example, the particular behaviors of different bird species (e.g., *Acc*: 28, 32). Ghost Bird's perspective construes perception that is habitually attuned to the nonhuman, which is often set in contrast with memories and opinions about the human world.

This ecologically entangled perspective is what *Acceptance* as a whole offers, as Control's anthropocentrism is repeatedly presented as delusional and dysfunctional in the context of Area X. After the more sympathetic depiction of Control in *Authority*, the slow destruction of the character in *Acceptance* appears to advance an underlying posthumanist agenda.

Ulstein (2017) notes how the horror and sensory confusion of the biologist's experience are missing from Ghost Bird's encounter with the Crawler: "There was none of the remembered distortion, no throwing back of her own fears and desires. It simply lay revealed before her, so immense, so shockingly concrete" (*Acc*: 284). The Crawler appears to Ghost Bird as "reassuringly corporeal" (*Acc*: 285). The description of the monster is precise and calm, and thus it appears to be just another strange organism, far more ordinary than the starfish in the biologist's tidal pool. Ulstein reads this naturalization as a result of Ghost Bird's nonhuman origin and proximity to the monster, concluding that "Ghost Bird's perception of the monstrous is thus in a position to evolve the reader's relationship with the monstrous" (Ulstein 2017: 88).

While I agree with Ulstein that Ghost Bird's perception definitely has some kind of effect on readers' relationship with the monstrous, I also want to discuss the specifics of this "evolution" further. Readers of the whole trilogy cannot accept this kind of kinesic and kinetic attunement to Ghost Bird and the monstrous as simply natural. Reading *Annihilation* has habituated readers, myself included, to doubt all feelings of personal strength and vitality, and consider them as effects of Area X, or, as the biologist puts it, as "brightness." Moreover, the flatness and naturality of the Crawler is questioned even by Ghost Bird herself (*Acc*: 286). The question is, then, how to engage the experientiality of a narrative perspective that embodies the very unreliability Area X from the inside—as a permanent and material "groundlessness"? To begin to answer this, we need to return to the question of how Ghost Bird invites interpretations of humanness and nonhumanness.

5.2.6 Is Ghost Bird "Just Another Creature"?

For some critics, Ghost Bird is both a stylistic lapse and a philosophical mistake. Faassen and Vermeulen (2019) criticize VanderMeer for turning his back on the Weird in the encounter between Ghost Bird and the biologist (*Acc*: 193–6), and abandoning "the engagement with the complexity of human/

nonhuman cognitive entanglement for an attempt to aestheticize and thereby sanitize otherness." For Faassen and Vermeulen, "Ghost Bird's status as … a fully nonhuman focalizer causes the weird effect to fall flat, and the biologist becomes just another creature, well-adapted to its different environments." They defend the unknowability of the nonhuman other as the core of the Weird tradition, as a philosophical stance that refuses "transcendence or a dissolution into ecstatic indifferentiation," which they claim is a move typical to new materialist thinkers.

This refusal (on part of both the Weird tradition and the critics in question) could be understood as "staying with the trouble," and specifically as staying with the friction and constraints of human subjecthood in a more-than-human world. But while such commitment to human limitations is commendable, I still agree with Ulstein that there is something potentially transformative in Ghost Bird's naturalizing experientiality. Rather than presenting this transformation as an easy feat of posthumanist imagination, I would propose that the figure affords a slow reconfiguring of a readerly choreography by way of amplifying the continuities rather than the contrasts between human and nonhuman life. Contrary to Faassen's and Vermeulen's reading, I do not think that the figure marks an abandonment of the complex cognitive entanglement between the human and the nonhuman. There are nuances between ineluctable difference and "ecstatic indifferentiation." While Ghost Bird's perspective foregrounds a conception of Area X's monsters as *organisms*, it does not completely erase the strangeness or difference of those organisms, or subject them to a totalizing knowledge, scientific or empathic. The same is true for the organism known as the human.

In other words, Ghost Bird's nonhumanness is construed not only in relation to Control's humanness, but also in relation to the nonhumanness of Area X, with which she is allied by way of her origin. During the hike through Area X, Control provokes Ghost Bird with a modern dichotomy, claiming that Area X "doesn't acknowledge machines" (*Acc*: 80). Ghost Bird then launches into an explicit monologue on the nature of Area X, which, to her mind, "can manipulate the genome, works miracles of mimicry and biology" and "*peer through things,* can surveil, and then withdraw" (*Acc*: 80–1, emphasis in original). Ghost Bird refers to humans as "incredibly blunt instruments" (*Acc*: 81) and cynically notes that humans cannot even understand the cognitive abilities of whales, bees, owls, or cormorants. Humans are "bound by their own view of consciousness" (*Acc*: 189) to the extent that even if an alien intelligence tried to contact them, they would not notice: "What if an infection was a message, a brightness a kind of symphony?" (*Acc*: 189–90). Ghost Bird views human blindness to such possibilities as a "lack of imagination" (*Acc*: 190).

In these conversations, the narrative negotiates Ghost Bird's status as a nonhuman creature. On the one hand, Ghost Bird is presented as a creature with inside knowledge of the strange nonhuman life of Area X and contrasted with insensitive and unperceptive humans. Yet, as VanderMeer's novels and the readers' capability of following his train of thought demonstrate, some humans *are* clearly capable of imagining infections as messages. Moreover, as I have noted earlier, Ghost Bird's perspective is narrated in ways that do not suggest anything other than an experientiality typical to human bodies and human narratives.

The "human" construed in Ghost Bird's ruminations must thus be a specific kind of figure, the human-centered human, the Anthropos of the Anthropocene: the kind of human that does not perceive or accept nonhuman forms of agency or intelligence. For the most part of *Authority* and *Acceptance*, Control acts as a figuration of such a human. Opposing such a figuration is an option available not only for fictional creatures but also for actual humans. If we choose to read Ghost Bird as nonhuman, then we should do so only against this particular background: treating "human" as a historically bound figuration. Rather than maintaining an opposition between the human and the nonhuman, I find it more productive to characterize Ghost Bird's perspective as *more-than-human* and consider how it can develop our understanding of the limits of human experience.

As Ghost Bird walks through Area X, her perceptions are laced with and partly constituted by the events in her environment, such as the flight of birds, the forms of the landscape, and the change of light. Toward the end of *Acceptance*, these perceptions come together as a *world*. The characters find that they are stranded in Area X, and that there might not be a border or a door to the outside world. Yet, they keep on walking, throwing pebbles ahead of them in an attempt to find the invisible border (*Acc*: 331).

In Ghost Bird's perspective, there is no nostalgia for the purely human world that the characters have left behind. Rather, there is an appreciation of Area X, which is full of all kinds of life, even if humans are few. While this might seem like a return to an idealized Nature, Ghost Bird's pragmatism allows that Area X is ineluctably strange: "The world went on, even as it fell apart, changed irrevocably, became something strange and different" (*Acc*: 328).

Maybe the impossibility of gaining a nonhuman perspective has to be accepted, as a necessary limit to human reach and control. Maybe it suffices that we acknowledge the existence of other life, strange as it is, and keep on living with the strangeness. Ultimately, *Acceptance* offers this insight as a figuration of walking through wilderness on a bright summer day, even as "the sun had decided to lodge itself behind her eyes and shine out so that the inside of her head felt burned" (*Acc*: 329). This perpetual brightness is weirdness to be lived with.

5.3 More-than-Human Writing and Reading

The conception of nature presented in *Acceptance*, and in *The Southern Reach* more widely, transgresses the boundary between the natural and the technological as well as the boundary between the conscious and the nonconscious. The obliteration of human technology from Area X gives room to another technology that is so advanced humans are not even able to perceive it: the surveillance and manipulation performed by Area X.[12] On the other hand, this kind of technology can just as well be biological, a part of the normal functioning of an "alien ecology" (*Acc*: 196). In his essays, VanderMeer has remarked on the amazing abilities of plants, such as the fact that plants use quantum mechanics in their photosynthetic processes, and characterized them as such imperceptible technologies (VanderMeer 2014d; see also Baluška and Mancuso 2007). Especially in the context of *The Southern Reach*, such functioning of ecologies may be characterized as "more-than-human writing"—a process in which nonhuman agencies inscribe meanings on human bodies and systems, thereby creating more-than-human meanings. Such meaning-making is often subtle, a matter of altering moods and motivations—in other words, it takes place on the partly nonconscious levels of affect and perception. *The Southern Reach* makes this subtlety explicit.

This view of more-than-human technologies is articulated through Ghost Bird in particular. In fact, and moving from the diegetic level to the dynamics of readerly engagement, we can consider the figure of Ghost Bird as one example of such more-than-human technologies. Through descriptions of bodily features, movements, and feelings, readers are invited to engage with the figure in kinesic and kinetic modes that feel easy and natural, and thus enter the cognitive ecology of the narrative. The figure exists only as part of a *figuration*, that is, as embedded in a context of potential movements, feelings, and perceptions. Ghost Bird thus affords a readerly choreography that involves a perceptual orientation toward the ecological dynamics of both Area X and the trilogy. Such a readerly choreography is made possible through the evocation of bodily feelings and perceptual dynamics that can be considered as emergent systemic properties rather than "real feelings" internal to the experiencing subject (see Warhol 2003: 23). Both phenomenology of moods (Ratcliffe 2010) and theories of affect (Ahmed 2004; Seyfert 2012; Vermeulen 2014) support such a view of bodily feelings.

Moreover, more-than-human technologies are distributed in the lived environments of the characters, and thus tracing them exactly proves impossible. *Authority*, in particular, tracks this futile attempt at the level of institutional inquiry. In *Annihilation*, Area X takes hold of the biologist's sensory perceptions and feelings, and it is impossible to know whether it is the beauty of nature or the effects of the alien spores that affect her so. The biologist's feeling of "a minor revelation"(*Ann*: 37) is entangled in her perceptions of the particular rough feel and brown color of the bark or the particular swooping movement of a woodpecker. It is impossible to objectively detect the exact source of the effect: rather, it emerges as a *mood* or an *atmosphere* that affects the entire orientation of the experiencing subject. In *Authority*, it is similarly impossible to tell whether Control's feelings of being watched are due to his paranoid psychological tendencies, the mind-control techniques practiced by his superiors, or the impending alien agency of Area X.

As such, the environmental affectivity of Area X comes close to Matthew Ratcliffe's (2010) characterization of moods as "spaces of possibility." In different moods, we experience the world as offering different kinds of possibilities. For Ratcliffe (2010: 357), mood "constitutes a phenomenological background in the context of which intentionally directed experience is possible." In such phenomenological terms, the biologist's heightened sensitivity (which is both sensory and emotional) or Control's paranoia are *contexts* for their perceptions. Accordingly, we could view such affective fictional contexts as *cognitive environments* (see Polvinen 2023; Section 1.2). Such a view is grounded on the readerly enactment of the bodily movements, feelings, and perceptions of the fictional figures, but the notion of cognitive environments also encompasses readerly engagement with the fictional artifact, that is, the trilogy of novels. Grounded on the analysis of the motif of *writing* in the novels, such a view gives rise to a more-than-human understanding of writing and reading.

This view of the more-than-human aspects of writing and reading complements Caracciolo's (2014c) network of experientiality by considering in more detail how the *experiential background* of a reader (or author) participates in the formation of experientiality. It also builds on the material ecocritical understanding of nonhuman meaning while refusing to conflate such meaning with *narrative* or *storytelling*. While it might be too much to suggest, as Iovino and Oppermann (2012) do, that nonhuman bodies and environments literally tell stories, an analysis of the bodily experientiality of mutant narratives such as *The Southern Reach* suggests that they participate in the formation of meanings that are traditionally considered as merely "human" or "cultural." Sometimes, as in the case of VanderMeer's experience of the Deepwater Horizon oil spill, the nonhuman exerts a significant force that influences and shapes the formation of narrative meaning. In this way, nonhuman agencies take part in processes of meaning-making.

5.3.1 More-than-Human Cognitive Environments

For characters, Area X functions as a cognitive environment within which they emerge as experiencing subjects. For readers, on the other hand, the fictional artifact of *The Southern Reach* trilogy functions as cognitive environment that draws on their familiarity with actual everyday environments while being remarkably different—especially due to its fictionality. As Merja Polvinen (2017, 2023) has argued, bodily and affective readerly engagement with such fictional artifacts can and does involve awareness of fictionality. In the case of reading *The Southern Reach*, the narrative strategies of the trilogy guide readers to adopt affective and reflective modes of reading that involve awareness of both aspects of literary cognitive environments—the mimetic and the synthetic.

On the level of kinesic intelligence, *The Southern Reach* evokes a cognitive environment through motifs and phrases at the edges of consciousness—the "hallucinations, reveries, epiphanies, and feverish dreams" Idema (2019: 106) mentions—and jarring shifts in narrative style. As I have argued earlier, such reiterations are part of the designed sensory flow of the trilogy, and as such they operate in the gray area between readers' conscious and nonconscious modes of engagement. Responding to such affective designs could be thought of as a kind of *pattern recognition* (see, e.g., Cave 2016; Hayles 2018). I propose that *The Southern Reach* trilogy presents the practices of reading and writing as such patterned activities, as part of organismic and environmental activity.

While literary practices definitely involve modes of thought and action that cannot be accounted for by such visions of the organism, *The Southern Reach* shows readers that sometimes they bear resemblance to eating, illness, or other bodily activities that are generally considered noncognitive. At moments of revelation, the characters utter as much, as when Ghost Bird comments that "an organism can have a purpose and yet also make patterns that have little to do with that purpose" (*Acc*: 189). While these explicit statements, often phrased in quotable sound bites that draw literary scholars like (rotten) honey, are readily available for thematic interpretations, VanderMeer's fiction also *demonstrates* how more-than-human writing might influence human cognition. Key passages in the trilogy can be seen to function as *contaminants* that push the reader to turn toward their own responses.

In terms of readerly engagement, the most important of such passages is the initial contamination scene, in which the biologist inhales the alien spores of the organism that forms the strange text on the wall of the underground tower. The moment also highlights the reading and writing as material and more-than-human technologies. From the moment of seeing the first words, "*Where lies the strangling fruit*" (*Ann*: 23, emphasis in original), the biologist is driven by an "impulse" (*Ann*: 23) to read the whole text, a "compulsion to keep reading, to descend into the greater darkness and keep descending until I had read all there was to read. Already those initial phrases were infiltrating my mind in unexpected ways, finding fertile ground" (*Ann*: 24).[13] She leans in closer "like a fool, like someone who had not had months of survival training or ever studied biology. Someone tricked into thinking that words should be read" (*Ann*: 25).[14]

Following the biologist, readers are easily tempted to lean closer to the strange text-shaped organism, tricked into thinking that words should be read. When they lean in, however, it is already too late: the affective and kinesic part of reading, "a high-speed response" that "needs to be 'slowed down' reflectively if one is to analyse it at all" (Cave 2016: 41), has already happened. The narrative technology has already contaminated them, and they are now left to deal with the consequences. In Pieter Vermeulen's (2020: 102) terms, we might describe the nonhuman affectivity of the narrative as *inscription*: the text turns around and *writes on the human body*, leaving traces that call for deciphering. Discussing *Annihilation*, Vermeulen (2020: 25) argues that "if we define agency as the capacity to have an impact, to leave traces for others to read, then it makes sense to figure agency as, precisely, a form of writing." Following Vermeulen's line of thought, it makes sense to state that both Area X (as a fictional entity) and *Annihilation* (as a narrative) have agentic powers.

Previous studies on the trilogy show surprisingly little interest in the theme of unconsciously effective narrative techniques. However, the analysis of such techniques can show how science fiction can estrange not just the intellectual notions of the everyday world but also the naturalized everyday modes of embodied experience—including the embodied experience of reading fiction.

In his monograph on VanderMeer's work, Benjamin J. Robertson (2018) proposes that *The Southern Reach* is not science fiction at all. For Robertson (2018: 39), science fiction assumes "a given world encoded in a symbolic structure," that is, a referential encoding of a given reality into a work of fiction. Robertson claims that this assumption has led science fiction scholars to focus on "decoding" the fiction as representative of the real world, thus dismissing the "fantastic materiality" afforded by the fictional worlds themselves.

> In the formulation of science fiction, the world and its allegedly immutable, discoverable truth provides a measuring stick for the quality of the story told about it. In contrast, in fantastic materiality, the narrative itself (the fantastic) modifies the world (materiality) in order to overcome such critical practices and thereby introduce to a world without predetermined notions of reality the means by which to change it. Fantastic materiality does not tell stories that are true in some way, according to a given materiality or empirical world out there against which they can be judged. It is a materiality that transforms by way of fantasies entangled with that world. (Robertson 2018: 41)

Robertson's fantastic materiality is a serious attempt at considering speculative fiction from a new materialist perspective while allowing that fiction itself holds a kind of material, potentially transformative agency. He also proposes a methodological step, "an abdifferent reading practice," which "requires a care or concern that allows fiction to be itself" and "involves imagining conditions that afford new ways of thinking and that do not assume a stable, grounding reality" (Robertson 2018: 135). Despite such promising formulations that successfully incorporate the notion of groundlessness, Robertson focuses his discussion of transformation "by way of fantasies" largely by juxtaposing it with historical-materialist readings that treat Area X as a representation of the Anthropocene. Thus, he explicates the fantastic logic of VanderMeer's fictional world, but does not delve into the material consequences of readerly engagement with the fiction.

Similar general claims about the power of VanderMeer's fiction are presented in Tom Idema's (2019) environmental posthumanist reading, in which he compares the paranoid tone of *The Southern Reach* to the work of Franz Kafka. Idema argues that the trilogy uses Kafkaesque means to disintegrate the human subject and give voice to nonhuman forms of agency and power.

> If Kafka's work raises the callous voice of social power, multiplied in so many personal and institutional incarnations, *The Southern Reach* amplifies a truly nonhuman voice reverberating through the wider environment. The human body becomes a soundboard for this nonhuman voice's messages of collapse and decay, broadcast in hallucinations, reveries, epiphanies, and feverish dreams. (Idema 2019: 106)

Do readers' bodies also become soundboards for a "nonhuman voice's messages of collapse and decay"? While Idema makes this claim, he stays on the level of the general theme of "human body," not going into the specifics of bodily reading. Just as Robertson, Idema evokes the potentially transformative power of language, but does not provide analyses on how such transformations could occur on the level of reading experience.

On the basis of the kinetic approach and posthuman feminist phenomenology, we can consider in more detail how transformation "by way of fantasies" or amplification of a "nonhuman voice" could happen in readerly experience. We can do so by returning to the strikingly material-ecocritical articulations of nonhuman writing in the trilogy. The bodies of the characters of Ghost Bird and Saul Evans, the lighthouse keeper, are figured as "messages from Area X," and the bodies of readers are exposed to affective narrative patterns that function with or without their conscious consent. Writing, a paradigmatic human activity, is thus reconfigured as a conduit for nonhuman agency. For readers, this inversion of human and nonhuman agency effects an uncanny sense of *becoming instruments*, or being recruited into the system of narrative and material meaning-making (cf. Kortekallio 2019). Such a technological aspect is inseparable of the notion of fictional artifacts as cognitive environments.

5.3.2 The Limits of Human Writing

In *Annihilation*, the journals of the explorers become representatives of their writers. Every explorer is instructed to keep a journal, hidden from the eyes of the others, and the novel is presented as the expedition journal of the biologist. In the course of her transformational experiences, the process of analytical writing functions for her as a tool for making sense of experience. It is an insufficient tool, as there seems to be no way of getting to the truth about Area X, but it is nevertheless presented as necessary for psychological purposes. In accounting for the oppressive vitality of Area X and the brightness that works its way in her body, the biologist makes a note of the impossibility of thinking about Area X without writing. As the sheer idea of Area X looms too large on her mind, she has to "leave it there, compartmentalized, until I could write it all down, and seeing it on the page, begin to divine the true meaning" (*Ann*: 93).

The most apparent mental strategy applied by the biologist, *compartmentalization*, protects the mind from shattering from the impact of Area X—for her, the threat is that letting herself consider the big picture would break her mood "like an avalanche crashing into [her] body" (*Ann*: 90). Instead of trying to consider the whole truth of Area X's possibly extraterrestrial nature, she focuses on analyzing specific details of her observations. That focus on detail is later echoed in the journals left behind by members of earlier expeditions. One particularly provocative journal focuses solely on the thistles that grow in the area and gives lengthy and detailed descriptions of them. This single focus is presented as "a way of coping" with the horror of there being a "terrible presence hovering in the background of these entries" (*Ann*: 114). Analytical thinking or writing thus emerges as an organizing technique that protects the illusion of existing in a normal, human-centered world, in which the explorers would be able to continue their research without being entangled in more-than-human monstrosities.

Further, the journals perform a more personal function that also evokes the theme of doubling. Finding the decaying mound of discarded journals, the biologist feels as if she has encountered a pile of "flimsy gravestones" (*Ann*: 110). From this pile, she finds the journal her husband, who had been part of the expedition immediately preceding the biologist's expedition. The journal is stuck to the back of another journal by something that at least resembles dried blood (*Ann*: 118). The material description of the journals makes them resemble dead bodies, a rotting mound that documents a history of unnamed expeditions gone awry, and they carry the traces of actual, familiar bodies: the blood and the handwriting of the biologist's husband.

Through the journal, the biologist finds a renewed connection to her deceased husband. She carries the journal with her for some time without daring to open it, and when she finally does, the experience becomes a resolution of a long-accumulated tension: "When I finally picked up my husband's journal and started to read, the brightness washed over me in unending waves and connected me to the earth, the water, the trees, the air, as I opened up and kept on opening" (*Ann*: 160). In reading the journal, the biologist has an experience of intimacy that years of shared living could not provide.

The biologist's reading experience dramatizes the issue of empathic engagement to first-person narrative, and thus speaks more to the affectivity of narrative than to intersubjective emotion. While the biologist could not empathize with her husband, his literary "ghost" or double makes her open up and connect with not just him but also the environment. *Annihilation* thus suggests that narratives can wield an uncanny power.

Speaking to such an effect, Caracciolo (2014b: 32) argues that the literary techniques of first-person narration can "take readers' empathic involvement with a fictional character to a higher level than would be likely in real life."[15]

While Caracciolo's claims about the exceptional power of first-person narration (compared to narration in the second or third person) might be exaggerated, his take on reading is interesting as it presents reading primarily as interaction with a kind of *amplifying technology* (cf. Neimanis 2017). The narrative technique of first-person narration can, Caracciolo claims, produce in us a deeply felt connection that is more intense than its equivalents in actual intersubjective relations. What this means, among other things, is that as readers and humans we are open to manipulation, including the simple, ubiquitous manipulation of texts convincing us that the "bundles of effects" (Caracciolo 2014b: 32) they present refer to coherent persons or even experiential selves.

The Southern Reach both evokes and estranges such readerly empathy and, more broadly, kinesic sense-making. The use of doubles is a central defamiliarizing device in the trilogy. Moreover, as these doubles gain metafictional aspects, they help to defamiliarize the very process of reading for character. This happens, for example, when Ghost Bird encounters "the moaning creature," a creation of Area X the biologist has also encountered previously (*Ann*: 15, 142; *Acc*: 162). For the biologist, the moaning creature has come to represent her fear of turning into a dysfunctional monster, "a mistake, a misfire by an Area X that had assimilated so much so beautifully and so seamlessly" (*Acc*: 162). Readers already know, at this point in the trilogy, that the biologist has since been turned into not just one but two monstrous beings: the mountain-sized creature capable of interdimensional travel (*Acc*: 193–6) and Ghost Bird. When Ghost Bird encounters the moaning creature, now in skeleton form, the encounter takes on an ominous quality as the dead creature seems to function as a conduit for Area X's perception.

> From those eye sockets, from the moldering bones, came a sense of a brightness still, a kind of life—a questing towards her that she rebuffed and that Control could not sense. Area X was looking at her through dead eyes. Area X was analyzing her from all sides. It made her feel like an outline created by the regard bearing down on her, one that moved only because the regard moved with her, held her constituent atoms together in a coherent shape. And yet, the eyes upon her felt familiar. (*Acc*: 37)

The image of Ghost Bird as an outline that moves along with the "regard" of the being that watches her is metafictional. Not only does the image present her as a creation of Area X, but it also presents her as a creation of readers, her coherence and movement dependent on their perception. The passage also puts readers in a curious position that aligns them with the dead creature, an obsolete dysfunctionally mutated human form through which a new kind of life *peers*. Rather than positioning readers as *objects to* nonhuman powers, then, the novel offers them a position as *conduits for* nonhuman powers. From a posthumanist perspective, I view this positioning as an invitation to the readers of the novel to amplify their experience of themselves as (part of) more-than-human assemblages, and more precisely to figure *contamination* as a *promise of more-than-human meaning* rather than a threat. When the isolation of human subjectivity in its "pure form" is disturbed, a material and ecological understanding of relational subjectivity can develop. Figurations of nonhuman writing in the trilogy support this view.

5.3.3 More-than-Human Meaning-Making

During her years in Area X, the biologist stays attuned to the present moment, since "to be taken out of the moment is dangerous—that is when things sneak their way in and then there is no present moment to return to" (*Acc*: 155). She is determined to "simply exist and live out whatever span was allotted to [her]" (*Acc*: 155). Despite this principle, she detaches herself from the present and writes an account of her life to unspecified recipients. The account is framed by another character as her "last will and testament" (*Acc*: 152), given before fully succumbing to monstrous transformation. The biologist associates the project of writing her biography with the human world, which to her has become an obsolete myth.

> Perhaps, too, hesitance overtakes me because when I think of writing I glimpse the world I left behind. The world beyond, that when my thoughts drift toward it at all, is a hazy, indistinct sphere radiating a weak light, riddled through with discordant voices and images that cut across eyes and minds like a razor blade, and none of us able to even blink. It seems a myth, a kind of mythic tragedy, a lie, that I once lived there or that anyone lives there still. Someday the fish and the falcon, the fox and the owl, will tell tales, in their way, of this disembodied globe of light and what it contained, all the poison and all the grief that leaked out of it. If human language meant anything, I might even recount it to the waves or to the sky, but what's the point? (*Acc*: 156)

In the antihumanist perspective of the biologist, the human world is construed as a strange sphere that "leaks" poison and grief, and as a condition that generally does not support life. There are no other potential addressees left for the biologist's account than the animals and environmental features of Area X, and they might not care for human language. The biologist's account continues to undermine human writing: the explorers leave their journals behind as most of them come to "recognize the futility of language" (*Acc*: 243). Human language marks a detachment from the immediate world of natural environments.

In contrast, toward the end of the trilogy, the nonhuman begins to write through the human. Ghost Bird characterizes herself, as well as the contaminations and transformations witnessed by other characters, as "messages" from Area X (*Acc*: 37, 190). This theme is also central to the storyline of lighthouse keeper Saul Evans, who turns into the monster known as the Crawler and acts as a conduit for nonhuman writing. In a transformational dream sequence that can be interpreted as the originating event of Area X (stars change form; a blood moon descends; mighty cities fall after ecological disaster, disease, and war; the lighthouse turns into a tunnel in the ground), Saul Evans descends the stairs into the tunnel, submerged in water, and sees "the fiery green-gold of words on the wall, being wrought before his eyes by an invisible scribe" (*Acc*: 107).

> He knew the words came from him, had always come from him, and were being emitted soundlessly from his mouth. And that he had been speaking already for a very long time, and that each word had been unraveling his brain a little more, a little more, even as each word also offered relief from the pressure in his skull. While what lay below waited for his mind to peel away entirely … . the words still lived inside of him, a sermon now coming out whether he wanted it to or not. Whether it would destroy him or not. (*Acc*: 107)

The trilogy thus loops back to its beginning, presenting the words on the wall as a result of a human conduit overtaken by the strange force of Area X, and as an unraveling of Saul Evans' contaminated mind. The same strange, perhaps-fungal words will eventually contaminate the biologist.

The brightness takes control of Saul Evans' body in a parasitic manner that echoes the invasion of ant bodies by the tropical fungus known as *Ophiocordyceps unilateralis sensu lato*. Such an invasion results in what are popularly known as "zombie ants." The fungus permeates the muscle fibers of the ants' bodies, leaving the brains intact, and "puppeteers" them onto tree branches and other elevated spots. After reaching their destination, the ants die, and the spectacular fruiting bodies of the fungus are unraveled out of the ant bodies, typically beginning from the head (Fredericksen et al. 2017; Zachos 2017). This image is also evoked in the biologist's speculations about the brightness: "I might find the brightness rising curious out of the top of my head, like a periscope—independent and lively, with nothing left beneath it but a husk" (*Acc*: 159). While there might be no direct link between the antics of the *Ophiocordyceps* and the creative mind of Jeff VanderMeer, the ant-puppeteering fungus serves as an apt figuration for thinking about the notion of more-than-human meaning-making.[16]

If we consider more-than-human writing as a theme, we can view the action of writing on the wall as bodily engagement between Saul and Area X. Neither of them is individually responsible for this action—even if it seems that Area X drives it. While in our regular lives it is rare that a single nonhuman entity exerts such a power on a person and completely reconfigures their cognition and action, similar agency exists in more dispersed forms: our minded bodies are constantly "driven" or "written" by ambient light and weather patterns, as in the case of winter depression (see Kortekallio 2020b), by the nonhuman creatures we encounter, as in the case of airborne microbes, and also by such simple constants as gravity and metabolism. Rather than figuring such agents as sovereign authors capable of single-handedly rewriting or even steering a body, we could think of them as participants in more-than-human processes of meaning-making, and thus as a subtler version of the uncanny power of the *Ophiocordyceps*.

In VanderMeer's fiction, such dispersed nonhuman agency is made accessible through the figure of Area X, which both rewrites the body of Saul as "a message" and drives the action of writing the text on the wall of the underground tower. While Saul experiences the words as not his own, their clerical style suggests that something of his personal history as a preacher participates in their formation. It is also his body and hand that carry out the act of writing.

In a narrative-theoretical line of thought, on the other hand, fictional narratives could be viewed as participants in such more-than-human meaning-making. As humans live their lives by enacting more-than-human cognitive environments, their minded bodies are impressed, influenced, and shaped by nonhuman beings and forces. Sometimes a particularly impressive force, such as the Deepwater Horizon oil spill, leaves a clear trace in the fiction of an author, such as Jeff VanderMeer (see VanderMeer 2014d). The fiction, in turn, can impress, inscribe, influence, and shape human bodies, mediating some of the force of the nonhuman being through layers of culturally established conventions of meaning-making. Fictional narratives can thus be understood both as traces left by nonhuman forces and as forces in themselves. By subtly shaping the bodily feelings, thoughts, and actions of humans, they also participate in shaping nonhuman bodies and environments.

A new materialist articulation helps to flesh out the notion of more-than-human meaning-making. Alison Sperling (2016), in her analysis of corporeal borders in *The Southern Reach*, evokes the notion of *trans-corporeality* (see Alaimo

2010) as crucial to the trilogy. Sperling makes note of how the contaminations in the trilogy take place through skin contact and that the experience of brightness involves sensations of heat, cold, and opening pores (Sperling 2016: 243–4). The novel thus figures the borders of individual human bodies as porous, and the skin as "the most vulnerable and open system of the body in its relation to the nonhuman environment as well as to others" (Sperling 2016: 243).

While Sperling's discussion of the skin as an "open system" is largely thematic, it can also inform a narrative-theoretical view of readerly dynamics. If we consider reading human bodies as such open systems, we can understand how they respond to both nonhuman bodies and narrative patterns, incorporating some of them into their functioning and rejecting others. As we have seen, VanderMeer figures this dynamism in terms of contamination and transformation that take place in both organs (such as the skin) and minds. Sperling (2016: 248) discusses VanderMeer's figures through new materialist theories of the body, claiming that the contaminated bodies in the trilogy can be understood as "a new kind of corporeality, a way of being at home in the body in the Anthropocene." Crucially, this kind of corporeality is open to the pervasive and toxic influences of spaces of ecological ruin (Sperling 2016: 251–2). In terms of narrative influences in VanderMeer's trilogy, we can understand the affects of horror, violence, and paranoia as examples of such toxicity. By staying with the human-centered resistance to more-than-human interactions, the trilogy creates a space in which readers can rehearse such troublesome bodily feelings instead of, for example, enacting a harmonious, difference-erasing return to Nature or imagining a posthuman fluidity between entirely open systems.

In my analyses of *The Southern Reach*, I have identified an array of narrative techniques, including depictions of perceptual peripheries, uncanny experiential motifs, and the use of doubles. Such techniques draw on the tradition of Weird fiction and collaborate in evoking bodily feelings of being haunted and contaminated by both systemic and nonhuman forces. VanderMeer's trilogy estranges the readerly choreography of engaging with fictional persons by revealing character perspectives as partially constructed by extrapersonal elements, most significantly the invasive influences of the Southern Reach organization and the alien locale known as Area X.

Gradually, after familiarizing its readers with such strange characters, the trilogy offers a more-than-human mode of experientiality by constructing an analogy between nonhuman affectivity and human writing. I have argued that this strategic narrative move is realized both through explicit metaphoric statements in which infections and even whole organisms are conceived as "messages" from Area X and by exposing readers to subtly affective narrative techniques. *The Southern Reach* thus offers readers an experiential position as bodily conduits for forces outside themselves: the narrative itself, and potentially also the nonhuman forces that VanderMeer identifies as the originating impulses behind the trilogy, such as the Deepwater Horizon oil spill. Such an openness to nonhuman forces may well leak into embodied experience beyond the literary context.

Notes

1 The expanding shape can also be experienced in a visual form, in the 2018 film adaptation, where it resembles and echoes cancerous growth.
2 David Tompkins (2014) mentions the American naturalist tradition, and Henry Thoreau, Rachel Carson, and Annie Dillard in particular. On the other hand, *The Southern Reach* has been compared to science fiction classics such as *Solaris* (1961), by Stanislaw Lem, and *Roadside Picnic* (1972, also known as *Stalker*), by the Strugatsky brothers, and to the work of Franz Kafka (Carroll 2015). For his part, VanderMeer has indebted himself to genre-defying works such as Leena Krohn's *Tainaron* (1985) and Weird precedents such as Michel Bernanos' *The Other Side of the Mountain* (1967) and, above all, "the true wondrous weirdness of nature" (cited in Spiegelman 2014).
3 I use a capitalized *Weird* when referring to the genre and *weird* when discussing the affect or atmosphere.
4 In his aptly named *Being No-One: The Self-Model Theory of Subjectivity* (2003), cognitive philosopher Thomas Metzinger articulates the phenomenal self as a transparent model:

> The phenomenal self is not a thing, but a process—and the subjective experience of being someone emerges if a conscious information-processing system operates under a transparent self-model. You are such a system right now, as you read these sentences. Because you cannot recognize your self-model as a model, it is transparent: you look right through it. You don't see it. But you see with it. (Metzinger 2003: 1, emphases removed)

Posthumanist philosophy has also incorporated this view and suggested that subjectivities can be considered as *fictional choreographies* (Braidotti 2002: 22).
5 The particular ecological significance of the "destroyer of worlds" lies in the fact that the starfish (*crown-of-thorns seastar* by its common name) destroys coral reef ecosystems. The phrase also resonates with the iconic words from the Bhagavad

Gita, recited by Robert Oppenheimer after the Trinity test: "Now I am become Death, the destroyer of worlds."

6 Thomas Metzinger thoroughly explores the source conflict of cognitive nihilism in *Being No One* (2003). The conflict is also central to recent popular fiction such as the television series *True Detective* (written by Nic Pizzolatto, 2014–17) and science fiction such as Peter Watts' novels *Blindsight* (2006) and *Echopraxia* (2014).

7 Sieg's analysis is supported by other research on monstrosity that argues that the horror of monster narratives is constructed upon a conceptual and experiential dualism between the pure subject/victim and the monstrous other (see Cohen 1996; Shildrick 2001).

8 Another line of interpretation would connect the biologist's encounter with the nonhuman to the romantic naturalist tradition in American literature. Posthumanist critics have argued that "the romantic tradition of US nature writing tends to preserve a conception of the self as becoming more 'in tune' with nature, both outside and inside, and therefore more human" (Idema 2019: 108, emphasis removed). As previous critics have noted, *The Southern Reach* plays with this tradition but ends up disintegrating the human subject rather than reinforcing it (Idema 2019; Ulstein 2017).

9 Tom Idema (2019: 109) connects the radical epistemological and existential uncertainty of *The Southern Reach* to postmodernist novels of J. G. Ballard, Thomas Pynchon, and Don DeLillo, claiming that the trilogy shares with them "a discrepancy between an unrelenting desire for truth and authenticity, and a structural inability to find it, an inability that the protagonist can barely fathom." In contrast to the postmodernists, Idema argues, VanderMeer presents this discrepancy not only as a social and scientific condition but as an environmental-posthumanist issue. He builds on contemporary research in ecology to claim that the continuous transmutations of ecosystems are philosophically just as radically unknowable as VanderMeer's Area X.

10 In her analysis of the second skin figuration in *The Southern Reach*, Alison Sperling (2016: 247–9) notes that when Ghost Bird perceives the Crawler, its "surface" is also doubled. Sperling links the "second skin" to Sara Ahmed's theories of locale and descriptions of a second skin as a leaky border zone between the subject and space.

11 However, I do not share Carroll's (2016) analytical contexts. While her psychoanalytical reading of *The Southern Reach* trilogy as a kind of "Mortonesque uncanny" (Carroll 2016: 76) is convincing and particularly revealing of *Authority*, I find that the particular constraints of psychoanalysis and historical materialism (which Carroll channels through the work of Jason W. Moore) operate on a level too general to contribute to my more-than-human reading.

12 In this regard, the intelligence present in Area X is similar to the alien intelligence in Peter Watts' *Blindsight* (2006): the manipulation affects perception directly, and therefore it cannot be opposed with any means that involve consciousness. (If a weapon targets your sense of reality, what do you do?)
13 The original contamination scene only includes a few lines of the words on the wall. Longer excerpts are provided in a later chapter, here reconstructed into one continuous excerpt: "*Where lies the strangling fruit that came from the hand of the sinner I shall bring forth the seeds of the dead to share with the worms that gather in the darkness and surround the world with the power of their lives while from the dim-lit halls of other places forms that never could be writhe for the impatience of the few who have never seen or been seen in the black water with the sun shining at midnight, those fruit shall come ripe and in the darkness of that which is golden shall split open to reveal the revelation of the fatal softness of the earth …*" (*Ann*: 46, 47, 50, italics in original).

   It is implied that the writing goes on indefinitely. Moreover, the biologist perceives a further "phantom script" in the gaps of the "living" lines (*Ann*: 48–9).
14 On her second reading, now descending into the tower with the surveyor of the group, the biologist notes that the words "infect" their own spoken language (*Ann*: 47).
15 While Caracciolo uses the term *empathic involvement*, his use of it contains an imaginative aspect. He uses *empathy* not just to denote "the capacity to experience another person's mental states in a first-person way" (2014b: 32) but as interchangeably with "mental simulation" (2014b: 32, 38). Empathy, construed in this way, does not imply an understanding of the experiences of the other, but rather the imaginative reconstruction or enaction of such experiences (see also Kortekallio 2019: 60–1).
16 Speaking to its popular appeal, *Ophiocordyceps unilateralis* has also featured as a central motif in the postapocalyptic television series *The Last of Us* (2023).

6

Conclusion: More-than-Human Reading and Subjective Experience

The authors this book has focused on—Greg Bear, N. K. Jemisin, Paolo Bacigalupi, and Jeff VanderMeer—have all responded to the destabilization of Enlightenment ideals of autonomy, rationality, and human exceptionalism, brought on most recently by developments in evolutionary and cognitive science as well as the global ecological emergency. While their mutant narratives reach for ecocentric or more-than-human perspectives, those narratives are ineluctably entangled in human-centered conventions in both theme and form. For this reason, mutant narratives do not offer emancipation through posthuman transformation, but rather invite their readers to stay with the trouble of living in messy and violent multispecies worlds.

Staying with such trouble has been the ethical and methodological starting point of this book. Resisting the call for transcendental modes of posthumanism, I have chosen to take the slow route out of the human-centered way of life. The first step has been an experiential analysis of what it feels like to live and read as a human organism in a more-than-human world. Given the persistent power that ideas of disembodied minds and human exceptionality still hold over common perceptions of human experience, this slow approach may still seem radical or speculative, and, indeed, posthuman. This is a tension that the book may not be able to fully solve.

I have argued throughout the book that reading is a bodily skill that can be developed in diverse directions, including a direction that attunes one to noticing the bodily feelings and perceptual alterations emerging in the process of reading. But how does more-than-human reading matter to subjective experience more generally?

Reading the mutant narratives presented in this book, I have imaginatively enacted hovering on the edge of an abyss, moving a mountain, going through perceptual confusion, and other such bodily feelings that I characterize as features of readerly choreographies. I have described the ways in which more-than-human experientiality emerges in my reading experience. The sense of becoming a conduit for nonhuman forces when reading *The Southern Reach* and the sense of being instrumentalized by the affective technologies of *The Windup Girl* are examples of such more-than-human experientiality.

The question still remains how much of such enactive attunement is due to the *attention* I direct at my bodily responses, and to the practice of *reflectively describing* such experiences. While I have already argued that such skillful actions as attention and reflective description are necessarily part of a more-than-human reading practice, the point is worth unpacking in some detail.

Some new materialist theorists have suggested that conscious orientation toward nonhuman material agencies—and toward embodied experience as an interface between the human and the nonhuman—can be employed as a means of developing posthumanist sensibilities (e.g., Coole and Frost 2010; Neimanis 2017). It is notable that their suggestion considers such a practice as a skill that unfolds in bodily interaction with material environments, and thus the exact outcome of the interaction always depends on the particular situation. Astrida Neimanis (2017: 61) has suggested that artworks can amplify our experiences of nonhuman forces and entities, serving as "mediating prostheses that open certain experiences for us, but foreclose or restrain others."

My dialogue with other critics of the same works of fiction points to the fact that some of the experiences rising from reading Bacigalupi or VanderMeer will make sense to other readers, while some will not. Even though I have, at times, suggested certain generalizations about the impressive force of particular narrative strategies, I do not intend to claim that all readers would experience the narratives in the same way. What I do claim is that particular narrative strategies, embedded in particular histories of production and reception, offer experiential patterns to be engaged with. As regards the movements and feelings of fictional bodies, I have described these patterns as *readerly choreographies* (see also Kortekallio 2022). My sustained engagement with such aspects of fictional narratives is bound to change the patterns of my feeling and thought.

While Neimanis (2017) would describe such a change as *amplification,* Robyn Warhol (2003) discusses it in terms of becoming more conscious of the intensities present in the engagement. Warhol's example is the context of watching soap-opera television as a daily routine:

> For some viewers, the intensities are a form of background noise in a life otherwise detached from the concerns of the soap-opera plot; for others—particularly

those who are moved enough by the story line to want to write about it … the intensities are more present, more vividly a part of daily consciousness. To watch every day is to be carried on that wave of intensities, to experience the build-up, the crisis, and the undertow of response as one of the structuring principles of daily life. (Warhol 2003: 118–19)

Warhol's account foregrounds the reciprocal relationship between readerly engagement and daily life. In Warhol's model, corporeal responses to narratives, such as crying or gesturing, *generate* feelings rather than *express* them. The body is understood "not as the location where gender and affect are expressed, but rather as the medium through which they come into being" (Warhol 2003: 10). While Warhol discusses the "buildup" of affective intensities that are both gendered and particular to watching sentimental television series, her discussion also supports the view of more-than-human meaning-making I have presented in this book. If the body serves as a medium, then affect is not subjective but somehow, as Pieter Vermeulen (2014: 122) puts it, an "impersonal dynamic principle that cuts across personal feelings and experiences." This view is generally accepted in affect theory, but according to Vermeulen (2014: 123), the "demise of feeling" is a particularly posthumanist project since it rejects the notion of subjectively "owned" feelings and emotions.

The nonsubjective view of affect, put forth by Warhol, Vermeulen, and other affect theorists, both recognizes affect as impersonal and pays close attention to the subjectively experienced feelings and emotions. I also view the analysis of subjective experience as a key point of departure for explorations of experiential change. Building on Warhol especially, I argue elsewhere that the bodily feelings that arise during reading also participate in everyday experience when one is not actively reading (Kortekallio 2020b, 2022).

Prolonged engagement with mutant narratives can amplify particular patterns of feeling that are highly relevant to the posthumanist reconfiguration of what it means to be human. It may not be wise to make strong claims about such effects, as both the narratives and the readerly experience vary significantly. Against this speculative background, however, I wish to make a more modest claim that prolonged engagement with VanderMeer's *The Southern Reach* amplifies a sense of perpetual uncertainty, or *groundlessness* as a lived condition. It does so by engaging our bodily sensitivities through affective narrative technologies, thus evoking a sense of contingency that extends to bodies, minds, and environments.

Whereas a humanist response to such a realization of contingency might be negative, even nihilist, as more-than-human agency is thought to undermine human agency and subjectivity, a posthumanist and enactivist response can parse contingency as an integral part of embodied experience. To repeat Haraway's (2016) motto once again, such a response encourages us to stay with the trouble. The acceptance of contingency is built on an understanding of embodied experience as both organismic and technologically induced, that is, as more-than-human.

Moreover, accepting contingency as a lived condition might be a direct demand placed by the material conditions of rapid environmental change, or, the Anthropocene. Anna Lowenhaupt Tsing (2017) articulates this condition through her ethnographic analyses of "precarious encounters," ways of life that emerge in the unlikely gaps left between capitalist commodity chains. Tsing's model for such precarious ways of life is the commercial picking of matsutake mushrooms, a practice that, due to both material and cultural reasons, requires a fair amount of flexibility and what Tsing calls "arts of noticing." I propose that mutant narratives are geared toward developing the kind of cognitive flexibility called for by precarious situations.

The naturalized notion of "human" as a sovereign entity is itself a particular experiential configuration enabled by more-than-human networks of matter and meaning. The notion may be defamiliarized by anomalous events such as particular readings. In my engagement with *The Southern Reach*, and *Annihilation* especially, the most instructive experience has indeed been the sustained failure of objective analysis (as performed by a sovereign rational subject; see Kortekallio 2019). The trilogy presents fictional figures and environments that cannot be approached by a naturalized attitude. The relationship to figures and environments like this necessarily involves mediating and technological processes: the psychologist's hypnotic suggestion, the characters' respective professional trainings (most of which assume "scientific objectivity"), or the joint practices of attentive observation and self-reflective writing. As the case of hypnosis demonstrates, mediation is also present in the moments of intuitive sense-making. As the case of empathic involvement with a journal (rather than with a living person) suggests, first-person narration can construct beings that feel, in some respects, more relatable than actual persons. This is embodied estrangement: the habituated bodily understanding of the environment is derailed by affective literary technology.

The bodily feeling of groundlessness is central to the understanding of life as mutual enfoldment of self and environment, as presented by Varela, Thompson, and Rosch (1992). Mutual enfoldment is, by definition, a complex process in which both perception and environment are in constant flux. The enactivist understanding of self, as an experiential structure that binds together the varying moments of experience, is neither a cultural construction that can be undermined and transformed by analysis nor a biological fact that reliably determines the behavior of a species or an individual. Rather, it resonates with the posthumanist formulation of subjectivity as *fictional choreography* (Braidotti 2002: 22). While neither the enactivist nor the posthumanist theorization of subjectivity properly *describes* more-than-human subjectivity as a lived condition, they can amplify the experiential traces that potentially develop into such a condition.

The relevance of mutant figures to this discussion of more-than-human subjectivity lies in their capacity to evoke affects and bodily feelings that both defamiliarize naturalized notions of human experience and suggest more-than-human modes of experience. They draw on our disposition as human animals, but they do so by employing and modifying cultural conventions of describing and narrating bodies and bodily experience. As the fictional figures of *The Southern Reach* evoke feelings in us, leading us to respond to fictional bodies like we would to real ones, they also make us aware of their manipulative force. While this awareness does not necessarily result in the emergence of more-than-human modes of experience, it can at least participate in practices of developing such modes. A posthumanist response to mutant figures would be to learn to cope with the awareness of our agency as entangled with other agencies, our actions not independent but always emerging and changing within different systems and assemblages.

Fictional narratives can participate in the development of posthumanist sensitivities not just by presenting new ideas but by offering new choreographies of feeling and attunement—even choreographies that involve destructive patterns such as derailment, disorientation, or infection. Both nonhuman environments and fictional artifacts are cognitive environments that, through attentive and extended engagement, can contaminate and transform human experiencers.

Perhaps the most useful contribution of my more-than-human take on readerly experience, and on experience more widely, is the fact that it does not treat the human-centered and destructive aspects of Anthropocene cultures as disembodied ideas or conceptualizations, but rather as *collective, more-than-human, material, and bodily habits*. In this book, I have argued that reading mutant narratives is an activity in which some destructive cultural habits, mainly perceptual and kinesic, can be reconfigured. I do not claim that such reconfiguration would be an automatic effect resulting from the exposure to mutant narratives. On the contrary, such reconfiguration should be thought of as a form of *bodily exercise*, in which readers, as it were, *wrestle* or *dance* with the fictional narratives, thus developing their skills in future engagements of the same sort. The particular choreographies and modalities of engagement depend, of course, on each work of fiction and its particular reader.

It is good to remember that the notion of mutant narratives is instrumental, coined to aid the particular reading practice of more-than-human reading. Living with the particular mutant narratives discussed in this book has been a personal learning process. I do not think others can iterate it as such, or go through it like a course program. However, I hope that reading about the process can offer some resonating insights that may contribute to the larger collective project of working toward a more ecologically viable culture.

Viewing cultural tendencies as collective, more-than-human, material, and bodily habits gives rise to practical questions that have to do with groundings, relations, and actions. In the context of fiction, the most relevant questions might be: How do particular works of fiction support or challenge the bodily habits of human-centered culture? How do those works participate in the moment-to-moment constitution of our feelings and perceptions? How might a particular work of fiction help us rehearse feelings and perceptions that develop our bodily understanding of ourselves as nodes in more-than-human networks of matter and meaning?

Such questions should be explored far more thoroughly than I have been able to do in this book, preferably by engaging in collective practices of reading, such as reading groups, empirical experiments, and seminars. In developing bodily and more-than-human reading practices, I also see it necessary to continue staging discussions between the frameworks of thought I have brought together here, and particularly between posthumanist feminism and the second-generation approach to literature and cognition. Such practices would also benefit from deeper engagement with phenomenology and reading studies, both of which I have only touched on this book, and with artistic work beyond literature. Moreover, while I here discuss only readers, reading, and literature, I intend the concept of readerly choreography to be inherently transmedial, as our experience of literature may also draw on or influence our experience of, for instance, film, games, graphic narratives. This transmedial aspect of experientiality could be explored further.

I have argued that science fiction is a particularly apt context for developing modes of more-than-human experience. Traditionally, science fiction both draws on and reaches beyond the conventions of human-centered culture, and as such it invites both its writers and its readers to become, in the words of

Ursula K. Le Guin (2007: 38), "realists of a larger reality." Even if you were not fully convinced by the specific flavors of experiential reality proposed by the particular works of science fiction I have discussed in this book, by enactively engaging with them you might nevertheless experience a relativization of your perception of everyday reality. By the sheer act of reading a work of science fiction, you may train yourself in accepting the uncomfortable, the implausible, and even the impossible. Even in its minimal form, such an engagement is an exercise in cognitive flexibility, which is in dire need in the rapidly changing environments of the Anthropocene.

References

Abram, David. (1996). *The Spell of the Sensuous: Language and Perception in a More-than-Human World*. New York: Vintage Books.
Ahmed, Sara. (2004). "Collective Feelings, Or, the Impressions Left by Others." *Theory, Culture & Society* 21(2): 25–42.
Alaimo, Stacy. (2010). *Bodily Natures: Science, Environment, and the Material Self*. Bloomington: Indiana University Press.
Alaimo, Stacy. (2016). *Exposed: Environmental Politics & Pleasures in Posthuman Times*. Minneapolis: University of Minnesota Press.
Alber, Jan. (2009). "Impossible Storyworlds—and What to Do with Them." *Storyworlds: A Journal of Narrative Studies* 1(1): 79–96.
Alber, Jan, Skov Nielsen, Henrik, and Richardson, Brian. (2013). *A Poetics of Unnatural Narrative*. Theory and Interpretation of Narrative series. Columbus: Ohio State University Press.
Aldiss, Brian Wilson, and Wingrove, David. (2001). *Trillion Year Spree: The History of Science Fiction*. London: House of Stratus.
Allen, William. (2003). "Plant Blindness." *BioScience* 53(10): 926.
Åsberg, Cecilia, Koobak, Redi, and Johnson, Ericka. (2011). "Beyond the Humanist Imagination." *NORA—Nordic Journal of Feminist and Gender Research* 19(4): 218–30.
Bacigalupi, Paolo. ([2004] 2008). "People of Sand and Slag." In *Pump Six and Other Stories*. New York: Night Shade Books.
Bacigalupi, Paolo. (2009). *The Windup Girl*. New York: Night Shade Books.
Badmington, Neil. (2004). *Alien Chic: Posthumanism and the Other Within*. London: Routledge.
Baluška, František, and Mancuso, Stefano. (2007). "Plant Neurobiology as a Paradigm Shift Not Only in the Plant Sciences." *Plant Signaling and Behavior* 2(4): 205–7.
Barad, Karen. (2003). "Posthumanist Performativity: Toward an Understanding of How Matter Comes to Matter." *Signs: Journal of Women in Culture and Society* 28(3): 801–31.
Barthes, Roland. (1974). *S/Z*. New York: Hill and Wang.
Bastian, Michelle. (2006). "Haraway's Lost Cyborg and the Possibilities of Transversalism." *Signs: A Journal of Women in Culture and Society* 43(3): 1027–49.
Bear, Greg. (1999). *Darwin's Radio*. New York: Del Rey.
Bear, Greg. (2003). *Darwin's Children*. New York: Del Rey.

Bennett, Jane. (2010). *Vibrant Matter: A Political Ecology of Things.* Durham, NC: Duke University Press.
Bernaerts, Lars, Caracciolo, Marco, Herman, Luc, and Vervaeck, Bart. (2014). "The Storied Lives of Non-human Narrators." *Narrative* 22(1): 68–93.
Bertetti, Paolo. (2017). "Signs and Figures: Some Remarks about Greimas' Theory of the Figurative." *Sign Systems Studies* 45(1/2): 88–103. DOI: 10.12697/SSS.2017.45.1-2.06.
Blish, James. ([1950] 1955). "Battle of the Unborn." In *Science Fiction Adventures in Mutation,* ed. Geoff Cronklin, 17–24. New York: Vanguard Press.
Bolens, Guillemette. (2012). *The Style of Gestures: Embodiment and Cognition in Literary Narrative.* Baltimore, MD: Johns Hopkins University Press.
Bollinger, Laurel. (2009). "Containing Multitudes. Revisiting the Infection Metaphor in Science Fiction." *Extrapolation* 50(3): 377–99.
Bollinger, Laurel. (2010). "Symbiogenesis, Selfhood, and Science Fiction." *Science Fiction Studies* 37(1): 34–53.
Boyd, Brian. (2009). *On the Origin of Stories: Evolution, Cognition, and Fiction.* Cambridge, MA: Harvard University Press.
Braidotti, Rosi. (2002). *Metamorphoses. Towards a Materialist Theory of Becoming.* Cambridge: Polity.
Braidotti, Rosi. (2013). *The Posthuman.* Cambridge: Polity.
Buell, Lawrence. (1995). *The Environmental Imagination: Thoreau, Nature Writing, and the Formation of American Culture.* Cambridge, MA: Harvard University Press.
Bukatman, Scott. (1993). *Terminal Identity. The Virtual Subject in Postmodern Science Fiction.* Durham, NC: Duke University Press.
Butler, Judith. (1990). *Gender Trouble: Feminism and the Subversion of Identity.* London: Routledge.
Butler, Octavia E. (1989). *Imago.* New York: Grand Central Publishing.
Cadigan, Pat. (2012). "The Girl-Thing That Went Out for Sushi." In *Edge of Infinity,* ed. Jonathan Strahan. Oxford: Solaris.
Callus, Ivan, Herbrechter, Stefan, and Rossini, Manuela. (2014). "Introduction: Dis/locating Posthumanism in European Literary and Critical Traditions." *European Journal of English Studies* 18(2): 103–20. DOI: 10.1080/13825577.2014.916999.
Canavan, Gerry, and Robinson, Kim Stanley (eds.) (2014). *Green Planets: Ecology and Science Fiction.* Middletown: Wesleyan University Press.
Caracciolo, Marco. (2014a). "Interpretation for the Bodies: Bridging the Gap." *Style* 48(3): 385–403.
Caracciolo, Marco. (2014b). "Beyond Other Minds: Fictional Characters, Mental Simulation, and 'Unnatural' Experiences." *Journal of Narrative Theory* 44(1): 29–53.
Caracciolo, Marco. (2014c). *The Experientiality of Narrative: An Enactivist Approach.* Berlin: De Gruyter.
Caracciolo, Marco. (2016). *Strange Narrators in Contemporary Fiction: Explorations in Readers' Engagement with Characters.* Lincoln: University of Nebraska Press.

Caracciolo, Marco. (2021). *Narrating the Mesh: Form and Story in the Anthropocene*. Charlottesville: University of Virginia Press.

Caracciolo, Marco, and Hurlburt, Russell T. (2016). *A Passion for Specificity: Confronting Inner Experience in Literature and Science*. Columbus: Ohio State Press.

Carroll, Joseph. (2004). *Literary Darwinism: Evolution, Human Nature, and Literature*. New York: Routledge.

Carroll, Siobhan. (2015). "The Ecological Uncanny: On the 'Southern Reach' Trilogy." Review of *Annihilation*, by Jeff VanderMeer. *Los Angeles Review of Books*, October 5, 2015. Accessed November 30, 2019. https://lareviewofbooks.org/article/the-ecological-uncanny-onthe-southern-reach-trilogy.

Carroll, Siobhan. (2016). "*The Terror* and the Terroir: The Ecological Uncanny in New Weird Exploration Narratives." *Paradoxa* 28: 67–89.

Cave, Terence. (2016). *Thinking with Literature: Towards a Cognitive Criticism*. Oxford: Oxford University Press.

Chakrabarty, Dipesh. (2009). "The Climate of History: Four Theses." *Critical Inquiry* 35(2): 197–222.

Chamovitz, Daniel. (2013). *What a Plant Knows*. New York: Scientific American.

Chu, Seo-Young. (2010). *Do Metaphors Dream of Literal Sleep? A Science-Fictional Theory of Representation*. Cambridge, MA: Harvard University Press.

Clark, Andrew. (2004). *Natural-Born Cyborgs: Minds, Technologies, and the Future of Human Intelligence*. Oxford: Oxford University Press.

Clark, Timothy. (2015). *Ecocriticism on the Edge: The Anthropocene as a Threshold Concept*. London: Bloomsbury Academic.

Cohen, Jeffrey Jerome. (1996). "Monster Culture (Seven Theses)." In *Monster Theory: Reading Culture*, ed. Jeffrey Jerome Cohen, 3–25. Minneapolis: University of Minnesota Press.

Cohn, Dorrit. (1999). *The Distinction of Fiction*. Baltimore, MD: Johns Hopkins University Press.

Colebrook, Claire. (2014). *Death of the Posthuman: Essays on Extinction*. Vol. 1. London: Open Humanities Press.

Colombetti, Giovanna. (2014). *The Feeling Body: Affective Science Meets the Enactive Mind*. Cambridge, MA: MIT Press.

Colombetti, Giovanna, and Thompson, Evan. (2008). "The Feeling Body: Toward an Enactive Approach to Emotion." In *Developmental Perspectives on Embodiment and Consciousness*, ed. W. F. Overton, U. Müller, and J. Newman, 45–68. New York: Lawrence Erlbaum.

Colombetti, Giovanna, and Torrance, Steve. (2009). "Emotion and Ethics: An Inter-(en)active Approach." *Phenomenology and the Cognitive Sciences* 8: 505–26.

Connolly, William E. (2010). "Materialities of Experience." In *New Materialisms: Ontology, Agency, and Politics*, ed. Diana Coole and Samantha Frost, 178–200. Durham, NC: Duke University Press.

Coole, Diana. (2010). "The Inertia of Matter and the Generativity of Flesh." In *New Materialisms: Ontology, Agency, and Politics*, ed. Diana Coole and Samantha Frost, 92–115. Durham, NC: Duke University Press.

Coole, Diana, and Frost, Samantha. (2010). "Introducing the New Materialisms." In *New Materialisms: Ontology, Agency, and Politics*, ed. Diana Coole and Samantha Frost, 1–43. Durham, NC: Duke University Press.

Crutzen, Paul J., and Stoermer, Eugene F. (2000). "The Anthropocene." *Global Change Newsletter* 41: 17–18.

Culpeper, Jonathan. (2002). "A Cognitive Stylistic Approach to Characterisation." In *Cognitive Stylistics: Language and Cognition in Text Analysis*, ed. Jonathan Culpeper and Elena Semino, 251–78. Amsterdam: John Benjamins.

Currie, Gregory. (2011). "Empathy for Objects." In *Empathy: Philosophical and Psychological Perspectives*, ed. Peter Goldie and Amy Coplan, 82–95. New York: Oxford University Press.

De Jaegher, Hanne, and Di Paolo, Ezequiel. (2007). "Participatory Sense-Making: An Enactive Approach to Social Cognition." *Phenomenology and the Cognitive Sciences* 6(4): 485–507. DOI: 10.1007/s11097-007-9076-9.

Djikic, Maja, Oatley, Keith, Zoeterman, Sara, and Peterson, Jordan B. (2009). "On Being Moved by Art: How Reading Fiction Transforms the Self." *Creativity Research Journal* 21(1): 24–9. DOI: 10.1080/10400410802633392.

Easterlin, Nancy. (2012). *A Biocultural Approach to Literary Theory and Interpretation*. Baltimore, MD: Johns Hopkins University Press.

Eldredge, Niles, and Gould, S. J. (1972). "Punctuated Equilibria: An Alternative to Phyletic Gradualism." In *Models in Paleobiology*, ed. T. J. M. Schopf, 82–115. San Francisco, CA: Freeman Cooper.

Faassen, Kahn, and Vermeulen, Pieter. (2019). "The Weird and the Ineluctable Human." *Collateral*, 15, Accessed December 3, 2019. http://collateral-journal.com/index.php?cluster=15.

Fialho, Olivia, Zyngier, Sonja, and Miall, David S. (2011). "Interpretation and Experience: Two Pedagogical Interventions Observed." *English in Education* 45(3): 236–53.

Fish, Stanley. (1980). *Is There a Text in This Class? The Authority of Interpretive Communities*. Cambridge, MA: Harvard University Press.

Fisher, Mark. (2016). *The Weird and the Eerie*. London: Repeater Books.

Fludernik, Monika. (1996). *Towards a "Natural" Narratology*. London: Routledge.

Forster, Edward M. ([1927] 1985). *Aspects of the Novel*. San Diego: Harcourt.

Foucault, Michel. (1984). "What Is Enlightenment?" In *The Foucault Reader*, ed. Paul Rabinow, 32–50. New York: Pantheon Books.

Fredericksen, Maridel A., Zhang, Yizhe, Hazen, Missy L., Loreto, Raquel G., Mangold, Colleen A., Chen, Danny Z., and Hughes, David P. (2017). "Three-Dimensional Visualization and a Deep-Learning Model Reveal Complex Fungal

Parasite Networks in Behaviorally Manipulated Ants." *PNAS* 114(47): 12590–5. DOI: 10.1073/pnas.1711673114.
Gallagher, Shaun, and Zahavi, Dan. (2007). *The Phenomenological Mind*. London: Routledge.
Gallese, Vittorio. (2011). "Embodied Simulation Theory: Imagination and Narrative." *Neuropsychoanalysis* 13(2): 96–200.
Gatens, Moira. (1996). *Imaginary Bodies: Ethics, Power and Corporeality*. London: Routledge.
Ghosh, Amitav. (2016). *The Great Derangement. Climate Change and the Unthinkable*. Chicago: University of Chicago Press.
Gibson, James Jerome (1979). *The Ecological Approach to Visual Perception*. Boston, MA: Houghton Mifflin.
Giddens, Anthony. (1990). *The Consequences of Modernity*. Stanford, CA: Stanford University Press.
Gilbert, Scott F., Sapp, Jan, and Tauber, Alfred I. (2012). "A Symbiotic View of Life: We Have Never Been Individuals." *Quarterly Review of Biology* 87(4): 325–41. DOI: 10.1086/668166.
Goldman, Michael A. (2000). "Evolution Rising from the Grave." Review of *Darwin's Radio*, by Greg Bear." *Nature* 404: 15–16. March 2. DOI: 10.1038/35003625.
Graham, Elaine L. (2002). *Representations of the Post/Human: Monsters, Aliens and Others in Popular Culture*. Manchester: Manchester University Press.
Greimas, A. J. ([1973] 1987). "Actants, Actors, and Figures." In *On Meaning: Selected Writings in Semiotic Theory*, translated by P. J. Perron and F. H. Collins, 106–20. Minneapolis: University of Minnesota Press.
Grosz, Elizabeth. (1994). *Volatile Bodies: Toward a Corporeal Feminism*. Bloomington: Indiana University Press.
Hakemulder, J. (2000). *The Moral Laboratory: Experiments Examining the Effects of Reading Literature on Social Perception and Moral Self-Concept*. Amsterdam: John Benjamins.
Haraway, Donna J. (1991). "A Cyborg Manifesto: Science, Technology, and Socialist-Feminism in the Late Twentieth Century." In *Simians, Cyborgs, and Women: The Reinvention of Nature*, ed. Donna J. Haraway, 149–82. New York: Routledge.
Haraway, Donna J. (1992). "The Promises of Monsters: A Regenerative Politics for Inappropriate/d Others." In *Cultural Studies*, ed. Lawrence Grossberg, Cary Nelson, and Paula A. Treichler, 295–337. New York: Routledge.
Haraway, Donna J. (1997). *Modest_Witness@Second_Millennium. FemaleMan©_Meets_OncoMouse™*. New York: Routledge.
Haraway, Donna J. (2008). *When Species Meet*. Minneapolis: University of Minnesota Press.
Haraway, Donna J. (2016). *Staying with the Trouble: Making Kin in the Chthulucene*. Durham, NC: Duke University Press.
Hayles, N. Katherine. (1999). *How We Became Posthuman: Virtual Bodies in Cybernetics, Literature and Informatics*. Chicago: University of Chicago Press.

Hayles, N. Katherine. (2006). "Unfinished Work: From Cyborg to Cognisphere." *Theory, Culture & Society* 23(7–8): 159–66. DOI: 10.1177/0263276406069229.
Hayles, N. Katherine. (2018). *Unthought: The Power of the Cognitive Nonconscious*. Chicago: University of Chicago Press.
Heidegger, Martin. ([1927] 1996). *Being and Time*. Translated by Joan Stambaugh. New York: State University of New York Press.
Heise, Ursula. (2008). *Sense of Place and Sense of Planet: The Environmental Imagination of the Global*. New York: Oxford University Press.
Hellstrand, Ingvil. (2016). "'Almost the Same, but Not Quite': Ontological Politics of Recognition in Modern Science Fiction." *Feminist Theory* 17(3): 251–67.
Hellstrand, Ingvil. (2017). "From Metaphor to Metamorph? On Science Fiction and the Ethics of Transformative Encounters." *NORA—Nordic Journal of Feminist and Gender Research* 25(1): 19–31. DOI: 10.1080/08038740.2017.1309456.
Herman, David. (2019). *Narratology beyond the Human: Storytelling and Animal Life*. Oxford: Oxford University Press.
Hochman, Baruch. (1985). *Character in Literature*. Ithaca, NY: Cornell University Press.
Hogan, Patrick Colm. (2003). *The Mind and Its Stories: Narrative Universals and Human Emotion*. Cambridge: Cambridge University Press.
Hurlburt, Russell T. (2011). *Investigating Pristine Inner Experience: Moments of Truth*. Cambridge: Cambridge University Press.
Husserl, Edmund. (1970). *The Crisis of European Sciences and Transcendental Phenomenology: An Introduction to Phenomenological Philosophy*. Translated by David Carr. Evanston, IL: Northwestern University Press.
Hutto, Daniel. D., and Myin, Erik. (2013). *Radicalizing Enactivism: Basic Minds without Content*. Cambridge, MA: MIT Press.
Idema, Tom. (2019). *Stages of Transmutation: Science Fiction, Biology, and Environmental Posthumanism*. London: Routledge.
Iovino, Serenella, and Oppermann, Serpil. (2012). "Material Ecocriticism: Materiality, Agency, and Models of Narrativity." *Ecozon@* 3(1): 75–91.
Iser, Wolfgang. (1978). *The Act of Reading: A Theory of Aesthetic Response*. Baltimore, MD: Johns Hopkins University Press.
Iser, Wolfgang. (1993). *The Fictive and the Imaginary: Charting Literary Anthropology*. Baltimore, MD: Johns Hopkins University Press.
Jackson, Rosemary. (1981). *Fantasy: The Literature of Subversion*. London: Methuen.
James, Erin. (2015). *The Storyworld Accord: Econarratology and Postcolonial Narratives*. Frontiers of Narrative Series. Lincoln: University of Nebraska Press.
Jannidis, Fotis. (2004). *Figur und Person: Beitrag zu einer historischen Narratologie*. Berlin: de Gruyter.
Jannidis, Fotis. (2012). "Character." In *The Living Handbook of Narratology*, ed. Peter Hühn, John Pier, Wolf Schmid, and Jörg Schönert, paragraph 15. Hamburg: Hamburg University. Accessed November 30, 2019. http://www.lhn.uni-hamburg.de/article/character.

Jauss, Hans Robert. (1982). *Toward an Aesthetic of Reception*. Minneapolis: University of Minnesota Press.

Jemisin. N. K. (2015). *The Fifth Season*. London: Orbit.

Jonas, Hans. (1966). *The Phenomenon of Life: Toward a Philosophical Biology*. London: Harper and Row.

Jones, Gwyneth. (2003). "The Icons in Science Fiction." In *The Cambridge Companion to Science Fiction*, ed. Edward James and Farah Mendlesohn, 163–73. Cambridge: Cambridge University Press.

Joshi, S. T. (1990). *The Weird Tale: Arthur Machen, Lord Dunsany, Algernon Blackwood, M. R. James, Ambrose Bierce, H. P. Lovecraft*. Austin: University of Texas Press.

Kaufman, Geoff F., and Libby, Lisa K. (2012). "Changing Beliefs and Behavior through Experience-Taking." *Journal of Personality and Social Psychology* 103(1): 1–19.

Keen, Susan. (2007). *Empathy and the Novel*. Oxford: Oxford University Press.

Kidd, David Comer, and Castano, Emanuele. (2013). "Reading Literary Fiction Improves Theory of Mind." *Science* 342: 377–80.

Koistinen, Aino-Kaisa. (2015). "'The Machine Is Nothing without the Woman'. Gender, Humanity and the Cyborg Body in the Original and Reimagined *Bionic Woman*." *Science Fiction Film and Television* 8(1): 53–74.

Kortekallio, Kaisa. (2019). "Becoming-Instrument: Thinking with Jeff VanderMeer's *Annihilation* and Timothy Morton's *Hyperobjects*." In *Reconfiguring Human, Non-human and Posthuman in Literature and Culture*, ed. Sanna Karkulehto, Aino-Kaisa Koistinen, and Essi Varis, 57–75. London: Routledge.

Kortekallio, Kaisa. (2020a). "Reading Mutant Narratives: The Bodily Experientiality of Contemporary Ecological Science Fiction." PhD dissertation. Helsinki: University of Helsinki.

Kortekallio, Kaisa. (2020b). "Seasonal Feelings: Reading Paolo Bacigalupi's *The Windup Girl* during Winter Depression." In *Narrating Nonhuman Spaces: Form, Story and Experience beyond Anthropocentrism*, ed. Marco Caracciolo, Marlene Marcussen, and David Rodriguez, 89–103. London: Routledge.

Kortekallio, Kaisa. (2022). "Dancing with the Posthumans: Readerly Choreographies and More-than-Human Figures." *Partial Answers: Journal of Literature and the History of Ideas* 20(2): 277–95. DOI: 10.1353/pan.2022.0016.

Kuiken, Don, Miall, David, and Sikora, Shelley. (2004). "Forms of Self-Implication in Literary Reading." *Poetics Today* 25(2): 171–203. DOI: 10.1215/03335372-25-2-171.

Kukkonen, Karin. (2014). "Presence and Prediction: The Embodied Reader's Cascades of Cognition." *Style* 48(3): 367–84.

Kukkonen, Karin. (2019). *4E Cognition and Eighteenth-Century Fiction: How the Novel Found Its Feet*. Oxford: Oxford University Press.

Kukkonen, Karin, and Caracciolo, Marco. (2014). "Introduction: What Is the 'Second Generation'?" *Style* 48(3): 261–74.

Kurzweil, Raymond. (2005). *The Singularity Is Near: When Humans Transcend Biology*. New York: Viking Penguin.

Kuzmičová, Anežka. (2016). "Does It Matter Where You Read? Situating Narrative in Physical Environment." *Communication Theory* 26(3): 290–308.

Lakoff, George, and Johnson, Mark. (1980). *Metaphors We Live By*. Chicago: University of Chicago Press.

Lakoff, George, and Johnson, Mark. (1999). *Philosophy in the Flesh: The Embodied Mind and Its Challenge to Western Thought*. New York: Basic Books.

Laland, Kevin N., and Brown, Gillian R. (2006). "Niche Construction, Human Behavior, and the Adaptive-Lag Hypothesis." *Evolutionary Anthropology* 15: 95–104.

Latour, Bruno. (1996). "On Actor-Network Theory: A Few Clarifications." *Soziale Welt* 47(4): 369–81.

Le Guin, Ursula. (2007). "The Critics, the Monsters, and the Fantasists." *Wordsworth Circle* 38(1/2): 83–7. DOI: 10.1086/TWC24043962.

LeMenager, Stephanie. (2014). *Living Oil: Petroleum Culture in the American Century*. Oxford: Oxford University Press.

LeMenager, Stephanie. (2017). "The Humanities after the Anthropocene." In *The Routledge Companion to the Environmental Humanities*, ed. Ursula K. Heise, Jon Christensen, and Michelle Niemann, 473–81. London: Routledge.

Levine, Caroline. (2015). *Forms: Whole, Rhythm, Hierarchy, Network*. Princeton, NJ: Princeton University Press.

Lewontin, Richard. (1983). "The Organism as the Subject and Object of Evolution." *Scientia* 118: 63–82.

Longden, Eleanor, Davis, Philip, Billington, Josie, Lampropoulou, Sofia, Farrington, Grace, Magee, Fiona, Walsh, Erin, and Corcoran, Rhiannon. (2015). "Shared Reading: Assessing the Intrinsic Value of a Literature-Based Health Intervention." *Medical Humanities*. 41(2): 113–20. DOI: 10.1136/medhum-2015-010704.

Lovelock, James. (2000). *Gaia: A New Look at Life on Earth*. Oxford: Oxford University Press.

Luckhurst, Roger. (2007). "Catastrophism, American Style: The Fiction of Greg Bear." *Yearbook of English Studies* 37(2): 215–33.

Lynch, Lisa. (2001). "'Not a Virus, but an Upgrade': The Ethics of Epidemic Evolution in Greg Bear's *Darwin's Radio*." *Literature and Medicine* 20(1): 71–93.

Maiese, Michelle. (2015). *Embodied Selves and Divided Minds*. Oxford: Oxford University Press.

Malm, Andreas. (2018). *The Progress of This Storm. Nature and Society in a Warming World*. London: Verso.

Mandala, Susan. (2010). *The Language in Science Fiction and Fantasy: The Question of Style*. New York: Bloomsbury.

Margolin, Uri. (2007). "Character." In *The Cambridge Companion to Narrative*, ed. David Herman, 66–79. Cambridge: Cambridge University Press.

Margulis, Lynn, and Sagan, Dorion. (2002). *Acquiring Genomes: A Theory of the Origins of Species*. New York: Basic Books.

McHale, Brian. (2010). "Science Fiction, or, the Most Typical Genre in World Literature." In *Genre and Interpretation*, ed. Pirjo Lyytikäinen, Tintti Klapuri, and Minna Maijala, 11–27. Helsinki: Department of Finnish, Fenno-Ugrian and Scandinavian Studies, University of Helsinki.

McHale, Brian. (2018). "Speculative Fiction, or, Literal Narratology." In *The Edinburgh Companion to Contemporary Narrative Theories*, ed. Zara Dinnen and Robyn Warhol, 317–31. Edinburgh: Edinburgh University Press.

Menary, Richard. (2009). "Introduction to the Special Issue on 4E Cognition." *Phenomenology and the Cognitive Sciences* 9(4): 459–63.

Mendelsund, Peter. (2014). "Describing the Indescribable with Jeff VanderMeer." *Boing Boing*, November 12, 2014. Accessed November 30, 2019. https://boingboing.net/2014/11/12/describing-the-indescribable-w.html.

Meretoja, Hanna, Kinnunen, Eevastiina, and Kosonen, Päivi. (2022). "Narrative Agency and the Critical Potential of Metanarrative Reading Groups." *Poetics Today* 43(2), 387–414.

Merleau-Ponty, Maurice. (2002). *Phenomenology of Perception*. London: Routledge.

Metzinger, Thomas. (2003). *Being No One: The Self-Model Theory of Subjectivity*. Cambridge, MA: MIT Press.

Miéville, China. (2009). "Weird Fiction." In *Routledge Companion to Science Fiction*, ed. Mark Bould, A. M. Butler, Adam Roberts, and Sherryl Vint, 508–15. Abingdon: Routledge.

Mikkonen, Kai. (2014). "Everyday Knowledge in Understanding Fictional Characters and Their Worlds." In *Narrative Matters 2014: Narrative Knowing/Récit et Savoir*, Paris, France.

Moore, Jason W. (2015). *Capitalism in the Web of Life: Ecology and the Accumulation of Capital*. Brooklyn: Verso.

Morton, Timothy. (2007). *Ecology without Nature: Rethinking Environmental Aesthetics*. Cambridge, MA: Harvard University Press.

Morton, Timothy. (2010). *The Ecological Thought*. Cambridge, MA: Harvard University Press.

Morton, Timothy. (2013). *Hyperobjects. Philosophy and Ecology after the End of the World*. Minneapolis: University of Minnesota Press.

Morton, Timothy. (2016). *Dark Ecology: For a Logic of Future Coexistence*. New York: Columbia University Press.

Nagel, Thomas. (1974). "What Is It Like Bat?" *The Philosophical Review* 83(4): 435–50.

Nayar, Pramod K. (2014). *Posthumanism*. Cambridge: Polity.

Neimanis, Astrida. (2017). *Bodies of Water. Posthuman Feminist Phenomenology*. London: Bloomsbury.

Noë, Alva. (2004). *Action in Perception*. Cambridge, MA: MIT Press.

Noë, Alva. (2015). *Strange Tools. Art and Human Nature*. New York: Farrar, Strauss and Giroux.

Nuismer, Scott. (2017). *Introduction to Coevolutionary Theory*. New York: Macmillan Learning.

Nussbaum, Abigail. (2008). "Review of *Pump Six and Other Stories*, by Paolo Bacigalupi." *Strange Horizons*, March 3, 2008. Accessed November 30, 2019. http://strangehoriz ons.com/non-fiction/reviews/pump-six-and-other-stories-by-paolo-bacigalupi.

Nussbaum, Martha. (1990). *Love's Knowledge: Essays on Philosophy and Literature*. Oxford: Oxford University Press.

O'Regan, J. Kevin, and Noë, Alva. (2001). "A Sensorimotor Account of Vision and Visual Consciousness." *Behavioral and Brain Sciences* 24(5): 939–1031.

Otto, Eric. (2012). *Green Speculations: Science Fiction and Transformative Environmentalism*. Columbus: Ohio State University Press.

Oulanne, Laura. (2021). *Materiality in Modernist Short Fiction: Lived Things*. London: Routledge.

Ovaska, Anna, and Kortekallio, Kaisa. (2021). "Reading Closely: Bodies and Environments." *The Polyphony*, November 24, 2021. Accessed November 24, 2021. https://thepolyphony.org/2021/11/24/reading-closely-bodies-and-environments/.

Pak, Chris. (2016). *Terraforming. Ecopolitical Transformations and Environmentalism in Science Fiction*. Liverpool: Liverpool University Press.

Pálsson, Gísli, Szerszynski, Bronislaw, Sörlin, Sverker, Marks, John, Avril, Bernard, Crumley, Carole, Hackmann, Heide, Holm, Poul, Ingram, John S. I., Kirman, Alan, Pardo Buendía, Mercedes, and Weehuizen, Rifka. (2013). "Reconceptualizing the 'Anthropos' in the Anthropocene: Integrating the Social Sciences and Humanities in Global Environmental Change Research." *Environmental Science & Policy* 28: 3–13.

Persson, Linn, Almroth, Bethanie M. Carney, Collins, Christopher D., Cornell, Sarah, de Wit, Cynthia A., Diamond, Miriam L., Fantke, Peter, Hassellöv, Martin, MacLeod, Matthew, Ryberg, Morten W., Søgaard Jørgensen, Peter, Villarrubia-Gómez, Patricia, Wang, Zhanyun, and Zwicky Hauschild, Michael. (2022). "Outside the Safe Operating Space of the Planetary Boundary for Novel Entities." *Environmental Science & Technology* 56(3): 1510–21.

Pettersson, Bo. (2012). "Beyond Anti-mimetic Models: A Critique of Unnatural Narratology." In *Rethinking Mimesis. Concepts and Practices of Literary Representation*, ed. Saija Isomaa, Sari Kivistö, Pirjo Lyytikäinen, Sanna Nyqvist, Merja Polvinen, and Riikka Rossi, 73–91. Cambridge: Cambridge Scholars.

Pettersson, Bo. (2016). *How Literary Worlds Are Shaped: A Comparative Poetics of Literary Imagination*. Berlin: De Gruyter.

Phelan, James. (1989). *Reading People, Reading Plots: Character, Progression, and the Interpretation of Narrative*. Columbus: Ohio State University Press.

Polvinen, Merja. (2012). "Being Played. Mimesis, Fictionality and Emotional Engagement." In *Rethinking Mimesis: Concepts and Practices of Literary Representation*, ed. Saija Isomaa, Sari Kivistö, Pirjo Lyytikäinen, Sanna Nyqvist, Merja Polvinen, and Riikka Rossi, 91–110. Cambridge: Cambridge Scholars.

Polvinen, Merja. (2016). "Enactive Perception and Fictional Minds." In *The Cognitive Humanities: Embodied Mind in Literature and Culture*, ed. Peter Garratt, 19–34. Gordonsville: Palgrave Macmillan.

Polvinen, Merja. (2017). "Cognitive Science and the Double Vision of Fiction." In *Cognitive Literary Science: Dialogues between Literature and Cognition*, ed. Michael Burke and Emily T. Troscianko, 135–50. Oxford: Oxford University Press. DOI: 10.1093/acprof:oso/9780190496869.003.0008.

Polvinen, Merja. (2023). *Self-Reflective Fiction and 4E Cognition: An Enactive Approach to Literary Artifice*. New York: Routledge.

Polvinen, Merja, and Sklar, Howard. (2019). "Mimetic and Synthetic Views of Characters: How Readers Process 'People' in Fiction." *Cogent Arts & Humanities* 6(1): 1. DOI: 10.1080/23311983.2019.1687257.

Popova, Yanna. (2015). *Stories, Meaning, and Experience: Narrativity and Enaction*. New York: Routledge.

Prendergast, Alan. (2010). "Sci-Fi Phenom Paolo Bacigalupi Has Seen the Future—and It's Scary as Hell." *Westword*, May 6, 2010. Accessed November 30, 2019. http://www.westword.com/news/sci-fi-phenom-paolo-bacigalupi-has-seen-the-future-and-its-scary-as-hell-5108064.

Prendergast, Finola Anne. (2017). "Revising Nonhuman Ethics in Jeff VanderMeer's *Annihilation*." *Contemporary Literature* 58(3): 333–60.

Raipola, Juha. (2014). "Inhimilliset ja postinhimilliset tulevaisuudet." In *Posthumanismi*, ed. Karoliina Lummaa and Lea Rojola, 35–56. Turku: Eetos.

Ratcliffe, Matthew. (2010). "The Phenomenology of Mood and the Meaning of Life." In *The Oxford Handbook of Philosophy of Emotion*, ed. Peter Goldie, 349–72. Oxford Handbooks Online.

Richards, I. A. (1929). *Practical Criticism*. Edinburgh: Edinburgh University Press.

Roberts, Adam. (2005). *Science Fiction: The New Critical Idiom*. 2nd ed. London: Routledge.

Robertson, Benjamin J. (2018). *None of This Is Normal: The Fiction of Jeff VanderMeer*. Minneapolis: University of Minnesota Press.

Rockström, Johan, Steffen, Will, Noone, Kevin, Persson, Åsa, Chapin, F. Stuart III, Lambin, Eric F., Lenton, Timothy M., Scheffer, Marten, Folke, Carl, Schellnhuber, Hans Joachim, Nykvist, Björn, de Wit, Cynthia A., Hughes, Terry, van der Leeuw, Sander, Rodhe, Henning, Sörlin, Sverker, Snyder, Peter K., Costanza, Robert, Svedin, Uno, Falkenmark, Malin, Karlberg, Louise, Corell, Robert W., Fabry, Victoria J., Hansen, James, Walker, Brian, Liverman, Diana, Richardson, Katherine, Crutzen, Paul, and Foley, Jonathan A. (2009). "Planetary Boundaries: Exploring the Safe Operating Space for Humanity." *Ecology and Society* 14(2): 32.

Roine, Hanna-Riikka. (2016). *Imaginative, Immersive and Interactive Engagements: The Rhetoric of Worldbuilding in Contemporary Speculative Fiction*. Acta Universitatis Tamperensis 2197, Tampere: Tampere University Press.

Rosenblatt, Louise. ([1938] 1995). *Literature as Exploration*. 5th ed. New York: Modern Language Association of America.

Rossi, Riikka. (2012). "The Everyday Effect: The Cognitive Dimension of Realism." In *Rethinking Mimesis: Concepts and Practices of Literary Representation*, ed. Saija

Isomaa, Sari Kivistö, Pirjo Lyytikäinen, Sanna Nyqvist, Merja Polvinen, and Riikka Rossi, 115–38. Cambridge: Cambridge Scholars.

Rucker, Rudy. (1982). *Software*. New York: Ace Books.

Ryan, John Charles. (2012). "Passive Flora? Reconsidering Nature's Agency through Human-Plant Studies (HPS)." *Societies* 2(3): 101–21.

Salminen, Antti, and Vadén, Tere. (2015). *Energy and Experience: An Essay in Nafthology*. Chicago: MCM.

Schell, Heather. (2002). "The Sexist Gene: Science Fiction and the Germ Theory of History." *American Literary History* 14(4): 805–27.

Shklovsky, Victor. (2012). "Art as Technique." In *Russian Formalist Criticism: Four Essays*, ed. Lee T. Lemon and Marion J. Reis, 18–28. Lincoln: University of Nebraska Press.

Selisker, Scott. (2015). "'Stutter-Stop Flash-Bulb Strange': GMOs and the Aesthetics of Scale in Paolo Bacigalupi's *The Windup Girl*." *Science Fiction Studies* 42: 500–18. DOI: 10.5621/sciefictstud.42.3.0500.

Seyfert, Robert. (2012). "Beyond Personal Feelings and Collective Emotions: Toward a Theory of Social Affect." *Theory, Culture & Society* 29(6): 27–46.

Sheehan, Paul. (2003). "Introduction. Contingencies of Humanness." In *Becoming Human: New Perspectives on the Inhuman Condition*, ed. Paul Sheehan, 1–12. Westport: Praeger.

Sheets-Johnstone, Maxine. (2011). *The Primacy of Movement*. 2nd ed. Amsterdam: John Benjamins.

Shildrick, Margrit. (2001). *Embodying the Monster: Encounters with the Vulnerable Self*. London: Sage.

Sieg, George J. (2009). "Infinite Regress into Self-Referential Horror: The Gnosis of the Victim." In *Collapse: Philosophical Research and Development*, Vol. IV, ed. Robin Mackay, 30–54. Falmouth: Urbanomic.

Sikora, Shelley, Kuiken, Don, and Miall, David S. (2011). "Expressive Reading: A Phenomenological Study of Readers' Experience of Coleridge's *The Rime of the Ancient Mariner*." *Psychology of Aesthetics, Creativity, and the Arts* 5(3): 258–68.

Sklar, Howard. (2013). *The Art of Sympathy in Fiction: Forms of Ethical and Emotional Persuasion*. Amsterdam: Benjamins.

Soper, Kate. (1985). *Humanism and Anti-humanism: Problems of Modern European Thought*. London: Hutchinson.

Sperling, Alison. (2016). "Second Skins: A Body-Ecology of Jeff VanderMeer's *The Southern Reach Trilogy*." *Paradoxa* 28: 230–55.

Spiegel, Simon. (2008). "Things Made Strange: On the Concept of 'Estrangement' in Science Fiction Theory." *Science Fiction Studies* 35(3): 369–85.

Spiegelman, Ian. (2014). "Jeff VanderMeer: 'Power of Nature' Inspired New Sci-Fi Novel 'Annihilation.'" *USA Today*, February 28, 2014. Accessed November 30, 2019. http://www.usatoday.com/ story/life/books/2014/02/28/jeff-vandermeer-annihilation/5902023.

Stewart John, Gapenne, Olivier, and Di Paolo Ezequiel, A. (2010). "Introduction." In *Enaction: Toward a New Paradigm for Cognitive Science*, ed. John Stewart, Olivier Gapenne, and Ezequiel A. Di Paolo, vii–xvii. Cambridge, MA: MIT Press.

Sturgeon, Theodore. (1953). *More than Human*. New York: Ballantine Books.

Suvin, Darko. (1979). *Metamorphoses of Science Fiction: On the Poetics and History of a Literary Genre*. New Haven, CT: Yale University Press.

Stableford, Brian. (2007). "The Cosmic Horror." In *Icons of Horror and the Supernatural: An Encyclopedia of Our Worst Nightmares*, Vol. 1, ed. S. T. Joshi, 65–96. Santa Barbara: Greenwood.

Stockwell, Peter. (2000). *The Poetics of Science Fiction*. Harlow: Longman.

Taylor, Charles. (1989). *Sources of the Self: The Making of the Modern Identity*. Cambridge: Cambridge University Press.

Thompson, Evan. (2007). *Mind in Life: Biology, Phenomenology, and the Sciences of the Mind*. Cambridge, MA: Harvard University Press.

Thompson, Evan. (2009). "Life and Mind: From Autopoiesis to Neurophenomenology." In *Emergence and Embodiment. New Essays on Second-Order Systems Theory*, ed. Bruce Clarke and Mark B. N. Hansen, 77–93. Durham, NC: Duke University Press.

Thompson, Evan. (2014). *Waking, Dreaming, Being. Self and Consciousness in Neuroscience, Meditation, and Philosophy*. New York: Columbia University Press.

Tidwell, Christy. (2011). "The Problem of Materiality in Paolo Bacigalupi's 'The People of Sand and Slag.'" *Extrapolation* 52(1): 94–109.

Tompkins, David. (2014). "Weird Ecology: On *The Southern Reach* Trilogy." *Los Angeles Review of Books*, September 30, 2014. Accessed November 30, 2019. https://lareview ofbooks.org/ review/weird-ecology-southern-reach-trilogy.

Trexler, Adam. (2015). *Anthropocene Fictions: The Novel in a Time of Climate Change*. Charlottesville: University of Virginia Press.

Troscianko, Emily T. (2013). "Reading Imaginatively: The Imagination in Cognitive Science and Cognitive Literary Studies." *Journal of Literary Semantics* 42(2): 181–98.

Troscianko, Emily T. (2014). "First-Person and Second-Generation Perspectives on Starvation in Kafka's 'Ein Hungerkünstler.'" *Style* 48(3): 331–48.

Tsing, Anna Lowenhaupt. (2017). *The Mushroom at the End of the World: On the Possibility of Life in Capitalist Ruins*. Princeton, NJ: Princeton University Press.

Uhall, Michael. (2016). "*Southern Reach* I: Cosmopolitics and Area X." *Environmental Critique*, February 2, 2016. Accessed November 30, 2019. https://environmentalcriti que. wordpress.com/2016/02/05/southern-reach-i-cosmopolitics-and-area-x.

Ulstein, Gry. (2017). "Brave New Weird: Anthropocene Monsters in Jeff VanderMeer's *The Southern Reach*." *Concentric: Literary and Cultural Studies*, 71–96. DOI: 10.6240/ concentric.lit.2017.43.1.05.

VanderMeer, Jeff. (2008). "The New Weird—'It's Alive?'" In *The New Weird*, ed. Jeff VanderMeer, ix–xviii. San Francisco, CA: Tachyon.

VanderMeer, Jeff. (2011). "Conversation #1: China Miéville and the Monsters." In *Monstrous Creatures: Explorations of Fantasy through Essays, Articles and Reviews*, ed. Jeff VanderMeer, 55–64. Bowie: Guide Dog Books.
VanderMeer, Jeff. (2014a). *Annihilation*. New York: Farrar, Strauss and Giroux.
VanderMeer, Jeff. (2014b). *Authority*. New York: Farrar, Strauss and Giroux.
VanderMeer, Jeff. (2014c). *Acceptance*. New York: Farrar, Strauss and Giroux.
VanderMeer, Jeff. (2014d). "The Uncanny Power of Weird Fiction." *The Atlantic*, October 30, 2014. Accessed November 30, 2019. https://www.theatlantic.com/entertainment/archive/2014/10/uncanny-fiction-beautiful-and-bizarre/381794.
VanderMeer, Jeff. (2016). "Hauntings in the Anthropocene: An Initial Exploration." *Environmental Critique*, July 7, 2016. Accessed November 30, 2019. https://environmentalcritique.wordpress.com/2016/07/07/hauntings-in-the-anthropocene.
VanderMeer, Jeff, and VanderMeer, Ann. (2011). "Introduction." In *The Weird: A Compendium of Strange and Dark Stories*, ed. Ann and Jeff VanderMeer, xv–xx. London: Corrus.
Varela, Francisco, Thompson, Evan, and Rosch, Elena. (1992). *The Embodied Mind: Cognitive Science and Human Experience*. Cambridge, MA: MIT Press.
Varela, Francisco. (1996). "Neurophenomenology. A Methodological Remedy for the Hard Problem." *Journal of Consciousness Studies* 3(4): 330–49.
Varis, Essi. (2019a). "The Monster Analogy: Why Fictional Characters Are Frankenstein's Monsters." *SubStance* 48(1): 63–86.
Varis, Essi (2019b). "Alien Overtures: Speculating about Nonhuman Experiences with Comic Book Characters." In *Reconfiguring Human, Nonhuman and Posthuman in Literature and Culture*, ed. Sanna Karkulehto, Aino-Kaisa Koistinen, and Essi Varis, 79–107. London: Routledge.
Vermeule, Blakey. (2010). *Why Do We Care about Literary Characters?* Baltimore, MD: Johns Hopkins University Press.
Vermeulen, Pieter. (2014). "Posthuman Affect." *European Journal of English Studies* 18(2): 121–34.
Vermeulen, Pieter. (2020). *Literature and the Anthropocene*. London: Routledge.
Vint, Sherryl. (2005). "Becoming Other: Animals, Kinship, and Butler's Clay's Ark." *Science Fiction Studies* 32(2): 281–300.
Vint, Sherryl. (2006). *Bodies of Tomorrow: Technology, Subjectivity, Science Fiction*. Toronto: University of Toronto Press.
Warhol, Robyn. (2003). *Having a Good Cry: Effeminate Feelings and Pop-Culture Forms*. Columbus: Ohio State University Press.
Weik von Mossner, Alexa. (2016). "Imagining Geological Agency: Storytelling in the Anthropocene." *RCC Perspectives: Transformations in Environment and Society* 2: 83–89.
Weik von Mossner, Alexa. (2017a). *Affective Ecologies. Empathy, Emotion, and Environmental Narrative*. Columbus: Ohio State University Press.

Weik von Mossner, Alexa. (2017b). "Vulnerable Lives: The Affective Dimensions of Risk in Young Adult Cli-Fi." *Textual Practice* 31(3): 553–66. DOI: 10.1080/0950236X.2017.1295661.

Wilk, Elvia. (2019). "Toward a Theory of the New Weird." *Lit Hub*. August 5, 2019, Accessed November 30, 2019. https://lithub.com/toward-a-theory-of-the-new-weird.

Wimsatt, William K., and Beardsley, Monroe. (1967). "The Affective Fallacy." In *The Verbal Icon: Studies in the Meaning of Poetry*, 21–39. Lexington: University of Kentucky Press.

Wolfe, Cary. (2010). *What Is Posthumanism?* Minneapolis: University of Minnesota Press.

Wolfe, Gary K. (2011). *Evaporating Genres: Essays on Fantastic Literature*. Middletown: Wesleyan University Press.

Zachos, Elena. (2017). "See What's Controlling These Zombie Ants." *National Geographic*, November 10, 2017. Accessed November 30, 2019. https://news.nationalgeographic.com/2017/11/ controlling-zombie-ants-fungus-spd.

Zunshine, Lisa. (2006). *Why We Read Fiction: Theory of Mind and the Novel*. Columbus: Ohio State University Press.

Zunshine, Lisa. (2008). *Strange Concepts and the Stories They Make Possible*. Baltimore, MD: Johns Hopkins University Press.

Index

Abram, David
 The Spell of the Sensuous 2, 12, 37–8, 103–4, 129
affect; *see also under* cognition, more-than-human
 as biological 65–6, 68–9
 emotion and 16, 41–2, 58–61, 65–6, 114–17, 120
 human-centered 58–61, 64–9, 70–1
 in literary analysis 4, 15–17, 39–44, 48–51, 71–3
 mood 58, 65–6, 153–4, 172
 nonsubjective 171–2, 189
 pleasure 65, 70–1, 113, 116–17, 140
 and reflection 41–4, 54, 71–3, 114–18, 124–5, 173
 violent 19, 113–17, 140–1
 weird 145–6
affective device 57, 114, 117–18, 174
affective fallacy 41–2
affective technology 17, 33, 50, 57–8, 110, 189–90
affordance 47–8, 58, 72, 94
agency; *see also* subjectivity; *see also under* more-than-human
 destructive 1–2, 20, 191
 material 70, 132–6, 162, 175, 188
 nonhuman 30, 132–6, 176, 181
 and writing 174, 176–7
the Anthropocene 1–5, 89, 134, 170, 190–2
anthropocentrism 2, 168, 170;
 see also anthropomorphism, human exceptionalism
 and character theory 89–91
 habitual 48, 72, 89, 187, 191
anthropomorphism 90, 104, 131, 135; *see also* anthropocentrism
attention 12, 39–40, 44, 48–51, 60–1, 188

Bacigalupi, Paolo
 The Windup Girl 18, 119–41

 "The People of Sand and Slag" 110–19
Bear, Greg, *Darwin's Children* 18, 55–73
biotechnology 85–6, 88, 117–18, 133
Blish, James, "Battle of the Unborn" 82
bodily feeling 13, 16, 48–51, 187–8;
 see also affect, kinesis, mood;
 see also under more-than-human
 amplification 48–51
 balance 152–8, 160
 disgust 115–17, 123–4
 disorientation 152–3
 and gender 33, 120–6, 140–1, 189
 genre-typical patterns of (*see* readerly choreography)
 hardness 96–7
 haunting 159–65
 and metaphor 96–7
 relational 39–40
 repetitive 163–5
 strange 14, 16, 47, 152–3
 tension 120, 132, 162
 warmth 65, 70–1, 96–7, 99
bodily movement 99–105, 119–27, 153–9
Bolens, Guillemette
 The Style of Gestures 101–2
Braidotti, Rosi
 Metamorphoses 30–2, 37, 51–2, 91, 191
 The Posthuman 33, 51, 91
Butler, Judith
 Gender Trouble 30–4, 37, 51
Butler, Octavia 64
 Imago 84–5, 94, 139

Cadigan, Pat
 "The Girl-Thing That Went Out for Sushi" 86–7
Caracciolo, Marco
 Experientiality 13, 26–7, 45, 57, 163, 172
 Narrating the Mesh 3–4, 48
 Strange Narrators 58, 93, 120
Carroll, Siobhan 149–50

Cave, Terence
　Thinking with Literature 49–50, 100–2
character 19, 58–60, 88–92; *see also* figure; *see also under* anthropocentrism, mimesis
　character-centered illusion 58, 93, 120
　and fictionality 130–1, 178, 182
　flat 94–5, 120, 127
　monstrous 131
　nonhuman 104, 166
　and perception 103–4
　and the posthuman 11, 115
　and realism 62, 93
　and science fiction 78–9, 88–92
　types 109, 121, 162–3
Chu, Seo-Young
　Do Metaphors Dream of Literal Sleep? 63, 69
Clark, Timothy, *Ecocriticism on the Edge* 2–4
climate change; *see* environmental change
cognition 5, 24; *see also* sense-making; *see also under* evolutionary theory, new materialism
　and affect 58
　conscious and nonconscious 44, 50, 54–5, 64–9, 157–63, 173
　embodied 13–15, 24, 46 (*see also under* subjectivity)
　enactive 14, 24–6, 28–9, 34–7
cognitive environment 17, 43–4, 46, 172–6, 191
cognitive estrangement 15–17, 93–4; *see also* defamiliarization, embodied estrangement
cognitive literary studies 13–17, 26–7, 43–4, 46–8, 192
　enactivism 28–9, 34–7, 39
　first-generation 41
　and posthumanism 13–17, 27, 29–31, 49
　and realism 93
　and science fiction 15–16
　second-generation 26, 29, 37, 42, 53
cognitive metaphor 97–100; *see also* corporeal concepts
cognitivist nihilism 144, 155–61; *see also* groundlessness
Colombetti, Giovanna
　The Feeling Body 53–4
contamination 148, 151–2, 163–5, 174, 182
corporeal concepts 99–100; *see also* cognitive metaphor
cultural transformation 4, 12–13, 32, 37, 52, 192
cyborg; *see under* figure

dance 40, 53–5, 99, 124; *see also under* reading
defamiliarization 15, 55, 60–1, 93–5; *see also* cognitive estrangement, embodied estrangement
designed sensory flow 53–4, 165, 173

ecocriticism 1–4, 26; *see also* material ecocriticism
embodied cognition; *see under* cognition
embodied estrangement 14–17, 94, 144–8, 190; *see also* cognitive estrangement, defamiliarization
The Embodied Mind (Varela, Thompson, and Rosch) 14, 25, 28–9, 34–5, 148, 155–6
enactive mind; *see under* cognition
enactivism; *see under* cognitive literary studies
environmental change 1–4, 8, 28, 190
　and science fiction 6–10, 56
evolutionary theory 2, 28, 80, 138; *see also under* humanism
　and cognition 34–5, 128
　and science fiction 8–10, 56, 64–70, 81–2, 88, 152
experience 1–4, 15–17, 23–39, 44, 187–93; *see also* experientiality, experiential change; *see also under* more-than-human, reading
　broad and pristine 44–5
　descriptions 65–7, 85, 95–7, 124, 143, 153
　environmental 37–9, 43, 45–8
　kinesic, *see* kinesis
　limits 147, 159, 170, 176–9
　mutant 84, 166
　nonhuman 91
　olfactory 60–2
　patterns 32–3, 53–5, 89, 163, 173 (*see also* experiential motif)
experientiality 15, 39, 45, 57–8, 92–5

experiential change 10–15, 23, 26, 29–39, 43, 48–51
experiential motif 163–5
experimentality 4–5, 17

Faassen, Kahn, and Vermeulen, Pieter
  "The Weird and the Ineluctable Human" 147, 168–9
feminist posthumanism; *see* posthumanist feminism
fictionality 23, 92–3, 95, 114–18, 127–32, 173; *see also under* character, mimesis
figuration 33, 51–2, 91–2, 113, 170; *see also* figure
figure 88–92, 104, 110–13, 118, 127–32, 139–41; *see also* character, figuration
  artificial woman 121–32, 140
  cyborg 51, 80, 87–8, 128, 137
  mutant 18, 80–8, 92, 115–17, 127–32, 166
  puppet 121–3
Fisher, Mark
  The Weird and the Eerie 146
Fludernik, Monika
  Towards a 'Natural' Narratology 45, 90

gender 30–4; *see also under* affect, figure, subjectivity
  female 120
  performative 30–4
  stereotype 138–9
Gibson, James Jerome
  The Ecological Approach to Visual Perception 47
groundlessness 27–9, 148–9, 154–6, 175; *see also* cognitivist nihilism, *The Embodied Mind*

Haraway, Donna
  "The Promises of Monsters" 23, 50, 54, 115–16
  Modest_Witness@Second_Millennium 51, 92
  When Species Meet 33, 38, 54
  Staying with the Trouble 11–12, 118, 158, 190
Hayles, Katherine N. 5, 11–13
horror 144–6, 152–9
human exceptionalism 2, 4, 33, 71; *see also* anthropocentrism, humanism
humanism 2, 10–13, 16, 190
  crisis of 2, 5–6
  evolutionary 68–70
  liberal 13, 28
  in narrative studies 88, 90–1, 128
  transhumanism 12, 86
  universal 70–1

Idema, Tom
  Stages of Transmutation 69, 144–5, 173, 175–6
instrumentality 95, 97, 109–10, 113–14, 119–27, 140
Iovino, Serenella and Oppermann, Serpil
  "Material Ecocriticism" 134–5, 172–3

James, Erin
  The Storyworld Accord 3–4
Jemisin, N. K.
  The Fifth Season 95–105
Jones, Gwyneth
  "The Icons in Science Fiction" 94–5

kinesis 49–50, 54, 100–105, 110–27, 154, 173–4; *see also* bodily feeling, bodily movement, kinetics
kinesic intelligence 101, 130
kinesic reading 49–50, 101, 120, 125
kinetics 53, 99–105, 110–27, 132–5; *see also* bodily movement, kinesis
kinetic portrayal 53
Kukkonen, Karin
  4E Cognition and Eighteenth-Century Fiction 42, 48, 53–4, 148, 165

Maiese, Michelle
  Embodied Selves and Divided Minds 35–6
Margulis, Lynn 68–9
material ecocriticism 11, 103, 134–5, 172; *see also* ecocriticism, new materialism
materiality 11, 15–17, 30–4, 39–40; *see also* new materialism; *see also under* agency
  bodily 31–2, 49, 105, 119–23
  and narrative 39, 117–18, 134, 176 (*see also* material ecocriticism)
  nonhuman 38, 49, 89, 97, 100, 132–6
  and reading 50, 92, 120, 126, 132 (*see also under* more-than-human)

and sense-making 99–100, 104–5, 134–6
materialization 30–4, 37, 40
meaning 13, 134; *see also* sense-making; *see also under* more-than-human
  cultural structures 50, 54, 88
  emergent 24, 100, 124
  meaning-making 26–7, 33, 44, 47, 102–4, 134
  narrative construction 101, 134
Merleau-Ponty, Maurice
  Phenomenology of Perception 50, 103
mimesis 78–9, 88–93, 102; *see also* realism
  in character theory 88–93
  ecomimesis 147
  and experientiality 99
  and fictionality 109–10, 127, 173
  and genre 78–9
mind-reading 59, 66, 90, 101
more-than-human 11, 171; *see also* posthuman, posthumanism
  affect 48–51, 127–32, 143–4, 174, 181–3
  agency 162, 167, 174, 181, 189–91
  bodily feeling 48–51, 102, 132, 152, 181
  ecology 14, 69, 166, 171
  ethics 11, 139
  experience 4, 17, 37–9, 48–51, 103–4, 187–90
  language 38
  meaning 37–9, 103–5, 171–3, 179–83
  reading 15–17, 39–55, 72, 92, 140, 191–3
  subjectivity 26–7, 29–33, 79, 187–93
  technology 14, 171–2, 174
  writing 171–2, 174, 181
mutant; *see also* mutant narrative; *see also under* experience, figure
  atomic 81–3
  embodiment 4, 61–4, 79–88
  genetic 80–1
  postmodern 83–4
  queer 84
  superhero 79
  teenage rebel 57–60, 70
mutant narrative 4, 5–10, 12–16, 94–5, 139–40, 187–92
mutual enfoldment 29, 35, 50, 190; *see also The Embodied Mind*

narrative; *see also* mutant narrative, narrative studies
  conventions 72, 113
  engagement 13–14
  experiential patterns 14, 55, 78, 188
  form 3, 5–6, 72, 93–4, 112–13, 147
  human-centered 10, 13–14, 88–90
  narration 61–2, 93, 121–2, 126–7, 147, 153, 157, 177–8
  nonhuman 134, 181
  political potential 3
  strategies 45, 93–5, 114–17, 123, 147
  as systems 5, 23, 174–6
narrative studies 17, 40–4, 88–90; *see also* narrative, mutant narrative
  cognitive approaches to narrative (*see* cognitive literary studies)
  econarratology 3–4
  feminist 33
Neimanis, Astrida
  Bodies of Water 33, 38, 48–51, 188; *see also under* phenomenology
new criticism 41–4
new materialism 14, 30, 133–5, 182
  and cognition 11
  critique of 11, 134, 169
  methodology 48–51, 132, 175
New Materialisms (Coole and Frost, eds.) 30–1
niche 37, 136–7
Noë, Alva
  Action in Perception 24–5
  Strange Tools 47–8, 54–5, 61, 72
Nussbaum, Abigail 116

objectification 82, 121–3
organized activity 25, 48, 50, 54

performativity 31–4, 39–40, 50–3, 140, 150
  enactive 118, 157–8
Pettersson, Bo
  How Literary Worlds Are Shaped 77–9, 92–3
phenomenology 12, 16–17, 25–6, 36–9, 44–5
  empirical 42
  of movement 99–100, 155
  posthuman feminist 38–9, 48–51

Polvinen, Merja 43–4, 95, 130, 173
Popova, Yanna 102–3
posthuman 4, 10–13, 80, 112–17, 187; *see also* more-than-human, posthumanism; *see also under* character, phenomenology
posthumanism; *see also* more-than-human, posthuman
  and feminism 30, 48–51
  and literary studies 1–5, 10–17, 27, 89–91
  and subjectivity 29–34, 72, 187–91

Ratcliffe, Matthew 39, 172
readerly choreography 19, 53–5, 109–10, 113–18, 156–7
reading 5, 26–7; *see also under* materiality, more-than-human
  close 1–2, 40–4
  as dancing 53–5
  empirical studies 41–3
  enactive 13, 17, 26, 42–3, 48
  experience 4–6, 10, 13–17, 26–8, 39–55, 176–9
  first-person 16–17, 26, 40
  genre 77–8, 110–1
  kinesic, *see* kinesis
  as niche construction 37
  performative 50–1
  situated 57–61, 77
  skill 13, 40, 44, 47, 132
realism 5–6, 58, 61–2, 72, 90–4; *see also* mimesis
Robertson, Benjamin J.
  None of This is Normal 174–6
Rossi, Riikka 61–2, 93
Rucker, Rudy, *Software* 122

science fiction 5–10, 15, 23, 77–8, 92–5; *see also under* character, cognitive literary studies, environmental change, evolutionary theory
  counter-imaginaries 51–2
  ecological science fiction 5–10
  history 5–7, 79–88, 151
  science fiction studies 5–7, 15–16, 62, 92–5
Selisker, Scott 121, 123
sense-making 35–6, 41, 46, 127, 165; *see also* cognition, materiality, meaning

bodily 99–105
nonhuman 46
participatory 102
social 59
sex 31–2, 80, 120–5, 139–40
Sheets-Johnstone, Maxine
  The Primacy of Movement 99–100, 102
Sperling, Alison 181–2
Sturgeon, Theodore
  More than Human 82–3, 84, 87
subjectivity; *see also* agency; *see also under* more-than-human, posthumanism
  decentralization 149, 162
  embodied 17, 25–6, 29–33 (*see also under* cognition)
  gendered 30–3
  human 6, 11, 34, 90, 169, 179, 190
  liberal humanist 13, 28
  posthumanist 10, 12, 29–30, 38
  rational 6, 155–8
  sensorimotor 35

Thompson, Evan 25, 68, 70; see also *The Embodied Mind*
Tidwell, Christy 114

Ulstein, Gry 145, 157, 166, 168–9

VanderMeer, Jeff 143–7, 172–6, 189
  Acceptance 158–9, 164–71, 178–81
  Annihilation 147–58, 164, 172, 176–8
  Authority 159–64, 172
Varis, Essi 89, 130–1
Vermeule, Blakey
  Why Do We Care About Literary Characters? 90
Vermeulen, Pieter 134–5, 174, 189

Warhol, Robyn
  Having a Good Cry 33, 37, 48, 53, 188–9
weird 145–7, 155, 157, 160–2
  New Weird fiction 143–9
  Weird fiction 144–9, 155–6, 168–9
Wilk, Elvia 152, 162
writing 134, 154, 164, 171–83; *see also under* agency, more-than-human

Zunshine, Lisa 128–32

www.ingramcontent.com/pod-product-compliance
Lightning Source LLC
Chambersburg PA
CBHW052109300426
44116CB00010B/1590